Aerial view of Sydney Harbour.

CITIES
of
VISION

ROLF JENSEN

B. Arch (Hons. Lvpl), B.E. Adel., F.R.I.B.A.,
F.R.T.P.I., F.R.A.I.A., F.R.A.P.I., M.Inst.R.E.

Dean, Faculty of Architecture and Town Planning
The University of Adelaide, South Australia

A HALSTED PRESS BOOK

JOHN WILEY & SONS
NEW YORK—TORONTO

PUBLISHED IN THE U.S.A. AND CANADA BY
HALSTED PRESS
A DIVISION OF JOHN WILEY & SONS, INC., NEW YORK

Library of Congress Cataloging in Publication Data
Jensen, Rolf.
  Cities of vision.
  "A Halsted Press book"
  Bibliography: p.
  1. Cities and towns—Planning—1945. I. Title.
HT166.J45   309.2'62   73–18279
ISBN 0-470-44191-7

WITH 201 ILLUSTRATIONS

© APPLIED SCIENCE PUBLISHERS LTD 1974

Printed in Great Britain by Galliard (Printers) Ltd Great Yarmouth

To my wife
Elfrida
and my sons
Peter
and
Rodney

Preface

In the pages which follow, the intention has been to try to bring clarity where, at present, complexity increasingly confounds or confuses. It has also been the purpose to argue a logical philosophy in relation to the city of the future; to its form, organisation and design.

Emphasis is laid on the importance—at one time generally recognised—of the city as a humane habitat, in which the architect–planner is restored to his uniquely creative, integrative rôle.

Without these ingredients there can be no real city, just a mere aggregation of parts, or, more often, simply chaos.

The writer makes a plea for a restored sense of perspective and balance, fired by a spirit of imagination, as the only means of ensuring that contemporary preoccupation with technology does not submerge creative efforts to improve the perceivable quality of our environment.

Some of the views expressed may, as yet, find limited acceptance at popular level or, at best, be the subject of mere lip-service. Sooner or later, however, it is certain that much of the argument put forward in this work must form the basis of rational urban planning and design policies if cities are to be retrieved from their present gadarene drive to destruction.

Contents

Acknowledgements

My immense gratitude is due to the very many fellow spirits who, particularly over a lengthy period of recent history, have sought to contribute something worthwhile to one of the major tasks facing civilised Man: that of creating or regenerating pleasurable and efficient urban settlements. From their written work, from their developmental programmes and from discussion, much of unique value has been gained to serve as a starting point for this book.

I am especially grateful to have been allowed to quote from a number of authors and to use various printed illustrations relevant to my text. Unfortunately, these are too numerous to mention individually.

However, special mention is due to the following for permission to use or adapt textual extracts:

J. Gottman, Economics, Aesthetics and Ethics, in *Modern Urbanization*, 20th Century Fund, New York, 1962.

J. Gottman, *Megalopolis*, Macmillan, New York, 1964.

N. Owings, Modern Living, *Time*, 2 August, 1968, Time Life Incorporated.

A. B. Gallion and S. Eisner, *The Urban Pattern*, Van Nostrand-Reinhold, New York, 1950.

C. Sitte, *The Art of Building Cities*, Van Nostrand-Reinhold, New York, 1945.

L. Halprin, *Cities*, Van Nostrand-Reinhold, New York, 1963.

E. Carritt, *The Theory of Beauty*, Associated Book Publishers, London, 1949.

E. Bacon, *Design of Cities*, Thames & Hudson, London, Viking Press, N.Y., 1967.

Jane Jacobs, *The Death and Life of Great American Cities*, Random House Inc. Alfred A. Knopf Inc., New York, 1961.

M. Meyerson, *Face of the Metropolis*, Random House Inc. Alfred A. Knopf Inc., New York, 1963.

M. C. Branch, *Planning Aspects and Applications*, Wiley, New York, 1966.

J. E. Burchard, The Urban Aesthetic, *Annals of the American Academy of Political and Social Science*, Philadelphia, November, 1957.

D. Crane, The Public Art of City Building, *Annals of the American Academy of Political and Social Science*, Philadelphia, March, 1964.

R. L. Meier, *Science and Economic Development*, MIT Press, Cambridge, Mass., 1956.

A. Rapoport and R. E. Kantor, Complexity and Ambiguity in Environmental Design, *AIP Journal*, July, 1967, American Institute of Planners.

D. Durden and D. Marble, The Role of Theory in Central Business District Planning, *AIP Journal*, February, 1961, American Institute of Planners.

S. M. Sherman, On Forming and Reforming Towns and Cities, *AIP Journal*, May, 1963, American Institute of Planners.

Green, Lowe and Walker (editors), *Man and the Modern City*, University of Pittsburgh Press, 1963.

L. Mumford, *The Urban Prospect*, Martin Secker & Warburg, London, 1956.

L. Mumford, *The Myth of the Machine*, Martin Secker & Warburg, London, 1967.

L. Mumford, *The City in History*, Harcourt Brace, New York, 1961.

Wingo (editor), *Cities and Space*, Johns Hopkins Press, Baltimore, 1963.
H. Carver, *Cities in the Suburbs*, Toronto University Press, 1962.
R. C. Weaver, *The Dilemma of Urban America*, Harvard University Press, Cambridge, Mass., 1965.
C. Abrams, *The City is the Frontier*, Harper & Row, New York, 1965.
R. Vernon, *The Changing Economic Function of the Central City*, Committee for Economic Development, New York, 1959.
J. Scott, *Journal of the Royal Town Planning Institute*, March, 1969.
J. Hochberg, *Perception*, Prentice-Hall, New York, 1964.
R. Moses, Are Cities Dead? *Atlantic Monthly*, January, 1962.
K. Lynch, in *Principles and Practice of Urban Planning*, International City Management Association, Washington, 1968.
J. Abercrombie, Design Methods in Architecture, *Arena*, February, 1968, Interbuild.
T. L. Blair and E. Leach, *Official Architecture and Planning*, February, 1969, Built Environment.
Checklist for Cities, Committee on Urban Design, American Institute of Architects, January, 1968.
L. Halprin, Motation, *Progressive Architecture*, July, 1965.
Exterior Volume, *Progressive Architecture*, June, 1965.
The New Town and Major Spaces, *Progressive Architecture*, June, 1965.
What Kind of City Do We Want? *The Nation's Cities,* Washington, April, 1967.
The Threatened City, Report of City of New York Mayor's Task Force, 1967.

Acknowledgement is due to the following for permission to use figures:

1 Brazilian Consulate, Sydney.
3 Bauen & Wohnen, Munich.
5 British Tourist Authority, London.
7 Hamburg City Planning Department.
8 Central Office of Information, London.
10 Philadelphia City Planning Commission.
11 KLM Aerocarto b.v., The Hague.
12 Crowell-Collier Publishing Co., New York.
14 Bureau Voorlichting en Publiciteit, Amsterdam and KLM.
15 Importhuis Gebr., Rotterdam.
16 Hamburg City Planning Department.
21 Japan Information Service, Sydney.
22 Los Angeles Goals Council.
23 US Information Service and Welton Becket.
24 Sakakura Associates, Tokyo.
25 'URBANISTICA', Turin.
28 Stockholm City Planning Department.
29 'l'ARCHITECTURE d'AUJOURD'HUI', Paris and Sam Lambert, London.
30 Nippon Beauty Card Centre Inc., Tokyo.
31 National Capital Development Commission, Canberra.
32 National Capital Development Commission, Canberra.
33 Cogetom, Paris and H. Baranger.
34 British Overseas Airways Corporation, London.
35 P. Ledermann, Vienna.
36 Central Office of Information, London.
38 Government of India Tourist Office, Sydney.
43 Port of New York Authority and A. Belva.
44 'FORUM VERLAG', Vienna.
48 Philadelphia City Planning Commission.
49 Cheng Ho-Choy, Hong Kong.
50 'l'ARCHITECTURE d'AUJOURD'HUI', Paris and Wurster, Bernardi & Emmons, San Francisco.
51 Stockholm City Planning Department.
52 Urban Renewal Department, Housing and Development Board, Singapore.
54 Canadian High Commission, Canberra.
57 'NATION'S CITIES', Washington.
59 British Tourist Authority, London.
62 H. Seidler, Sydney.
63 Qantas Airways.
66 ENIT, Rome.
68 Hamburg City Planning Department.
70 Crowell-Collier Publishing Co., New York.
74 Central Office of Information, London.

75 Thames & Hudson Ltd., London, ARTEMIS, Zurich and Panda Associates, Toronto.
77 Thames & Hudson Ltd., London, ARTEMIS, Zurich and Strüwing, Copenhagen.
79 Tokyo Metropolitan Government.
80 TWA
81 US Information Service, Sydney.
82 Central Office of Information, London.
83 Canadian High Commission, Canberra.
85 Central Office of Information, London.
88 Ministry of Reconstruction, Paris.
89 Qantas Airways.
90 University of California Press.
91 British Tourist Authority, London.
92 ENIT, Rome.
93 Greater London Council.
94 Greater London Council.
96 'l'ARCHITECTURE d'AUJOURD'HUI', Paris and Studio Orop.
97 EPAD, Paris.
99 H. Seidler, Sydney.
100 Clarke, Gazzard Pty. Ltd., Sydney.
101 Central Office of Information, London.
105 Edition's 'CHANTAL', Paris.
111 'JAPAN ILLUSTRATED', Tokyo.
115 Aerofilms and Aeropictorial Ltd, London.
116 Nakladatelsvi Pressfoto, Prague.
117 British Tourist Authority, London.
119 British Overseas Airways Corporation, London.
120 Hanover City Planning Department.
121 Urban Renewal Department, Housing and Development Board, Singapore.
122 Hamburg City Planning Department.
123 Thames & Hudson Ltd, London, ARTEMIS, Zurich and Jane Doggett and Malcolm Smith, New Canaan.
125 Intourist.
126 US Information Service, Sydney.
127 Cheng Ho-Choy, Hong Kong.
128 Tuna Kartpostal, Istanbul.
129 Stockholm City Planning Department.
130 Austrian National Tourist Office, Sydney.
131 'JAPAN ILLUSTRATED', Tokyo.

134 US Information Service, Sydney.
137 Ministry of Public Buildings and Works, London.
140 Hamburg City Planning Department.
141 Singapore High Commission, Canberra.
144 Hilton Hotel, Amsterdam, and 'GOING DUTCH'.
145 National Capital Development Commission, Canberra.
146 EPAD, Paris.
148 National Tourist Organisation of Greece, Athens.
151 Hanover City Planning Department.
152 Hamburg City Planning Department.
153 Stockholm City Planning Department.
157 Central Office of Information, London.
158 British Tourist Authority, London.
159 National Tourist Organisation of Greece, Athens.
162 National Capital Development Commission, Canberra.
163 Crowell-Collier Publishing Co., New York.
165 Crowell-Collier Publishing Co., New York.
166 Historic Urban Plans, Ithaca, N.Y.
168 French Embassy, Canberra.
170 E. D. Khazravi, Isfahan.
171 Columbia University Press.
174 Qantas Airways.
175 US Information Service, Sydney.
176 US Information Service, Sydney.
177 John W. Reps, Cornell University, Ithaca, N.Y.
178 Crowell-Collier Publishing Co., New York.
179 US Information Service, Sydney.
180 Senator for Building and Housing, Berlin, and Reinhard Friedrich.
182 Princeton University Press, N.J.
183 'URBANISTICA', Turin.
184 Qantas Airways.
185 KLM Aerocarto b.v., The Hague.
191 Hungarian Tourist Office, London.
193 US Information Service, Sydney.
195 Rockefeller Centre, Inc., N.Y.
196 Qantas Airways.
197 Qantas Airways.
200 US Information Service, Sidney.
Frontispiece: Exportad Pty Ltd.

Needless to say, the views expressed in this work are, in all cases, my own, for which I accept full responsibility.

List of Figures

Chapter I

Introduction and hypothesis

Today's cities are in a serious plight. That they are in urgent need of help no one would deny. Uncontrolled noise, air and water pollution, inconvenience, discomfort, congestion, traffic dangers, visual assaults and a lack of any evident sense of order are just some of the symptoms of the malaise afflicting them.

That these conditions can exist in civilised communities is surely an indictment of the most serious kind, whether such conditions arise from apathy, inefficiency, or a collective unwillingness to learn from experience and apply the lessons thus learned in a practical manner.

Whether we simply retreat into an admission that we do not have more efficient ways of governing our affairs so as to assure a decent, humane environment as an automatic by-product in our cities, or whether, because of the impact of other issues and interests, we have become genuinely unaware of the urban squalor and untidiness which so frequently surrounds us, is immaterial.

These cities, it must be accepted, are here to stay and, unless some natural disaster or unforeseen cataclysm overtakes them, we must conclude that they are likely to continue to grow and proliferate in number. Certainly there can be no question of abandoning our cities, as some have quite seriously advocated!

Notwithstanding the analogy that certain of today's scientists claim to make between rats and urban Man, the present situation cannot continue if we are to retain any claim to our self-designation, *homo sapiens*.

Rather than, therefore, continuing to exist among the squalor, degradation and ugliness of our cities, if the will and the means which have made interplanetary travel a practical possibility can be directed to the more immediate problems of this planet, then, surely, it can be assumed that civilised beings, who, in most other respects, can normally be shown to enjoy and prefer a sense of order and who demonstrate a degree of sensibility in direct proportion to their degree of civilisation and cultural development, will do something, individually and collectively, to rectify matters.

Perhaps we may take as our starting point here the assumption that there are enough people who care, who will insist on seeing that the present decline in the city is halted by one means or another, and who are convinced that such means exist if collective action can be taken and the will to take it is strong enough.

Only through a process of increasing awareness can the will be implanted on a wide enough scale to ensure that remedial action is undertaken without further delay. The sort of action that is undoubtedly needed is of the kind which led a former President of the United States to create special machinery and a Cabinet-level appointment to deal with the problem of cities, and the present President to make such an appointment his first responsibility after his election. If some feel that the present situation in our cities is all but hopeless, their feelings could well be a continuation of that movement which led to the creation of the garden cities and, subsequently, the New Towns, and which arose from an understandable reaction against the cities of the industrial revolution era.

Turning our backs on these social misfortunes has, however, never appeared to answer the need, especially as we have little or no guarantee, in an age of *laissez-faire*, that the same sad story of the older cities will not be repeated in the New Towns.

There is little to convince us that they *will* be any different unless, in the meantime, we discover the secret of how to guide and control the development of the older cities in a beneficial way for all concerned.

It has also been suggested that the present-day phenomenon of the flight from the cities forms a part, at least, of the impetus to reach new planets. Perhaps, if we continue to foul our earthly urban nest as we are doing at the present time there will be no other alternative but to colonise other planets. If we also continue, at the same time, in the belief that we can absorb indefinitely increasing areas of this planet for new urban developments, such extra-terrestrial colonisation may seem a logical conclusion!

We are reminded of Krushchev's first visit to the United States and his trip down one of the urban freeways at peak travel time, when he commented that at least he could now understand the haste of the Americans to reach the moon.

We cannot, however, put the urban clock back to the days of the rural Utopia for all—our highly-developed and sophisticated commercial and industrial system and our complex socio-economic relationships render this quite impracticable. The inroads we are already making on our vital metropolitan recreation 'lungs' and food-growing areas, in the absurd pretence that suburbs can be rural communities, is both suicidal and misplaced.

This process cannot continue, since, even on the great continents of North America and Australia, all too little of those precious areas immediately adjoining the cities, for which there is no alternative or substitute, remains to be absorbed.

More and more people are moving into cities and this process will inevitably continue. Civilised countries have settled for an urban life apparently as a matter of choice—now we must see that the cities are replanned and revitalised and all the causes of discomfort and inconvenience removed, as they can be.

In order to undertake these tasks effectively and soon, we need, amongst other things, not only determination and the allocation of funds as a top priority in national budgets, but also trained, experienced and *imaginative* planners, as well as career professional politicians. This combination of people and conditions could undoubtedly achieve results where, today, little can any longer be expected from the untrained part-time amateurs at government and local government level, or from the professional services at their present mediocre level.

It is entirely illogical to most thinking people that cities in highly-developed and civilised communities, with advanced cultural levels and attainments, can become such an affront to the visual and other senses and that the organised assault of traffic, with its concomitant noise and pollution, continues unabated. At the same time the city is under continued economic attack from the dispersionists and the decentralists, inevitably leading to a further undermining of its structure.

Perhaps for too long we have heeded the arguments that the city, as it exists, is incapable of improvement; or, alternatively, all that can be expected will be through the negative approach implied by the application of statutes, bye-laws, regulations and the like, although, only too clearly, in spite of the application of such remedies, the ailing city continues to suffer.

If for no other reason, the need for political, social and economic survival should suggest, as a matter of extreme urgency, the necessity of putting our cities in order—even though this problem becomes ever vaster as the years go by. Nothing less than the type of programme being devised for space travel, or applied to wartime emergencies, is required and nothing less than this can be expected to achieve worthwhile results.

Unless the construction of New Towns and cities—which is preoccupying many people to the exclusion of all else—is required as a means of dealing with population overspills from existing cities or of getting urban renewal programmes underway, it should be halted until the priority task of dealing with existing cities has been effectively carried through.

The quixotic prodigality of leaving existing cities to deteriorate still further, while, at the same time starting the whole unenlightened process afresh by building new cities by negative regulation is hardly worthy of serious support and, moreover, a staggering drain on the resources which should be concentrated where the need is paramount—namely, in the established city cores.

The social chaos and disruption at present taking place in a number of countries is likely to continue until the necessary remedial treatment is applied to the wound itself, instead of to some remote part of the regional body.

No longer can urban programmes and policies be dictated primarily by past history, but rather must the future inevitabilities of continued growth and decline be seen clearly, as well as the vital importance of halting this process through constructive planning programmes.

Such programmes must make a new and fundamental approach to the overall problem of planning cities and the absurdly trite stereotypes—particularly of the last twenty-five years—must be rejected as entirely unsuitable models for future urban environments.

Even the totalitarian approach presented by Brasilia (Fig. 1) and Chandigarh (Fig. 2) for example, follows an entirely conventional disposition of land-use and physical development, motivated by two-dimensional compartmentalisation theories. In place of this, however, something as radical as the thinking underlying the Japanese metabolists' proposals (Fig. 3) is required, although applied in a way that shows a much greater recognition of the need to plan for the future, with a continuity from the present, in all renewal operations.

In outlining the hypothesis forming the basis of this work, the first point that must be made is that means can be found to achieve an orderly visual environment in the city, while, at the same time, maintaining the widest possible variety of treatment with individual buildings, thus avoiding a too-stereotyped overall appearance. This process may well be described by the familiar formula of diversity within uniformity, or, alternatively, as guided *laissez-faire*.

It is further believed that, with the attainment of a satisfactory visual environment, a more compact, lively city is also a practical possibility—this without, in any way, implying unwanted congestion. In order to achieve this ideal, a consistent policy of concentration needs to be pursued throughout the city, such as has already been postulated elsewhere by the present writer for urban housing developments.

Uncontrolled *laissez-faire* or piecemeal development cannot possibly provide (as is to be seen at the present time in so many cities) a unified whole, and has little prospect of creating many of the city-wide advantages and attributes only possible with truly comprehensive and cohesive development with a benign overall form of control.

It is becoming increasingly clear that flight from the city or policies of dispersal cannot be expected to contribute to the solution of this problem and, rather than effecting a cure for the undesirable aspects of city life, tend, with the removal of the urban cancer, to eliminate also some of the vital organs of the city structure, such as inevitably spells their death-knell.

Many contemporary cities, zoned on a two-dimensional set of land-use packages, can now be seen to have lost certain of the desirable qualities and vitality of earlier traditional models and to have become impossibly inconvenient to use.

A satisfying visual environment must be seen as the ultimate achievement for which all city planners, from whatever specialisation or discipline, need to strive. Only the attainment of this quality can justify the continued existence of the city as we know it.

Well-tried techniques of city planning and control have proved ineffectual in achieving the desirable environmental character, mainly because they are negative and cautionary, rather than positive and creative. New techniques are urgently overdue and, it is believed, are now available as a means of providing cities which are at least equal, in visual impact and environmental quality, to some of the fine earlier examples.

As one of the initial practical measures all the elements tending to disrupt city life at the present time, or to mar its more positive attributes, must be eradicated in conjunction with enlightened renewal programmes. This measure would be the first major step towards halting urban decline.

A return to beauty in the city—a quality evident in some of the best historic examples —is by no means inconsistent with efficient functioning to meet today's and tomorrow's needs; always provided that an approach involving mere eclecticism is firmly shunned.

Meeting the stated goals requires considerable changes in the political and administrative machinery concerned with every aspect of city planning and development, at every level, since, otherwise, no significant results can be expected. This will involve, in many cases, new or streamlined legislation and plenipotentiary planning powers, wielded by trained specialists at executive, professional and administrative levels.

Finally, it is intended to show that negative policing rules, embodied in planning or building legislation, will never produce beautiful cities and may seriously inhibit worthwhile contributions to such an overall objective.

Nothing short of creative, positive judgement and guidance is likely to achieve the desired ends, and this is only practicable with trained, experienced master planners, endowed with more than usual taste, judgement and powers of perception—as well as the patience and foresight to work within an extended time-scale without a consequent loss of a sense of continuity.

The only satisfactory answer to fragmentation, disunity or chaos in our cities is a workable system of coordination through a master mind. All the experiences and efforts directed towards city development, particularly in the last fifty years, have demonstrated quite clearly that rules-of-thumb, intended to be applied by bureaucratic automata, have failed lamentably, and any fresh attempts to generate more positive results through similar techniques are also doomed to failure.

Systems analysis, operations research and all attempts to produce rational methodologies, while at best playing a valuable part in assisting in the creation of a substructure for the city, must inevitably fall far short of the essential creative act required to produce a humane environment. It was neither the plumbers, nor the engineers, the surveyors or the economists who provided the physical entity of the traditional city we admire, but the architect in his extended capacity as an urban designer. Recognition of this fact and the revival of this form of machinery is likely to be the surest method of creating the livable city of the future, rather than the mechanistic urbanism which otherwise seems to be our destiny.

The cities of vision, to which we should aspire, would thus become the creative masterpieces of enlightened individuals, endowed with foresight; as well as a reversion to urban areas with a highly-developed visual emphasis as the essential prerequisite for the habitat of urban Man.

Chapter II

New directions in city planning and design

It is a regrettable fact that we have yet to create or experience a city which, in any substantial way, measures up to contemporary needs. Nor have the increasing numbers of urban dwellers been able to enjoy a really fine modern city—indeed one that even begins to use our knowledge and experience in urban planning and design. So far we have yet to see a city which has been planned specifically for the pedestrian, and particularly for those who prefer to walk to work.

We have not yet experienced the pleasures of a city planned to take full advantage of the opportunities of building high and compactly; nor of a city where full utilisation of the centre at high density allows those who prefer low density to enjoy it relatively close to the city. There are few, if any, modern cities whose best central locations are not cluttered with obsolete and inadequate old buildings which should have been replaced long ago—buildings that continue in occupation only because urban decay is now subsidised by under-assessing and under-taxing obsolescent properties.

Few in our generation have seen a city where busy streets are not choked with parked or moving cars, or where the air is clean enough to breathe and the water fit to swim in. Rarely do we find a city that provides plenty of usable open space for recreation where it is most needed and where children, particularly, can play safely out of doors reasonably close to home—or without leaving their own building. Yet it is a fact that, with present-day technology, such a city would cost much less to live and work in than the obsolete urban sprawls occupied by so many people today.

These comments can be applied with equal justification to most of the cities of the world. Certainly the objectives and goals of the good city, which we should now be able to expect as we progress towards the twenty-first century, are applicable in almost any country. They are objectives and aspirations with which no one could possibly quarrel, and yet how rarely are they being achieved!

It has been argued that nobody can be really satisfied with the form of the modern city, and that neither as a working mechanism, nor as a social medium or a work of art does it fulfil the high hopes that modern civilisation has nurtured for it.

It is also true that the city is necessarily a collective product and one that can never be regarded as completed. It is the medium for Man's artistic endeavour and the visual framework within which he lives. Increasingly, however, it is an inhuman environment. Accordingly, the city is the major aesthetic problem confronting us—but, even more, it is the problem of the politics of aesthetics. The methods whereby the aesthetic quality we desire in a city can be attained is a crucial question to which more space will be devoted later.

Putting the whole seriousness of the problem of ordering and reorganising our cities —so as to make them places fit for people to live and work in—into better perspective,

6

the *World Health Organisation*[231] has recently emphasised that the tremendous in-crease in urban populations clearly justifies the warning that, after the question of keeping world peace, metropolitan planning is probably the most serious single problem faced by Man in the second half of the twentieth century. We can add the cautionary comment that maintaining human values in the solution of this particular problem is far and away the other most important objective and one to which, even at the present time, scant attention is being paid. Only if we can remember this can we hope to find an answer to the charge that while we are irretrievably and inescapably heading towards an urban world, on present indications it may not be a world worth living in.

Lyndon Johnson underlined the problem, shared by other world cities, when he said, 'It is harder and harder to live the good life in American cities. There is the decay of the centres and the despoiling of the suburbs. . . . Our society will never be great until our cities are great'.[176] In historical times cities were great only when the communities that created them were a positive force, and where the form of the city was a direct reflection of the degree of enlightenment of the whole community.

We have only to reflect, very briefly, on the place of the city in the national economy to realise that, in this age of ever-increasing industrialisation, the city is, in a very real way, the economic and social core of national life and it is here that the whole impetus towards national development must be initiated, however important the rural com-munity and its products. A healthy urban core implies, in turn, the means of assuring a sound metropolitan and regional strategy and, ultimately, a firmly-based national planning policy.

In setting about this task we must remember that urban development implies a continuing responsibility, with all forces acting together and interdependently. The degree to which these forces are integrated reflects the aspirations, ambitions and convictions of an entire community, and the initiative and sense of responsibility of its people at whatever level they are manifested. When the forces that contribute to city building become unbalanced, inequities develop and the city declines; its collective energy is undermined and it no longer encourages sound and continuing business investment, while the total environment degenerates. This imbalance is one of the significant symptoms of present urban development activity where such activity occurs; and coincidently, and more particularly, where there is an absence of due regard for the renewal of desirable aesthetic standards.

It is only too apparent that, in such circumstances, the drab, uninspiring appearance of our cities approaches almost inhuman ugliness. This prevalent malaise can only be due to the lack of a virile artistic tradition in our present day society which has dulled our awareness of the visual decadence of our surroundings.

In offering some practical suggestions as to ways in which this aspect of our urban problems may be tackled it is emphasised that there are two spheres in which the public could directly assist. One is in the public domain proper—the significant part of a city area in the form of streets, pedestrian areas, parks and civic reserves. These provide broad scope for the creative treatment of space arrangement, landscaping, street furniture, lighting, signs and structures.

The other area of activity relates to public regulation of three-dimensional volumes as an expression of community design. This involves the integrated use of land, open space, landscape, buildings—with due regard to uniformity in the design of façades—advertising media, ingress and egress for pedestrians and vehicles and the provision of public rights of way. Close concern with the formulation of such regulations may accomplish some useful results without resort to judgements involving taste. In the final analysis, however, the creation of beauty is the result of determination, as well as the employment of the necessary talent to produce such beauty. This, it is argued, demands the cultivation of cultural values.

While a city consists of more than buildings, streets, services, steel, concrete and glass, these are, nevertheless, the basic raw materials of the physical structure. They are static by nature and tend to be quite inelastic. Once in place they cannot readily be moved to suit either fancy or changing conditions, in spite of 'plug-in-city'* notions or some of the more dramatic engineering feats which have been carried out from time to time. The width of the street cannot fluctuate in accordance with the volume of traffic, nor are buildings, in practice, to any extent really flexible, so that, if viewed critically, the often-made analogy of the city to a 'living organism' is pure fantasy.

As has already been pointed out, moreover, it is becoming ever clearer that, whatever the direction taken in the search for a new urban form and however persistent the lobby in favour of decentralisation, the idea of the city must always be paramount. The complex and manifold urban functions may be reorganised or restructured, but the basic elements of the city must always remain. The commercial and social institutions upon which our communities depend for both spiritual and physical progress are of fundamental importance and, even though the traditional advantages of the city have often been exploited anti-socially, or simply allowed to lie fallow, they are rendered no less important.

It is essential to be continually alert to the fact that democracy in city building provides the scope within which the multiple functions of contemporary urban life may be accommodated with a considerable degree of freedom of expression. Such freedom in organised society, as we must come to realise, implies self-discipline and respect for the dignity of others.

Building laws not only permit, but have practically forced, enormous building volumes and bulk to be loaded on to sites. Thus the city has been reduced to a network of streets and pavements, lined with the façades of unrelated buildings. In such circumstances architectural mediocrity and chaos are almost inevitable. The right to build as one wishes has become an abuse of licence, and has made some form of architectural control an inevitability. Such control is, of course, far from being the sole answer to the problem, unless the techniques of control provide for the maximum degree of flexibility in operation and are accompanied by constructive forms of appraisal.

Because the form of the city is always changing as it responds to the creative endeavours of many people attempting to give concrete form to their spatial needs, accommodation and movement patterns, the city is in a continuous state of flux and its planning must be flexible enough to accommodate a variety of forms. The harmonious integration of these varied forms is the art of planning urban areas. It is here,

* Term used by 'Archigram' group in Britain to express ultimate in urban flexibility.

in establishing an effective method for dealing with the contributions of a 'thousand designers' that the whole essence of the problem of urban design lies.

In a worthy attempt to illuminate the problems posed, and referring to constructive attempts to meet the needs of the consciously-ordered urban core, a recent publication by the *American Institute of Architects*[211] describes urban design as, 'the form given to the solution of the city's problems', and points out that it is, 'the professional process that finds practical answers to these problems', wherein the 'answers take physical shape: the shape of the city itself'. The best solutions, therefore, are creative; combining delight and utility; evolving beauty from function. Urban design is thus, in consequence, 'neither esoteric nor purely aesthetic'.

This perceptive and authoritative statement also makes the plea: 'the time has come to put urban design into practice through a wider partnership of concern in cities throughout the country—through each architect and environmental designer, through local government, and through an interested citizenry'. Urban beauty is, it is pointed out, 'more difficult to programme as a specific and attainable end in itself. Consequently reliance on urban design as a term-defining process, as well as end product, is recommended'.

In what can be described as an exceedingly timely document, reference is made to a 'checklist of factors which articulate the evolving form of the city'. This is the 'form which constitutes the design as an end product, which may be appraised qualitatively, in whole and in its component parts, as to its aesthetic merit or demerit and its responsiveness to our needs'. Thus it is that, 'first, it will reveal how these factors interrelate to make up the form of the city—"the urban design"—and second, as an action-oriented framework, it will reveal the decision-making process by which the form of the city is actually determined'.

The need for the environmental design professions of architect, planner, engineer and landscape architect is stressed 'to accomplish qualitative appraisals of urban form; to make known the results of such professional appraisals and to initiate and encourage the mobilisation of public and private urban forces to take corrective actions indicated by these appraisals'.

However, a warning is given that, at the present juncture, so far as the United States is concerned, over the nation as a whole there is a grossly insufficient pool of environmental design professionals to meet the need. This holds good, unfortunately, in very many other countries faced with similar problems.

In a reference to the need to ensure that the necessary strategies must recognise social, economic and political realities within each community, we are reminded that, 'our cities do not suffer so much from ugly design as from non-design. The first aim, therefore, must be to incorporate design into the decision-making process that shapes our urban environment and to incorporate it from the very beginning of this process'. This should then, in time, 'remedy the chaotic happenstance which pervades the urban scene and which is perhaps the chief contributor to urban ugliness'.

It is emphasised that the form of the urban environment—the city and its segments—should give evidence that it is deliberately designed, guided and co-ordinated by urban Man. Design need not violate the requirements of variety and flexibility which must accommodate future changes. By comparison the evidence in our present urban environment is often of 'rational but unrelated pieces grouped into an irrational and formless whole'. In contrast, 'the ideal behind a rational design process is that it creates coherence and unity within a physical environment, while providing for variety and choice; for flexibility, and for responsiveness to the needs of each of us'.

The objective of urban design, it is clear, is to produce physical forms and systems that are rational, coherent and responsive to the needs and expectations of those who use them. Above all, its highest achievement must be the creation of an aesthetic quality in the environment able to give satisfaction to all.

It is obviously one of the working parameters that until radical changes are brought about, much of the physical development in our cities is regulated by government, through planning regulations such as zoning, and through building codes and other devices which directly influence the forms produced. These are however, in general, entirely negative and non-creative, and must in the course of time yield to more flexible systems.

We therefore have to recognise that, in substituting desirable levels of urban design for non-design, we shall need to be concerned not least with an enlightened administrative process.

It is extraordinary to reflect that, with so many examples of beautiful old cities which still exist, the urban creation of Man has reached such a parlous condition, more especially when we recall that, long before significant cultural developments had taken place, nature had provided Man with a series of prototypes of creativity, in which chance gave way to organisation and organisation reflected needs and priorities.

It is very difficult, in a great many modern cities, to see the obvious evidences of such guidance and even less any confirmation that Man really prefers to express himself 'through the creative arts or through the medium of constructive organisation; the deliberate forming of patterns, or the comprehensive and comprehensible establishment of order'.[139] It is rarely evident that this principle is in any obvious way basic to either civilised society or to planned development, any more than it is easy to see the creative order and meaning which should be expected from deep seated and fundamental human needs.

Unfortunately, formalistic order has now largely been supplanted by mechanical order, but even this has been accompanied by a contemporary revolt by the younger generation against the machine, and, even worse, a hankering after a general state of disorder and complexity which has itself become a type of conformity.

Perhaps, then, it is not altogether surprising that earlier formalisms and an older pattern of conformity have tended to yield, certainly in most of the arts, to a new philosophy based on what often appears to be a deliberate policy of complexity and confusion. In city building, however, this complexity and lack of order is already an accidental and abiding manifestation and our only hope is that formalistic order may be restored as the basis of a constructive organisation, and the concrete evidence of a positive application of creativity on a macro-scale.

Only in this way can we hope to restore a situation such as that where historical cities 'expressed a visible unity which bound together even the more complex forms into the total life of the community; and where the face and form of the cities still recorded that which was desirable, memorable, admirable'.

We must recognise a fact, already increasingly recognised by many, that 'neither architect nor planner can alone from the background of their own professional skills generate the conditions necessary for building or recreating satisfactory urban communities'. Nevertheless, it is to be hoped that their influence, training and experience in these matters will be felt throughout the operation, involving at various stages many other groups, professions and institutions.

It is all the more regrettable, therefore, that all too little collaborative effort is to be seen in many current proposals and projects for further urban 'improvement' which, almost inevitably, tend to follow a mechanistic pattern: through the process of carving new expressways into the city, and the associated parking garages, both above and underground. Covering entire urban areas with a geodesic dome has even been seriously suggested.[138] So long as the main human functions and purposes of the city are ignored these techniques and systems, which should be the means to an end, tend to dominate the whole concept of the city.

It is a part of the restoration of balance and perspective we are currently facing that, while of late an immense amount of literature on cities has appeared, it frequently consists of economic and social analyses of limited scope, dealing with many and varied aspects of urban life, some significant, others less so. Most of these studies have been entirely lacking in any appreciation whatsoever of architectural implications and rarely of the historic evolution of a city.

Unfortunately it is a fact that 'the effect of this literature has been to clarify the economic and technical processes in western urban society but from the standpoint of the architect and city planner such analysis would be useful only if it were directed to a formative idea of the city: where such an idea of the city is precisely what is lacking'.[138]

The term 'idea' in this context is synonymous with 'image'. It is thus relevant that: 'current proposals for city improvement are so imageless that city planning schools in America for the last half-generation have been turning out mainly administrators, statisticians, economists, and traffic experts'.[138] Parallel processes can also be traced in which, sadly, trends in America have too often had a direct effect on unquestioning thoughts and ideas in other countries.

At a time when it is all too abundantly obvious that the visual aspects of the city are being almost entirely neglected, or going by default in so many countries, it was alarming to be informed recently, in Los Angeles, that the City Planning Authority was employing no more architects—who surely must be the prime contributors to a visual urban environment—but that, 'instead, social scientists would be employed in future'.

In Great Britain the position is hardly different since, over the years, architects and planners in government and local government have worked under immense difficulties and restrictions and, too often, under the inhibiting influences of the Treasury or legal and administrative departments, as well as, in some instances, in the purely technologically-oriented engineers' departments.

Recent recommendations, which will inevitably lead to the production of even fewer qualified architect-planners, due to deflection of government funds into the social sciences fields, will aggravate the urban problem and ensure that the visually trained urbanist or environmentalist will have even less executive power and responsibility than hitherto.

In considering some of the reasons why we so rarely achieve satisfactory standards of urban design in our city centres and some of the ways in which we may hope to rectify this situation, we should reflect that urban design, architecture, and, to some extent, landscape architecture, are 'inescapable and the only arts that cannot be avoided'[131] in contrast, for example, to painting, sculpture, music or literature. We are, moreover, 'patrons of urban design, whether we like it or not, in our role as voters and taxpayers', and yet, too often, we pay little heed to our responsibilities or interests and appear unconcerned about the kind of urban design we have.

Perhaps the real fact of the matter is that the enlightened members of the public at least are patiently awaiting results in the belief that the best and the most professionally competent city planning professionals have been systematically undertaking the necessary studies and enquiries so as to provide a logical relationship between human needs and patterns of development. Sadly, however, the truth is that any such expectation is entirely at variance with the facts, as anyone familiar with the actual state of investigations into the creation of a desirable physical environment will be well aware.

Yet this inertia is taking place at a time when the centres of all our big cities are assuming an even more urgent importance. The central city may have discarded some of its functions, transferring them into the suburbs, but in the economy of the big city the nucleus or core must tend to become more concentrated as it becomes more valuable.

It has been suggested that, logically, in the composition of cities two qualities establish form and give it definition. The first quality is that related to order or system, in the disposition or location of the component sections, and the other quality is the almost indefinable one of townscape and the landscaping which create the unique identity of a city, just as other art forms bear the unmistakable stamp of the creative master craftsman responsible for them. These are, indeed, the qualities at which, once again, we should be aiming in the recreation of viable city centres, but which are, unfortunately, all too obviously absent in most modern cities.

It is also undeniably a fact that while, to a certain extent, cities can be explained in engineering terms, there are other aspects of their character that cannot be given such a mechanical explanation. It is particularly true that the places in some of the historic cities which captivate our fancy and remain memorable appear often to have come into being almost by accident (Fig. 4). However there are other similar localities which have, just as clearly, been consciously contrived (Fig. 5).

One of the outstanding problems relative to most central area renaissance operations and well typified by the majority of North American cities going into decline through obsolescence and deterioration, is that a major part of the rehabilitation and renewal work involved necessarily implies rehousing large numbers of occupants of substandard dwellings—from which the original owners have moved out some years earlier into suburban areas.

The whole operation is vast in terms of money and complexity and is not made easier by the overtones of racialism existing in certain parts of the world. Unfortunately these areas have too often become the residential sinks of underprivileged groups, where poverty, squalor and blight are inevitable by-products.

Massive rehousing operations are therefore an essential prerequisite to any reordering or replanning of the central areas of such cities (Figs. 6, 7 and 8), but these, at the same time, provide the potential and the opportunities for developing enlightened forms of high density living, thus creating homes where they are needed, near places of employment, and in a manner that will help much in reviving the city itself.

It becomes abundantly clear, when this matter is examined closely, that the problem of redeveloping and renewing city centres is almost inseparable from that associated with the creation of better forms of urban housing. The one is an essential counterpart of the other, and even those residential areas not actually forming a part of the city centre are affected by the renewal of the core, since their health is mutually sustaining.

A typical example of this sort of operation has taken place in the cities of Pittsburgh (Fig. 9) and Philadelphia (Fig. 10), where it has been claimed that 'men of imagination have reoriented the rather reluctant and desultory programmes of slum clearance into a major renaissance of the hearts of these lively cities'.[37]

It thus becomes apparent that the core of the city is one indivisible composition. Restoration is not just a matter of clearing slums in one place, solving traffic problems in another, or replacing obsolete office buildings in a third. The revival of these city centres during the last decade has given something of new vitality to city planning, if only in a moderate degree, because it has shown the importance of the city core as 'the energy centre' of every urban community. It is the further extension of these at present all too limited cases, involving positive programmes of urban renewal, that is now so desperately needed.

Chapter III

Urban form and structure

While our immediate interest must primarily be with the city centre, this cannot be logically separated from some concern for the metropolis as a whole. Much earlier in history these two terms would have been virtually synonymous, but with the modern city this is less and less the case.

Because the prosperity of the metropolitan area, and, for that matter, of the metropolitan region, are intimately linked with the city, the planning and design of the city must inevitably be tied to that of the larger urban metropolis, of which it is in reality an integral part. It is therefore not possible to give closer consideration to the problem of the city centre, or core, without relating it to its urban context, as many of the changes that have taken place in city centres are the direct result of changes in metropolitan developments, land-use and communications.

Many of the aggravated symptoms of congestion which occurred in the mediaeval city were a direct consequence of its having to grow within the straitjacket of the city wall (Figs. 11 and 12). With the limited building technologies available in those days, leading inevitably to closely packed horizontal forms of development, this process continued until even pedestrian communication became almost impossible.

The next stage involved the disorganised clutter of ill-planned buildings, growing on an *ad hoc* basis outside the city wall, in response to particular local pressures and as land market values and speculation made it feasible, and apparently worthwhile.

This second stage considerably compounded and intensified the original problems of congestion and bad planning, and many of the older cities still retain this legacy, in part at least. This renders the whole process of renewal infinitely more difficult notwithstanding the old-world charm, which, superficially at least, may exist in some of the highways and byways.

Even a major conflagration and nearly 300 years of redevelopment and growth, followed by bombing attacks and a further disastrous fire have not entirely solved this problem in the city of London (Fig. 13). Other cities, such as Rotterdam (Fig. 14) were, perhaps, in retrospect, more fortunate, in being presented with a clean start (Fig. 15). However, the problems associated with the design of the reconstructed, or entirely new city, are, in many ways, not a great deal easier to solve as can be seen from some of the rather sterile treatments given to these rebuilt cities. The lack of a historical continuity and variety must rob any city of one of its potentially most attractive qualities.

In modern cities possibly the most significant elements relating to the form of their development have been those concerned with communications. First the tramcar, then the railway and, subsequently, the motor car, have all had a disruptive effect, both physically in their penetration to, and, in many cases, through, the city centre (Fig. 16); introducing a scale and element entirely at variance with the traditional pedestrian-oriented compact development.

The mobility these forms of transportation provided in turn led to concerted moves away from the city centre and, in the case of the fixed rail systems, along well-directed radial routes; but in relatively compact forms of ribbon development.

Only when the motor vehicle, with its universal mobility, made its appearance was the whole city structure burst wide open and the formless amorphous urban sprawl—which, today, we see as its inevitable consequence in so many western cities—was bound to follow.

How far these changes have affected the city centre is well expressed by Kenzo Tange, who, referring to the contemporary city of ten million, which are the nucleus of contemporary civilisation, has argued that, 'the speed and scale which have been made possible by modern technology, are destroying traditional patterns of spatial order. By contrast, in the Middle Ages, cathedrals and city halls had a mass human scale which was suited to the numbers of people gathered in the open centres, and which harmonised with the human scale of the roads radiating from them' (Fig. 17).[179]

Today, however, huge highways, carrying high speed traffic, have intruded themselves into the old system (Fig. 18). 'They represent a super-human scale. The centripetal hierarchy of the cities of the Middle Ages will no longer serve, for it represents an order determined by the fact man walked on his own two feet. In the moving, flowing cities of our time pedestrian traffic and automobile traffic intersect, and the direction of both is variable. Movement is not closed and centripetal but open and fluctuating'.

It is therefore clearly necessary, while organising the city in such a way as to give order to the various levels of urban space—from private to public—to arrange these spaces in a clear pattern within the urban structure. The telephone, the radio, television, the portable telephone, the video-telephone—all these indirect means of communication will doubtless continue to develop and to cause changes in the social system and in the structure of life. However, it is beyond the bounds of possibility that the need for, and the wish to have, direct communication between human beings, and, in turn, the close and intimate link with human activities, will diminish in any degree simply because of the availability of technical aids.

Transportation, which makes direct communication possible, is therefore a vital part of the basic physical foundation of the city. It is the arterial system which helps preserve the life and human drive of the city; it can be likened to an essential part of the nervous system which links with the brain. The requirements of mobility determine the structure of the city, for good or for ill.

With these reflections Tange has concluded that his task in replanning Tokyo (Fig. 3) involved finding 'a new urban spatial order which will reflect the open organisation and the spontaneous mobility of contemporary society'. Most contemporary planners would be inclined to agree with him about this inseparable relationship between physical development and social needs. Included in this number would be Japanese 'Metabolists', British 'Structuralists' and, in essence, probably most American planning theorists although, in this instance, with the establishment of principles which have led to diametrically opposed systems in practical application.

These conclusions are also consistent with those of Meier who states that: 'after examining human settlements as they emerge from the beginnings of civilisation, following the changes as they might be seen by an archaeologist, historian, anthropologist, or natural scientist, and after considering man's behaviour in cities, looking at human activities, as the economist, social psychologist, human ecologist and political behaviourist might, the one common element in all of these perspectives is human communication—whether viewed in the very concrete terms of market-place transactions or in the more abstract notion of the transmission of culture'.[233]

Undoubtedly the major problem of all the complex and difficult questions confronting the urban planner and designer is the impact of the motor vehicle on the central city area. This is having, in most instances, profound effects, including the removal or displacement of some of the traditionally more important commercial and business interests, as well as many private houses, into outlying areas, and the disruption and dissection of the remaining central area as the motor vehicle attempts to burrow its way into the city (Fig. 19). There are, moreover, the effects created by large parking facilities, either at ground level or in multistorey structures, or even within the basements of buildings, and the arterial road system with which an attempt is made to serve these.

Generally speaking, retail sales have decreased in the core, as evidenced by a wide cross-section of investigations which have taken place in many cities of North America, and, although new office buildings are going up in many city centres, the total provision of office space has decreased on a *per capita* basis. The net effect on property values is that any increment in value on central property is in doubt and may, in fact, not exist. It is, indeed, much more probable that there has been an overall diminution in values where access to the city centre depends on the motor vehicle alone. Only in those cases where rapid transit systems have been introduced is a converse situation likely to occur (Fig. 20).

Urban expressway systems have, of course, played a very considerable part in this decline of central city areas over a period of approximately twenty years. Sad to relate, however, a number of countries other than North America are all too tardily learning the lessons which are there for them to see and are still, in disregard of the evidence, bent on introducing such urban expressway systems on the advice of itinerant consultants.

The expressway, as a regional, inter-urban, inter-city highway, often makes good sense, provided that it is planned with due regard to the areas it intersects and is not, as has all too often been the case, located so as to cut up single properties and seriously damage irreplaceable sections of the natural environment.

This, however, is not to be compared, in so far as the seriousness of its effects is concerned, with the effects the urban expressway has in almost all instances, and it matters little whether this invasion and destruction of the urban structure is rationalised in the form of a 'transportation corridor', or simply effected by means of the more usual crude surgery (Fig. 21).

This is not the place to argue at greater length the incompatibility of the unrestrained use of the motor vehicle and the fabric of a humane, attractive city, designed primarily for pedestrian use and access. The assumption will have to be made that commonsense will prevail, in a sufficiently large number of cities, soon enough for all those involved to see that there can be no possible virtue in attempting to discuss questions of renewal or redevelopment of city centres until the destructive influences of the motor vehicle are curbed, and this modern marvel of mobility relegated to its proper place as a servant of Man, rather than retaining the master role it at present occupies.

The serious decline of central areas has, of course, been greatly accelerated through positive policies of decentralisation, aided to a large extent by the mobility of the motor vehicle. Many business organisations and department stores have taken out insurance policies during this operation in the form of a share in regional and district centre developments.

We cannot, however, have our cake and eat it, and in contemporary circumstances we must recognise that the city will remain as a viable entity only so long as everything possible is done to bolster up its economy. Alternatively, if cities persist in fragmenting and dispersing a vital part of their economic life, this can only have serious and deleterious effects in the long term.

It should only need one Los Angeles to convey the lessons of how deadly such a city centre can be, when its essential purposes become confused with the functions of a metropolitan motor race-track (Fig. 22). At non-peak hours one can certainly travel very rapidly along the Los Angeles expressways but, on arriving at the city centre one finds, as Gertrude Stein pointed out, 'there is no there there', and so the exercise appears entirely without point (Fig. 23).

Usually rather belatedly, certain other American cities are now facing up to these problems in a realisation that accessibility and communication through the medium of the motor vehicle has utterly failed, and that, in consequence, the city is in a serious plight. In some instances action may have been taken just in time to introduce rapid transit and efficient public transport systems (Fig. 24), with a view to retaining some vestiges of the city proper in the more dynamic or attractive downtown centres, as these offer a unique, magnetic quality which is valuable. This, of course, is true not only in terms of real estate but also as regards the physical components of the city and in the contribution they make to the liveliness of the environment.

It has recently been increasingly apparent that American central business districts, for example, will remain, with luck and good planning, as the most interesting, historically and architecturally, of a number of competing centres and that one way by which the urban cores can be kept alive is good planning. Another is by retaining all the governmental and public employment uses in the centre, an idea in direct contrast to policies which have applied in many cities for far too long. These functions will, in turn, support a range of ancillary uses and services, and because the central area is the heart of the urban community and its commercial, civic, social, cultural and psychological centre, it is there that the highest land values, the tallest buildings, the greatest intensity of development will occur. The city centre is, moreover, the nucleus of the city region.

There is little difference in principle between the functions of a modern centre and those of the ancient and mediaeval worlds. Throughout the ages men have flocked to the centres of their communities: to the agora or forum, market-place or plaza (Fig. 25). Man is essentially gregarious and the central area of the city is his meeting place—the place for major shopping, the market-place, a centre for conferences, education, recreation, culture and pleasure. The typical historic centre has a mixture of almost every type of land-use, all clustered together, one above the other, changing according to the slow processes of economic change. This pattern reflects the age-old linkages between different land-uses and the reciprocal relationships between various land-uses.

It is therefore of timely interest that one of the most significant changes in European planning practice, manifesting itself in urban renewal and reconstruction projects, is the restoration of multiple land-use to its earlier place in city design (Fig. 26). In a revolt against the indiscriminate, chaotic and often obnoxious and incompatible mixtures of urban land-uses which became common after the industrial revolution and which sometimes extended well into the twentieth century, planners in recent decades have been inclined to go to the other extreme of excessively orderly land use segregation.

Now planners recognise increasingly that some land-uses, while different, are not necessarily incompatible. This point will be developed further later, but suffice it to say, for the moment, that it is dependent on performance and zoning standards, rather than through the application of rules-of-thumb, for the workability of compatible uses to be made effective.

Under the impact of the motor vehicle, both in its passenger carrying and goods carrying capacities, the city centre is increasingly seen not only as a multiple land-use concept but also, inevitably, a multi-level access pattern (Fig. 27). One of the better known attempts to define the ways in which this system might be applied through the use of environmental precincts—as they have been termed—is in the Buchanan Report entitled 'Traffic in Towns'. These environmental precincts have a hierarchy of traffic systems to meet the needs of through traffic, local traffic and service vehicles within an overall cellular system. However, in all probability, something much more modest is likely to be needed in most cities undergoing renewal, if anything of the existing fabric is to remain, since the almost total replanning implied in this set of proposals would probably only have been practicable in a new city or one undergoing the massive reconstruction that Rotterdam experienced after the war.

While the full benefits of multi-level forms of traffic access and the environmental precinct may not be feasible without total replanning, many of the comprehensive renewal projects being undertaken in various cities have shown that the principles are, in many ways, applicable and have produced beneficial results—much greater than could be expected where the problem is tackled at a single level by means of traffic segregation (Fig. 28).

Although no one should confuse the growth and changes in a city with those of a living organism, there is, in some ways, an interesting parallel with an organic structure in that the city's health growth can be judged by increased stature; that is preferably in height, rather than in breadth, to which we assign such pejorative terms as middle-age spread, obesity or *embonpoint*. As the natural and desirable form of growth occurs, the limbs and arteries, the nervous systems—analogous to buildings, roads and services—extend, but none of these can be permitted to grow disproportionately or we may find a form of hyperthyroidism or 'megalopolis'. In less severe, more localised, cases it may be merely a question of 'varicose veins'.

Uncontrolled growth at any point can obviously be serious in both the case of the human body and the city and suburban spread appears to have similarities to the onset of cancer which may have the effect, if not checked, of strangling normal growth elsewhere and leaving a 'dead heart'.

Even in less serious cases, atrophy of a particular area can occur due to lack of a viable nervous and arterial system (as, for example, where mains services such as water, sewerage, electricity or telephones are not available in a given location).

Clearly the cure to these problems must be prophylactic or therapeutic, rather than surgical and least of all can we visualise a successful implantation of new arteries or nervous systems into an already afflicted urban body. Rather is a restrictive diet, aimed at curbing the intake of unwanted automobiles, likely to produce the only long-term and entirely satisfactory prognosis.

Even though this analogy may, in some respects, seem to border on the frivolous, referring, as it does, to matters of serious moment, the apparent similarity between the two processes suggests what we know to be a fact: that we have ignored important aspects of growth of the supreme human artifact—the city—and the implication that it must reflect, in many ways, human growth processes. Perhaps here we can most clearly see a vital role for the medical scientist in urban planning, in competition with the systems analyst and his very dubious mathematical model. Certainly a closer regard for the biological aspects of the urban ecology can only have increasing significance and validity if we are to concern ourselves with a truly humane environment.

Chapter IV

Economic and social factors in the changing city

In spite of the great changes which have been brought about, particularly in forms of communication, and, more especially, in the adoption of the motor vehicle both for the great majority of intra-urban travel and carrying roles as well as for inter-urban journeys—and with the very serious, and in many ways, unfortunate decline in the use of the railway system which has accompanied these changes, the importance of the central city area as a commercial and, to some extent as an industrial, heart of the whole metropolitan complex, continues.

Notwithstanding the competition which city centres are now having to meet from comprehensive regional or district centres and from planned policies of decentralisation, both of which are tending to pull population and business away from the traditional city core, the economic advantages of concentration and location which originally brought the city into being, are likely to ensure its continuance even though undergoing changes and modifications through the continuous process of growth and redevelopment.

Undoubtedly one of the most important ways in which the city may be revitalised in future is for renewal to take place in such a manner that larger numbers of the urban populations are offered the choice of in-city living, as was traditionally the case, but, in this instance, planned in an entirely different manner with regard for past experience and an understanding of the causes underlying the flight from the city.

Where sub-standard dwellings already exist near city centres, they must be progressively moved as a high priority task; not, however, to make way for further commercial and industrial premises, but, above all, to re-establish residential areas and city-living opportunities of the right kind (Fig. 29). This is not to say, however, that these may not be combined on a multi-use basis with other suitable commercial and professional types of land-use where the latter can be shown to be compatible with residential use, and which may often, in fact, be entirely advantageous as positive contributions to a more lively environment.

A second important contribution to the revival of city centres must rest on a discontinuance of present widespread policies, sapping the strength of the city itself —and setting up district centres of an all-purpose type, sufficiently close to the metropolitan centre to offer serious competition with it.

This absurd and utterly illogical strategy, which can only be called suicidal, is being practised by many city governments or with their connivance and as a perpetuation of the initial blunder of permitting cities to spread, sprawl and scatter over the face of the land, rather than pursuing policies of compact planning for convenience, through renewal programmes, in the vitally important central areas.

Even though it has been comparatively easier to develop new areas at low densities in the broad acres surrounding existing metropolises, this is now being seen by many enlightened people as a disastrously mistaken policy, and one which tends to brush a large number of urban problems 'under the carpet'.

These problems, however, have to be faced, and this is now increasingly being realised, after the wasteful extravagance and misallocation of both private and government resources into programmes of urban sprawl. These programmes have greatly aggravated the overall problem of metropolitan planning and, whether or not compounded by the complications of racial problems, have allowed a continuance of an intolerable situation in most older city centres.

The enforced use of the automobile, the lack of essential services, and the inconvenience and expense forced on the commuter, are just some of the symptoms of this suburban spread which will be discussed later. Suffice it to say here that, in terms of economics, these attempts to have the best of both worlds—namely, a viable city centre, as well as a suburban paradise—will not work. In a very short time, unless urgent and drastic action is taken to accelerate and greatly enlarge urban renewal programmes, we shall find ourselves confronted with enormous suburban metropolitan rings as the future pattern of the city, with all radial journeys ceasing to have any meaning, since there will be little or no heart left. We shall then be confronted with an entirely different communications problem to which no obvious solution exists since the ring routes, which are implied, will necessarily involve intolerably long circuitous journeys for those who, for one reason or another, do not find employment within the district in which they live.

This is, of course, not in any sense to condemn the policy of development of new towns or urban settlements as a means of opening up and making better use of some of the at-present vast, unoccupied, areas of continents like Australia and North America. If such policies are to be pursued, in the most effective and logical way, however, they must be directed to the establishment of new centres in entirely new locations where they cannot parasitically act in competition with established urban centres.

Reference has already been made to the importance of communication systems on the pattern of urban development. In particular it is clear that during the earlier part of this century, the railway systems led to the establishment and reinforcement of radial routes and forms of linear radial development which were not without serious disadvantages.

In most cases, to bring these routes into city terminals involved considerable destruction of existing properties, increasingly so as they came nearer to the centre. Apparently as an almost inevitable consequence, the worst type of sub-standard properties were those most affected; whether residential, commercial or industrial. Railway routes notoriously became the most depressingly tawdry introductions to any city. History has incredibly repeated itself, however, with the urban highway, and more especially with the freeway. If anything, the latter has been even more destructive and disruptive of the social pattern of the city.

The introduction of the railways also tended to enforce a degree of concentration or even of ribbon development, in outlying areas, since most of these necessarily had to be within walking distance of the suburban stations. However, the one sovereign advantage of these systems was that they were able to carry large numbers of people in a comparative degree of comfort and, even fifty years ago, at appreciable speeds, due to the monopoly they enjoyed on their fixed, designated routes. Some of these advantages have tended to disappear with the economic decline which has occurred through loss of patronage.

There is nothing, however, to prevent the initial advantages enjoyed by these systems being restored, if a reallocation of the enormous subsidies, which go into the construction of highways, takes place in favour of supporting the systems we already have, and into which heavy capital investment has been made.

There is no use thinking we can entirely put the clock back, however, and we must recognise that suburban sprawl has already taken place to an alarming extent, and a great many of those involved have already been forced to take to the road and invest in motor vehicles. This is all part of the wastemakers' economy of the contemporary world, with its built-in obsolescences, increasingly evident each year, in which many motor vehicles are being 'traded-in' annually in the United States, or, at maximum, given a three-year life before finding their way on to one of the enormous scrap heaps which litter the countryside.

This pattern is, inevitably, likely to spread to other countries as a part of the American way of life, steadily and remorselessly being implanted everywhere to the accompaniment of high pressure advertising and selling campaigns.

There can be no room for despair, however, and if we can look ahead, and in particular if the railway systems can be re-equipped and brought up to date with all the technological innovations now to be seen in some of the most recent developments in Japan (Fig. 30) and America, they are fully capable of reasserting their vitally important role of intra-urban communication for the masses. Already 'kiss-and-ride' and 'park-and-ride' facilities in the United States have shown that the wider introduction of public transport feeder services could play a decisive ancillary role to the reintroduction of better suburban rail services and, at the same time, assign to the motor vehicle its preferable 'supporting' role in urban transportation systems.

It will be argued by some, and especially those with highway interests, that this is the age of the automobile and that the 'highwayman's Autopia' is here to stay. Even if this were an inescapable fact, which is not the case, it is a pity that some of the lessons derived from the earlier development of the fixed rail systems were not learned.

How especially unfortunate it is that some of the essential differences in the increased mobility provided by the motor vehicle, as against the fixed rail system, were not better understood.

The railways created enormous damage, as has already been pointed out, in carving their way into cities, and some of this was undoubtedly an inseparable part of acceptance of the role that the railway was to play in urban planning and communication, in which there was no alternative to the concentration of routes into major urban terminals.

With the motor vehicle, however, there is no need or justification for this form of concentration, which inevitably leads to a series of expressway bottlenecks as traffic enters the central city area. The widest possible degree of dispersal of this traffic obviously has every conceivable advantage, in the extent to which the city could be hoped to assimilate the increasing volumes of automobiles. This was the obvious means of making use of the mobility of the car and its non-dependence on fixed routing systems.

FIG. 1.   Brasilia.

24

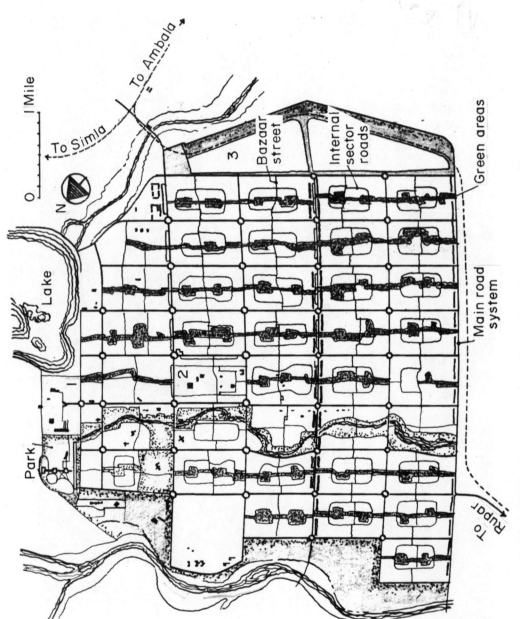

FIG. 2. Plan of the city of Chandigarh, India: 1, capitol group; 2, business centre; 3, industry.

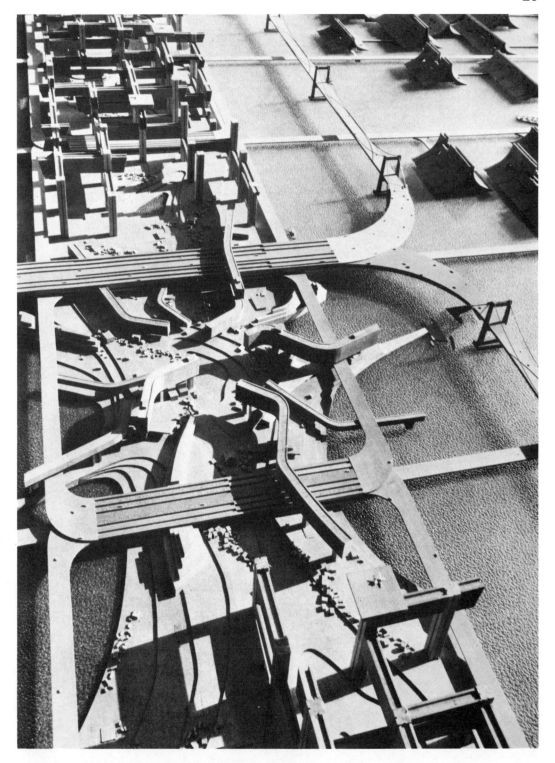

FIG. 3.   A section of Tange's proposed redevelopment of Tokyo.

FIG. 4. Santillana, Spain.

FIG. 5.   'The Pantiles', Tunbridge Wells, England.

FIG. 6.   Urban housing, Paddington, London (adjoining the Old Roman Watling Street).

FIG. 7. Siedlung Osdorfer Born, Hamburg, West Germany.

FIG. 8. 'The Barbican' development, City of London.

FIG. 9. Office development: 'The Golden Triangle', Pittsburgh, USA.

FIG. 10.   Society Hill and Independence Mall, Philadelphia.

FIG. 11.   Naarden, Holland.

FIG. 12. Avila, Spain, from the Salamanca Road.

FIG. 13.   The Stock Exchange area, City of London.

FIG. 14.   Rotterdam after clearance of bomb damage.

FIG. 15. 'Lijnbaan' renewal area, Central Rotterdam.

FIG. 16. 'Deichtorplatz', Hamburg—concentration of railways and roads.

FIG. 17. Notre Dame Cathedral, Paris.

FIG. 18. Shepherd's Bush area, London.

FIG. 19.   Macquarie Street, Sydney.

FIG. 20.   Vällingby, Stockholm.

FIG. 21.   Transportation corridor (road and railway), Tokyo.

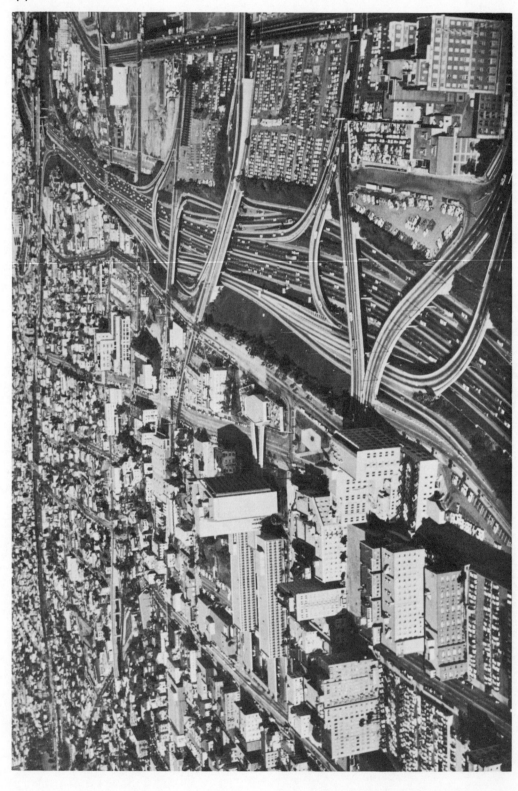

FIG. 22. Los Angeles downtown freeway.

FIG. 23. An attempt to bring life into Los Angeles City Centre.

FIG. 24. Shinjuku transportation interchange, Tokyo.

FIG. 25.   The Plaza Mayor, Madrid.

FIG. 26.   'Beaugrenelle' area renewal, Paris.

FIG. 27.   North Hamburg development.

FIG. 28. Norrmalm area, Stockholm.

51

FIG. 29.   Housing project, Bloomsbury, London.

FIG. 30.   'The Hikari' train, Tokyo.

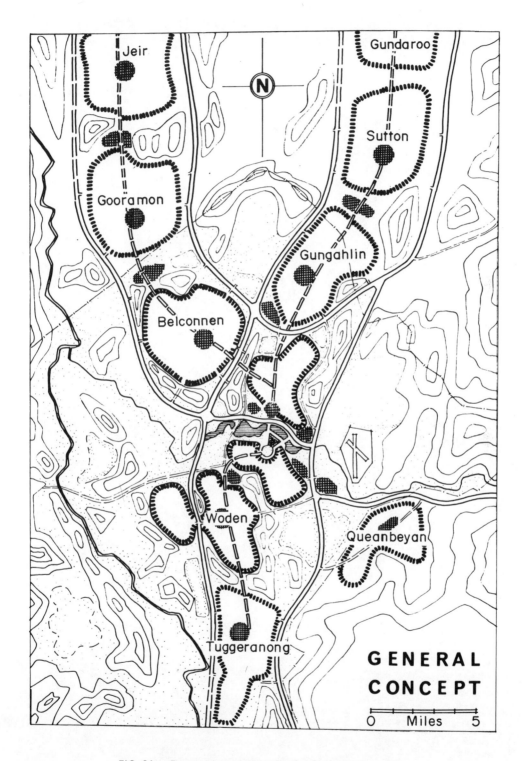

FIG. 31.   Proposed expansion plan for Canberra, Australia.

FIG. 32.   Canberra, panorama.

In consequence of the breakdown of urban expressway systems in almost every instance in which they have been constructed, a return to public transport systems, including rapid rail transit, is, it seems, inevitable. Even those American cities where strong pressure is exercised by the automobile lobbies are having to face this fact of life.

The battle is, however, not being conceded very willingly, and perhaps the most paradoxical and absurd situation is to be seen in the efforts now being made to introduce automatic control systems for the motor vehicle, by which it can then find its way along fixed routes: probably on pre-programmed, computerised networks. The apparent hope is that this may provide at least some of the advantages of the fixed rail systems, with their well-developed and sophisticated signalling methods, and the automatic or electronic control now coming increasingly into use.

In other words, the mobility of the motor vehicle, which has been claimed as its one single outstanding attribute and the justification for its choice as against fixed routing systems, is now likely to be sacrificed. This is primarily because, in practice, it has utterly failed to solve the problem of mass urban communication, instead rapidly bringing many cities either to a progressive stalemate or a state of destructive fragmentation.

Of course the supreme absurdity in this interlocked matrix of urban/suburban policies, which is greatly facilitated by the breakdown of urban government itself, as well as by the lack of adequate town planning land-use control and legislation, is the multiplicity of ways in which suburban spread and its accompanying evils are assisted and encouraged. In too many Western countries, including Australia, America and Canada, it is very much easier to borrow money, from whatever source, in order to build a suburban cottage, than it is to participate in a flat or apartment development condominium or to purchase a stratum title for such a dwelling.

In most of these cases the illusion persists that, because the capital cost of an apartment near the city centre is somewhat higher than that of a dwelling in the suburbs, this is a decisive argument for favouring suburban construction. It has already been shown conclusively elsewhere by the writer that this is far from being the case. On the contrary, when all social costs relative to suburban development are taken into account, a totally different picture is presented.

Public services need to be brought into these outlying suburban areas, in most cases at public expense. Regrettably it is apparent that far too many such developments take place without the simultaneous provision of essential services. These, when provided, present direct and indirect forms of subsidy, either from the city governments or their agencies, or with their connivance or support. The largest subsidy of all, however, is probably that devoted to highway construction for the benefit of the motor user commuting to and from his suburban home and his place of employment in the city.

It is just as absurd to argue that money expended in this way, which is probably largely derived from purchase or sales tax on motor vehicles, tax on oil and petrol, drivers' licence fees and motor vehicle registration tax, should be earmarked and only used for the motor vehicle. These are, nevertheless, the arguments used by most of the motoring organisations in what has, to date, been most effective lobbying of public

authorities and government departments. Similar arguments have been put forward
from time to time regarding the earmarking of parking fees for the development of
off-street parking facilities, with what may seem to be an equal lack of logic.

It is just as reasonable to suggest that revenue derived from the sale of beer and
liquor, or that from cigarettes or tobacco, should only be used for financing more
and bigger tobacco farms and factories, breweries, or bigger and better vineyards.
Clearly, however, broad public interest would indicate that no such argument could
possibly be sustained. As for parking on the highways—there can never be justification
for a continuance of this practice and certainly not for official approval, since
highways are justified where they are built only for the movement of traffic and for no
other purpose, and then only where no other form of urban transportation is feasible.

It has often been pointed out that the overall economic advantages presented by the
established urban areas, as against the newer and more dispersed forms of settlement,
spring from the fact that, with larger populations, there can be greater division of
labour or specialisation among the inhabitants, and a greater variety in the goods and
services provided. Generally, therefore, the larger the population the greater the
specialisation which can take place. However, with a given population size, the degree
of specialisation depends on two other factors: first, the compactness of the population
itself and, second, the ease with which it can circulate. It is likely that the town with
the more compact population will achieve a greater specialisation in the provision of
goods and services and be the more prosperous, having a higher real income per
inhabitant.

While it seems likely that the most compact population will be in disc formation,
since this will provide, other things being equal, the greatest ease of accessibility for
the largest number of the population to the town centre, as well as to the recreation
areas and open space surrounding the metropolis, it must be emphasised again that
transport systems will have some bearing on the otherwise ideal pattern of development, to a greater or lesser extent. Only in the case of the assumed widespread use of
the motor vehicle is it ever feasible to consider the possibilities of an amorphous
spread, although, even here, freeway planning is tending to dictate lineal forms of
development in the shape of transportation corridors which are just exactly the
patterns and forms best suited to public transport and rapid transit systems.

If we bear in mind that the location of industry is itself likely to have an equally
important bearing on the pattern of urban development, whether this is distributed
centripetally round the metropolitan area or in a concentrated series of industrial
parks, it will tend to favour lineal spurs radiating from the central city area, with green
open space wedges intervening.

The move of a great deal of urban industry from the traditional central locations
out to the urban fringes—where there is more space for expansion, where it can usually
function with greater efficiency, and where communication and transportation are
often very much easier—provides the most promising way, through the release of
inner area sites, of substantial reorientation of land-uses—and, through constructive
policies of renewal, the means of expanding the central business district functions which
cannot operate other than in the core.

Intensification of the use of valuable inner city sites during renewal activities, accompanied by the introduction of multiple land-use concepts, is the other way in which necessary healthy growth and change may be permitted to take place within the city proper. Any other desirable and necessary expansion will then be located in the radial spurs.

The extent to which this tightening up process can take place, accompanied by peripheral expansion, is considerable in most established cities. The economic justification for pursuing such a programme was very well documented some considerable time ago by one major Australian city.* Unfortunately, too few cost–benefit comparative studies of this type have been undertaken—or rarely have the results of such studies been published.

The stage must, however, be reached in every city, of whatever size, when continued growth is likely to take it beyond the availability of the necessary resources or facilities or what could have conceivably been planned for, even with some degree of 'open-endedness'. Increasingly, these considerations must weigh at national policy and planning level, when firm measures will need to be instituted to initiate new settlements in order to absorb further expansion in non-competing areas with, however, the guarantee that they may expect to enjoy, at an early date, the same advantages and opportunities as presented by the established urban areas.

Unfortunately, to date, few countries or cities have found the practical means of curbing the expansion of particular city areas; rather, most politicians and many planners wring their hands helplessly in the face of what they believe to be an inevitable train of events, leading to such phenomena as 'megalopolis'. In close family relationship to this concept, which is entirely at variance with any idea of conscious planning, or the control and guidance of our destinies, is the contemporary cliché of 'continuous-growth' (Fig. 31).

There is, clearly, a minimum size for the city below which its economic viability is in question, although precisely what this size should be varies greatly in estimates put forward within our current planning orthodoxy. There are those who seriously hold to the view that a population of fifty to sixty thousand is adequate to establish a self-contained urban settlement. This, indeed, was the basis of the post-war New Towns in Britain.

Ideas have, however, changed greatly in the course of some twenty years and a number of these New Towns, neatly planned to the sixty thousand population package —and presumably with the facilities to suit these needs—are now being expanded to double the original population with the same arguments now being put forward to justify this figure as the essential minimum.† The lack of consistency or logic, and the implications with regard to the facilities and services being asked to undertake double their original task, do not appear to have caused much concern to those who confuse these circumlocutions with planning.

The case of the comparatively new Australian federal capital, Canberra, is interesting in this connection (Fig. 32). Here the original population target of the government of the day was for what was believed to be an optimistic estimate of 10 000. Painful

* 'The Economics of Urban Expansion' by Cumberland County Council, December, 1958.

† An example is Stevenage, England.

disagreements took place with Burley Griffin, the planner for the new city, who held that the right population to be planned for would be about 75 000. In consequence of this disagreement Griffin was dismissed. Today the population of Canberra has reached nearly 120 000 and the Government is talking in terms of an inevitable growth to half a million by the turn of the century, and one million shortly thereafter.

No suggestion appears to have been made to date that any of these estimates was wrong, but clearly they cannot all have been right. Perhaps this is a typical example of the difference between conscious guided and controlled planning in the modern city and rationalising or putting the best face on what is, in reality, uncontrolled growth, justified by the use of such terms as 'continuous-growth'.

While this extraordinary process of 'flywheel' growth continues in so many cities, including the new capitals and New Towns, where it should usually have been feasible to plan for, and adhere to, ideal standards, there are those planners and others who point with justification to the fact that only where there are urban populations in the millions, such as in London, Paris (Fig. 33), New York and Tokyo (Fig. 34), do we expect to find the full range of cultural activities and outlets, as well as the whole gamut of specialised commercial and industrial activities. These simple facts would argue for more realistic growth patterns in city planning on a long-term basis into which shorter term objectives may be interlocked and related to ascertainable intermediate goals.

Looked at from another angle, it may be said that a city of 50 000 can have a satisfactory medical system, schools, a supermarket, a highway system, the requisite industry, a good cinema, churches for most denominations, adequate housing and a clean atmosphere. It might also be expected to have traffic segregation, a range of public utilities, if not too scattered, trees, lawns and flowers and reasonable peace and quiet. It is unlikely to be able to afford a significant museum or art gallery, nor a worthwhile library, symphony orchestra or theatre. It may be without a first-class newspaper, good parks and recreation areas, a zoo or botanical garden. It may never see opera and only possess mediocre restaurants. If we are not very careful decentralisation of our big cities could occasion a decline to the uninspiring level of the 50 000 city without, however, getting rid of any of their metropolitan disadvantages.

On the other hand, as Burchard puts it; 'the big metropolis can make all the greater joys possible. That is because it presents the statistical probability that within its boundaries there are enough potential customers for each experience which may be "caviare to the general". But, if the big metropolis is just an accumulation of contiguous communities of 50 000 populations and if it does not maximise the opportunities for diversity, then it really has no reason to exist at all. Its disadvantages are so great that the sooner it is destroyed the better. Living in Manhattan is meaningless if you never visit any of the foci of Manhattan's culture and excitement'.[32]

All this helps in putting this aspect of the problem of city size into the clearest possible perspective, and we can only agree with the statement that, 'the most humane cities would perhaps be produced by a set of urban dictators, each benign, each of good taste—so that each city had a special flavour'. Indeed, it is equally true that we will certainly never have the best if we continue to let the forces of technology be guided primarily by economics. We cannot lose sight of the human values—however difficult these values may be to assess or cost they must continually be set alongside economic virtues.

In this restoration of human values, not the least important factor is the creation of a satisfying visual environment. Underlining and giving emphasis to the truly metropolitan character and the unique qualities of major cities is a prerequisite to any closer examination of their purpose, function, and structure.

Clearly, larger cities are still, and are likely to continue to be, the major centres of political power (Fig. 35), the seats of government (Figs. 36 and 37), of international authorities and government institutions, of professional organisations and the headquarters of industrial and trade union organisations. Trade organisations will necessarily be located in such centres and, because of the important parts industry and communication have played in their development and growth, it is likely that major cities will be associated with major ports. For the same reasons they are likely to be the focus of road and railway communications and the home of banking, finance and insurance companies, as well as the sites of international airports.

All the largest teaching hospitals are likely to be in, or associated with, major cities, as well as the majority of teaching and research institutions, the headquarters of the country's legal profession and its High Courts (Fig. 38), national libraries and museums, and the preferred location of publishers.

It is extremely difficult to imagine any of the foregoing functions or institutions, facilities or installations, being located in the suburbs, or, for that matter, anywhere other than as near as practicable to the centre of the city itself—any more than would be the case with radio and television centres, major departmental stores, theatres, opera houses, the best restaurants, the largest hotels (Fig. 39), or the most convenient and popular conference centres.

The suburbs have been undergoing a very rapid growth, in many cases at the expense of the central city area, and the sooner it is realised what folly continuation of such a policy is bound to be, the better for city and metropolis alike. Only when the situation is seen in its true light can we expect the necessary restoration of full vitality in the city centre and a clearer recognition of the importance of planning and redeveloping suburban areas in a more compact form so that they can continue to function as part of the metropolis, rather than being forced to hive off into separate quasi-self-contained communities.

In spite of these trends it is reassuring that a least one valuable report—'The Changing Economic Function of the Central City'[192] emphasises that significant and important functions are still performed in central cities. These include headquarters office functions where communication is a vital factor, and many types of small operations which depend upon supplementary activities in the central city. For example, this study indicates that there is 'a high proportion of employment remaining in eight central cities (in the USA) in business services, finance, insurance, real estate, wholesale trade, retail trade, and manufacturing of special types and size'. It also demonstrates that, of the total employment in business services, finance, insurance and real estate, wholesale trade, retail trade and manufacturing, and in the eight central cities referred to, between sixty and eighty per cent of the total for the whole metropolitan area in each instance was provided in the city centre itself.

A number of other considerations, many of major significance, arguing the case for concentration, as against dispersal and sprawl, have been developed at length in a previous work. Some further reference will be made to these in a subsequent chapter but it should not be necessary to repeat these arguments in detail at this juncture since, if anything, their importance has been emphasised and underlined every year since the writer's earlier publication. To touch on one or two points, however, the true economic comparisons between high density and low density development require the full inclusion of the social and services costs, as well as those for buildings and land. The increasing misuse of agricultural and recreational land—more especially that immediately adjoining metropolitan areas and on which they depend—represents a total and irreparable loss which can never be made good.

The true savings in land requirements, if a consistent policy of higher densities is pursued throughout all aspects of development—including not only the residential sectors but also the commercial and industrial areas, and with a relocation policy of open space and recreational areas—is so significant as to completely refute earlier fallacious claims such as: 'nothing gained by increases in density'.*

Finally, there is the question of ease of accessibility, both within the city itself and between the city and the outlying recreational and open space areas—that is, the natural habitat which must increasingly form a vitally important part of humane urban planning. No fulminations or rearguard actions on the part of the garden city adherents can controvert these facts which point conclusively to the benefits of the compact city.

If we need further confirmation of the importance of the vested interest we all have in maintaining the stability and growth of the central city—provided that this is in a healthy, planned form, we might remember, as the extreme case, that by 1980 over ninety per cent of the American people will be living in urban areas, where, in 1920, the figure was fifty-one per cent and, in 1962, under seventy per cent. Other countries can be expected to follow this pattern. Five metropolitan areas in the United States accounted for twenty per cent of the nation's total population in 1960—at which stage it was approximately 190 million. While this is not to say that all these people inhabited the central city areas proper they lived in metropolitan areas in support of business, commerce and industry being undertaken in the central areas. Without the impetus of such commerce and industry there would have been no point in their moving into the metropolitan areas at all.

'Men come together in the cities', said Aristotle, 'in order to live. They remain together in order to live the good life'. As the alternative, however, it is evident that the consequences of sprawl will include streets overcrowded with commuter traffic, ineffectual public transit, the spreading of blight, increasing air and water pollution, delinquency and crime, inequalities in educational opportunities and convenience, neglect of park space and other community facilities, such as libraries and museums, and a significant lack of that range of government services and facilities which should be regarded as the minimum essential for civilised community well-being.

* This is to paraphrase Unwin's aphorism which is answered in detail in, 'High Density Living'.

These deprivations and defects, which most people who know cities at first hand will recognise, have formed the basis of a useful study which warns us of many of the anti-city elements at work today. These, together with fallacies about decentralisation, must be eradicated if the city is to be given a healthy future.

Other important city problems, all capable of solution, are lack of privacy through unsatisfactory environmental planning, lack of recreation and landscape spaces adjoining but in contrast to building masses, the unsightly clutter of badly-designed advertisements and signs and of what is often entirely unnecessary street furniture, refuse and litter in the streets, tedious and endless street layouts and canyon types of development, overhead cables and poles to support them (Fig. 40) and the social and physical disruption already referred to, as the result of the introduction, at an earlier period, of railways and, more recently, of freeways.

To these we must add the creation, or aggravation, of ghetto conditions as a result of similar human artifacts, a lack of sun, air, and shade or shelter to meet varied climatic conditions, indifferently or badly-designed buildings not related to one another, to the street or the city as a whole (Fig. 41) the dangerous fire hazards posed by badly-designed and overcrowded building, badly-designed or related anti-social building masking or obscuring other adjoining buildings (Fig. 42), the noise, fumes, smell and risk to pedestrians of the motor vehicle *en masse*, the all too frequent loss of activity during evenings and at weekends, and last, but by no means least, all-pervasive noise.

In spite of the astonishing capacity of urban Man to adapt himself to his conditions and circumstances this last factor must be considered by many people as far and away the most serious. Already it has been demonstrated that the continued impact of the urban cacophony will inevitably, 'jar the human nerves, sabotage concentration, rob the weary of needed rest, impair human health and performance, and in general trespass on man's most prized and private possession—his mental preserve'. It has to be recorded that, far from this problem being in sight of early solution, noise levels are increasing annually at an alarming rate, and no one can view lightly the early introduction into service of new, bigger and noisier types of jet aeroplane, which will have particularly serious effects. As most airports are now located some distance away from city centres, much of this increased noise level will be felt in the suburban areas, so that a possible effective remedy may lie in the direction of rigid land-use policies which will prevent the development of residential communities within at least five miles of modern airports.

Much more can be done, still, in the way of research into silencing systems for aircraft, and the application of even more stringent policies with regard to take-off and landing areas. There is everything, moreover, to be argued in favour of the VTOL and STOL types which localise the impact of the bulk of the serious noise to the airport area itself.

The problem of noise is, however, by no means confined to emanations from airports or aircraft. Motor vehicles and motor-cycles are powerful generators of entirely unnecessary noise and, undoubtedly, noise reduction techniques must accompany the many new safety factors likely to be built into motor vehicles in future, as a consequence of increasing government vigilance. At the same time, the absurdity of ambulances with sirens whose din must cause untold harm to patients, and fire engines with sirens blaring impotently on congested roads, must be regarded as anachronisms which society should no longer tolerate.

A further potent source of unnecessary annoyance in city residential areas is that created by the use of outmoded refuse disposal vehicles. If modern equipment, such as is already available and in use in a great many cities, were to be insisted upon, this nuisance could be totally eliminated overnight.

These are all problems capable of solution and which must be solved since, in the past, they have undoubtedly played a considerable part in the flight from the city and in formulating the belief that many, from Ebenezer Howard onwards, have shared, that the city is no place for people to live in! A failure to solve or eradicate these objectionable features can only result, in the long run, in their being repeated in the New Towns or cities being developed now, presumably with the consequence that, in due course, their populations will take flight to some still more remote rural area, if such a place still remains on this planet.

It is, however, vitally important if appropriate long-term planning is undertaken that such planning be within an ultimate, defined limit. Whether this limit is initially dictated by considerations of creating a truly metropolitan city, it is, in any event, likely to be influenced to a considerable degree by considerations of what we now know to be the maximum size of an urban unit which can continue to function with any reasonable degree of convenience for its inhabitants. It will also be affected by local geographical and topographical considerations, especially in regard to availability of suitable land, without making serious inroads into food-growing areas and, by no means least, by the availability of natural resources, such as water, and the means of disposing of human wastes.

Furthermore, at all stages during this progressive long-term development there must be a basic economic viability in the city which presents, at any given stage, an apparent quality of completeness in its urbanity. This is only possible if tightening up and intensification of development take place through progressive renewal over the years, and neither of the alternatives of leaving vacant large areas in the city centre for future development, nor of creating district nuclei of new settlements, is likely to prove satisfactory, for reasons which have already been touched upon.

All these arguments point to the conclusion that the most difficult part of the problem, which the urban designer is set to solve, of creating a more worthwhile visual environment in the city centre, will surely come about in the older cities through a continuous process of renewal and redevelopment—and, equally certainly, if new towns and new cities are planned intelligently, as has been suggested, they must be expected to undergo a similar process.

In sum it can be said, therefore, that assembling, at any given time, a number of properties adequate to permit the advantages of comprehensive redevelopment, and the ability to redevelop these continuously in a way that keeps them in context with their surroundings, regardless of any changes made, together with the ability to retain the whole city as a single functioning entity with an overall sense of unity during the process of growth and change, is the essence of the urban designers' and planners' tasks.

Apart from the evident determination of most cities to continue in being and to grow, there may still be some which need reassurance that this will be the case in future, despite the often unpropitious indications to the contrary.

A previous Commissioner for Urban Renewal in the United States, William Slayton, has confirmed that, 'while the economic functions of our larger cities are changing, they are not disappearing'. Manufacturing and wholesaling may continue to move from the urban core to more outlying areas where they can function with greater efficiency, but the core of the central city and its environs still remain as the only parts of the metropolitan area that can properly support the facilities and services dependent upon a metropolitan area-wide clientele. Such facilities as concert halls, museums, theatres, central libraries, speciality shops and larger retailers can survive only in the central business district. The fine restaurants, amusement facilities and hotels dependent, in large part, upon visitors, must be concentrated at the centre, and, 'since most of these activities tend to cluster, each being more strongly supported by virtue of having the others there, they naturally fit into a central location'.*

This point of view is increasingly one that most thoughtful urban planners will be inclined to accept as irrefutable, and a confirmation, if such is needed, must come from the continued activity in the commercial sector in cities such as New York, London and Sydney, accompanied by equally dramatic growth in industrial activity in the same general metropolitan areas. The importance of the cultural facilities and entertainment provided in these established cities has certainly in no way diminished and most countries are recognising the increasing importance of such facilities in their tourist potential, the revenue from which no country can afford to ignore.

In the long run, however, the prime considerations are those relating to the use by, and the convenience of, the city's inhabitants, and to this end only a redeflection of more funds into central area residential development can hope to bring about a greatly improved use of this enormous investment capital in the form of employment opportunities and cultural facilities in the city centre: a process which can only be to everyone's benefit.

Cybernation and automation are seen by some people as likely to lead to the further decline of the city as we know it in favour of widely-dispersed centres with much smaller populations. It is argued that such centres, together with the improvement in communications systems, must lead to a smaller number of people being required, certainly in the city centre itself, but also, ultimately in many of the peripheral industrial locations.

It may, on the other hand, be argued as much more probable, that before the economy of any country can permit widespread unemployment to occur through the introduction of mechanical systems and methods, whatever retraining schemes may be applied, the use of these new technologies would be better harnessed to improvements in efficiency and the future growth and extension of business and commerce.

Whatever the effects of these innovations, there can be little doubt that many commercial operations will need to continue to function on the basis of face-to-face contacts and it will certainly be a very long time indeed before the customs of the market-place give way to more remote forms of control and exchange.

* Monograph—limited circulation by H.U.D.

Judging from cities as they are, and the enormous capital investment supporting the present economic and social structure and our current business methods, it is equally unlikely that significant changes will occur even under what to many people is the more serious threat of a future all-out nuclear war: which might suggest the possibility of a new pattern of troglodyte cities; if this were to be allowed to govern our thinking.

Looking, however, at more imminent and positive developments likely to affect the city centre, one principle must be kept in the forefront of all our city and metropolitan planning. Whatever technical developments take place in the form of more efficient central city area transportation systems, ultimately the city core has to be thought of as a predominantly pedestrian area, for the simple reasons that people in vehicles cannot conduct serious business, go on shopping expeditions, or visit galleries or museums.

These functions are, after all, what the city is about and the reason for it being where it is. That is why the planning of the core must continue to be on a pedestrian scale of accessibility, with the physical development of buildings and intervening spaces being carried out with due regard to the scale and needs of the city's inhabitants. It is also the reason why the automobile must be very firmly kept in check and, above all, out of the city centre, in which it can have no place and is unable to function at all without detriment to the essential needs of pedestrians.

To accept any other policy is to relegate the pedestrian to the undignified role of an automaton, functioning or moving only when the correct signal is applied by some inhuman mechanism and, equally importantly, to condemn the city centre itself to becoming one large, untidy motor vehicle museum—in which, if guided, automated systems come into operation, as is being currently predicted, even the human being will not be needed, and certainly not in his erstwhile role as driver.

The form of urban centres, as of settlement generally, has evolved over the centuries as a result of social and economic pressures for growth. The geography of each site will affect the feasibility and direction of growth, but, ultimately, it is the value of land which influences the form of growth—upwards or outwards.

Manhattan, New York (Fig. 43), grew upwards because it could not grow outwards and because its commercial importance made its land values high enough to justify the erection of skyscrapers, as soon as techniques of high rise construction and the elevator became available. These basic considerations will not change in relation to development in any city centre now or in future: rather they may tend to produce answers in many cases similar to those of the past, reflecting the same factors.

These considerations also stress the importance of relating the form of the city centre to that of the whole metropolis and demonstrate the overall advantages of compaction. Land-saving, ease of access and contact with the surrounding country are such advantages.

The design of some city centres has admittedly been influenced by intellectual and artistic efforts to create or reconstruct them according to scientific or architectural principles, such as in Vienna (Fig. 44), Karlsruhe, Coventry, and most New Towns (Fig. 45) and new capital cities. In other places urban designers, like those commissioned by the Popes of mediaeval Rome; John Nash in central London (Fig. 46), and

Haussmann in Paris (Fig. 47), as well as Edmund Bacon in contemporary Philadelphia (Fig. 48), deliberately set out to improve the design of a city centre so that it functioned and looked better.

Landlords of central area properties have traditionally redeveloped their sites when the financial returns reasonably to be expected on rebuilding justified the destruction of the old building and the cost of the new one. A site is theoretically ripe for redevelopment when its value cleared is greater than with the existing buildings.

Normally it has been usual to construct new buildings with more lettable or usable floor space than in the previous buildings on any site—so that, by more intensive redevelopment, and thus by increasing rental returns and capital value, the owner is reimbursed for the costs of redevelopment and assured profit commensurate with his risks and enterprise. Values which are linked to turnover and, in turn, to accessibility, traditionally reach a peak in central areas.

There are drawbacks in this national economic evolution. As the centres have become more intensively developed, the modes and speeds of access have been affected by the traffic congestion in the centres. Carried to its ultimate extreme this means that eventually central area values start to fall and the forces which give rise to decentralisation begin to take effect. This is likely to continue unless a fundamental reorganisation of the planning takes place on a more rational, multi-purpose basis, with either the planning of environmental zones or the simple restriction of unwanted vehicular traffic into business areas.

Another problem of overdevelopment is that, as buildings become taller and bulkier, so the environmental conditions within and around them deteriorate unless skilful planning is brought to bear. Less sunlight and daylight may penetrate, natural vegetation and open spaces can become crowded out and traffic nuisances dominate. As the buildings grow larger they accommodate and attract more people and vehicles. Then, unless the necessary safeguards are applied, congestion—as can be seen in so many contemporary cities—will inevitably occur.

A further problem inherent in allowing economic criteria to be the sole yardstick of the form and rate of growth and renewal of urban centres is that this results in individual landowners redeveloping their own properties without regard for adjacent buildings and sites—indeed, without regard for the overall land-use transportation strategy for the total urban system.

To prevent 'unneighbourly' schemes and to ensure that all new developments conform to the development plan proposals, planners must concern themselves with the detailed control of all new buildings. Such control must, however, be undertaken and administered in an enlightened way, permitting the best forms of development without unnecessary or unwanted restrictions.

Chapter V

Decentralisation or intensification?

Substantial arguments have already been put forward elsewhere, some of which have been touched upon in the previous chapter, underlining the importance of redeveloping and renewing our cities in a much more compact form. A policy which has been increasingly adopted in recent years, is that of similarly treating, from the outset, new cities and towns which can be shown to be part of a desirable pattern of urban growth.

Surprisingly this question forms an area of disagreement, and of polemic of the most bitter kind, where, logically, there would seem to be no possible alternatives. The conclusions and inferences are only too clear and can no longer be gainsaid, notwithstanding the fact that cities and governments still tend to persist with the application of urban growth planning policies in which it has for long been evident that a serious misdirection of energy and resources is taking place.

We simply have to recognise that however fragmented it may appear to be, the metropolis is a single entity. We must therefore do everything possible to integrate and urbanise it. While this is increasingly becoming the accepted view of enlightened urbanists, as well as many critical writers, social scientists, architects, renewal promoters and even development economists, it has to be admitted that the number of adherents to these policies is still small. On the other hand, it is a fact that the enlightened few have often turned out to be the precursors of much larger movements, and the growth of this philosophy seems inevitable. Its potential should not, therefore, be underrated.

Many will agree that great, concentrated cosmopolitan cities, with their close contacts and stimulating diversity, have always been the 'source' of civilisation. The metropolitan community is still, in essence, a city, no matter how many people there are in it; but it is disintegrating through the stupidity of sprawl and the illusory escapism of suburbia and the automobile.

The sooner, therefore, that the intelligent, although often unfashionable, view held by a comparatively small number of new urbanists, can be seen at its true worth, the better, since it provides the only hope and solution for the future of the cities. By the same token, the sooner destructive inroads into urban civilisation, threatened by suburbia and the automobile, can be halted, the sooner can we hope to begin to tackle this priority problem of urban revival.

As a step in the right direction perhaps we should hope to discourage the eternal drives for personal space and land ownership, which no longer make much sense. Instead, recognition of increasing urbanisation as a fact in the world's metropolises could lead to more profitable diversion of effort to worthwhile and beneficial use of land in and around the cities themselves.

It is also relevant to observe the serious misuse of valuable agricultural land adjoining cities which continues unabated. However, it is a matter of simple geometry that the space immediately surrounding most urban settlements is limited. Even with the availability of modern transportation techniques, having regard to the cost implications, close-in space obviously has greater potential than distant space. This is, indeed, the situation confronting practically every modern western city, whether it be in the wide open spaces of Australia and North America, or in the more congested areas of Europe. In either case it is metropolitan land—quite irreplaceable once it has been absorbed or used for the wrong purposes—that is of the greatest value.

It is one of the significant virtues of the traditional city that it shows that gregariousness is not merely a thing of the past as has sometimes been suggested. Rather is it the essence of urban life. The compact community is not a product of a philosophical theory or an aesthetic ideal; it is undeniably the physical expression of basic social needs. The tragic error of spread-city is, for all these and other reasons, beginning to disturb many thinking people and this process will gather force as the city increasingly fails to provide the satisfaction its occupants seek and expect.

In spite of the fulminations of the anti-city school—and whatever the reasons advanced in support of their arguments, it is an inescapable fact that even if, by a stroke of the pen or through some unforeseen disaster, we were induced to write-off all our existing cities as bad investments—the apparent chance to start again would present little or no advantage. We would, on the contrary, be losing the best and most logical sites for urban development, built on a basis of human and economic values. We would also lose that essential continuity of human experience which underlies civilised living. The point, therefore, which has to be re-emphasised is that, if we cannot marshal the resources and ingenuity to reorganise and rebuild our existing cities, there must be serious doubt as to the availability of sufficient wisdom and ability to create new urban settlements which will be any better.

When he was Secretary to the Department of Housing and Urban Development in the USA, R. C. Weaver stated the policy which he advocated, and which many believe to be the inevitable answer to the urban problem, when he argued: 'a case for preserving and renewing our cities really rests on what I consider the keystone of our national housing policy. It is concerned with maximising choices for the American people. Some of us prefer to live in a central city, others prefer to live in the suburbs. In order that these preferences may find realisation the central cities must be economically strong, as well as attractive and functional. Urban renewal . . . is a tool to achieve these objectives'.[198] The emphasis is, once again, necessarily on the importance of undertaking greatly increased programmes of urban renewal as, of course, this is significantly where present choices are likely to be widened from the inevitability of the suburban cottage.

Many people will undoubtedly prefer and insist on a dwelling in the outer suburban areas, in spite of the very obvious problems of long-distance commuting and the 'New Town blues' which would deter others. Many, on the contrary, as has been pointed out, 'will not find a garden city a welcome relief from the chaos of the modern city', but rather feel that the city itself should be tidied up and the more obvious advantages of urban life restored.

Some of those who have tried suburban life will always prefer it, but many others who have made the move, possibly for family reasons or as a reaction against some of the less attractive qualities of the downtown areas of the city, realise that they have not achieved a solution and would return to the city without delay, were this economically feasible.

All too often, however, the lack of suitable middle or lower income developments on high value central area land presents many people with little or no basic choice. Yet in support of a policy of urban consolidation and in rejection of a continuance of flight from the cities an increasing number of intelligent people have pointed out that the existing cities can be reorganised more cheaply, more efficiently and more quickly than we can build new cities. We could double their populations simply by better use of the existing area and, at the same time, organise in a way that would eliminate the present chaos.

This approach at the same time confirms the potential seen by many people for worthwhile urban renewal, not only in terms of visual satisfaction but also in intensifying the development in such a way as to allow the city to expand and breathe and to do so, moreover, twenty-four hours a day, with the transfusion of life which comes from a restoration of living opportunities and the presence of people in the city itself.

This process of compaction, of course, only takes place under certain conditions and it is this which creates the major problem confronting the urban planner and designer. This problem can only be solved satisfactorily if we accept the view that the present illogical, and often anti-social, competition between building owners, vying with one another through their prestige edifices, will eventually give way to the recognition of common concerns.

Inevitably we must soon reach the point where environment planning on a collaborative scale will be the accepted policy. Recognition of this change of front is immensely important and, as a starting point, the indications are that a significant proportion of the best contemporary architects, who are undertaking the more worthwhile work in the cities, will be ready to coordinate their several efforts as soon as the lead is given by city planning organisations.

A number of authorities are on record in regard to the alternative choices of concentration or dispersion. Robert Moses, as one such, has pointed out that: 'there is indeed much wrong with cities—big and little—but the answer is not to abandon or completely rebuild them on abstract principles. Only on paper can you disperse concentrations of population and create small urban stars with planned satellites around them. In the course of many years devoted to reclamation of waterfront, manufacturing of topsoil to cover thousands of acres of new parks, buying and preserving large areas of natural woodlands and shores, in advance of the realtor and subdivider, planting thousands of trees along parkways and expressways, building hundreds of playgrounds, planning cultural centres in place of decaying tenements, tightening zoning and building laws, restricting billboards, opposing entrenched power companies and other utility corporations, and stopping water pollution, I never caught a glimpse of the breastbeaters who are now touted as pundits in this field'.[135]

Many practical planners would agree that the programmes undertaken under the authority and initiative of this politician have played a vital and important part in preserving and improving one of the world's major cities. It would be nothing less than sheer folly to attempt seriously to disperse any of the essential elements of this admittedly enormous city and metropolis—one which is still in urgent need of mammoth renewal operations. Nevertheless, the proponents of 'spread-city' do advocate such a process. They consequently show a great deal less realism than Moses, or those who are presently pursuing, in the same city, a much wiser policy of clearing up what problems already exist by an orderly sequence of urban renewal operations, aided by reclamation and redevelopment of some of the harbour front areas. Such areas form a part of the most valuable real estate in the world and it would be entirely irresponsible not to use them in a way beneficial to everyone.

It is abundantly obvious that many, even now, fail to appreciate fully the economic and other effects of programmes of dispersal such as have given rise to the extra-ordinary belief that while the economic advantages of urban concentration are un-deniable and still continue to pressure population in the direction of urbanisation, the effect of metropolitan dispersion is to minimise the disadvantages of this con-centrated urban growth. Another fallacy is the view that motor transport has made it possible for large agglomerations of population to continue to grow without the inconveniences of increases in density.

Of course the major flaw in this argument is the confusion which exists in the minds of many people between concentration and congestion, whereas, in fact, concentration is the hallmark of a city. Some people seem to think, however, that in order to eliminate congestion we should also get rid of concentration. However, concentration—the reason for the city's being—existed long before the special kind of congestion caused almost entirely by modern means of transportation in the form of the motor vehicle. Dispersion, in contrast, is the chief characteristic of suburbia. Therefore those who imagine that the inconveniences of urban congestion are likely to be overcome through the creation of 'regional districts' or 'metropolitan districts', however they choose to describe them, are offering a contradiction in terms, since these concepts are nothing more than suburbs under another name. They are not a basis for planning cities and are unlikely to present any solution to the current problems of the real cities.

Obviously the low densities implied in suburban dispersion are in direct contrast to the conditions in which most highly specialised activities or services flourish and in which they can draw on a large area and still be near the centre of the traffic system. Not only are there inherent weaknesses in the suburban development itself, but the spread of the suburbs in turn led to, and is still leading to, growth in the peripheral metropolitan shopping areas and similar facility areas. It has induced many indus-trialists to move further out for business expansion than would otherwise have been warranted.

New Towns are, in many respects, merely special versions of this dispersed pattern of urban growth, and it does not confer any special virtue on them to argue, rather disingenuously, that if people are, in some cases, willing to move from badly-planned and over-crowded central city areas it is because the city has no further purpose for them and presents them with no advantages. The real remedy in such circumstances is, of course, to renew the city itself and provide better living conditions where they are most needed.

The further inevitable corollary in this New Town policy, which attempts to set up self-contained employment facilities in order to avert the otherwise unavoidable commuting to and from the city centre, is that it only makes matters infinitely worse for the metropolitan job-seeker.

The underlying assumptions both of the need for dispersal and of the pattern this should follow, are basically wrong—as only the established city centres which have persisted can hope to provide many of the necessary business and cultural purposes and opportunities. Also, as has already been pointed out, it is impossible to both decentralise these facilities and to permit the urban economy to continue on a viable basis.

The other self-evident point regarding the New Town or Metropolitan District concept, with its underlying hope that these areas might be made entirely self-support-ing and independent so as to defeat the planners' spectre of the dormitory suburb, is the fact that even in the first generation of 'immigrants' such self-support and independ-ence will not be feasible: certainly not in times of high employment mobility such as those through which we are at present passing. In the second generation it is even less likely that people who live in a particular area will be able to obtain the full range of employment close at hand, or that employment will be available in all its wide com-plexity of contemporary specialisations, considering the relatively small populations involved.

Slumps in one industry and booms in another are also likely to have very significant local effects on employment prospects. These are difficult to overcome unless and until some rationalisation of industrial location is achieved. To date this has rarely been possible, any more than the obtaining of a full enough range of industry and commerce in a particular town.

As for metropolitan dispersion assisting the established urban centres, it should, by now, be clear that the very reverse is likely in the conditions of quite undesirable competition which grow up as an inevitable consequence of such a policy.

Surely it is better to agree here with Lewis Mumford that: 'We must now conceive the city accordingly, not primarily as a place of business or government, but as an essential organ for expressing and actualising the new human personality'. . . and that: 'The innovations that beckon urgently are not in the extension and perfection of physical equipment: still less in multiplying automatic electronic devices for dispersing into formless suburban dust the remaining organs of culture'. On the contrary: 'significant improvements will come only through applying art and thought to the city's central human concerns'.[138]

FIG. 33.   Montparnasse Maine, Sector III, Paris.

FIG. 34.   The Ginza, Tokyo.

FIG. 35. Parliament Building and the Ring, Vienna.

FIG. 36. The Royal Exchange and Bank of England, London.

FIG. 37.   Parliament Square, London.

FIG. 38.   Queen Victoria building, Calcutta (relic of the British Raj).

FIG. 39. 'The Hilton Tower', Park Lane, London.

FIG. 40. Urban clutter.

FIG. 41. Unrelated discordant buildings.

FIG. 42. Anti-social crowding.

FIG. 43.   The upward thrust of Lower Manhattan.

FIG. 44. The central area of Vienna.

FIG. 45. Cumbernauld Centre.

FIG. 46. Nash's Regent's Park terraces, London.

FIG. 47. Paris boulevard.

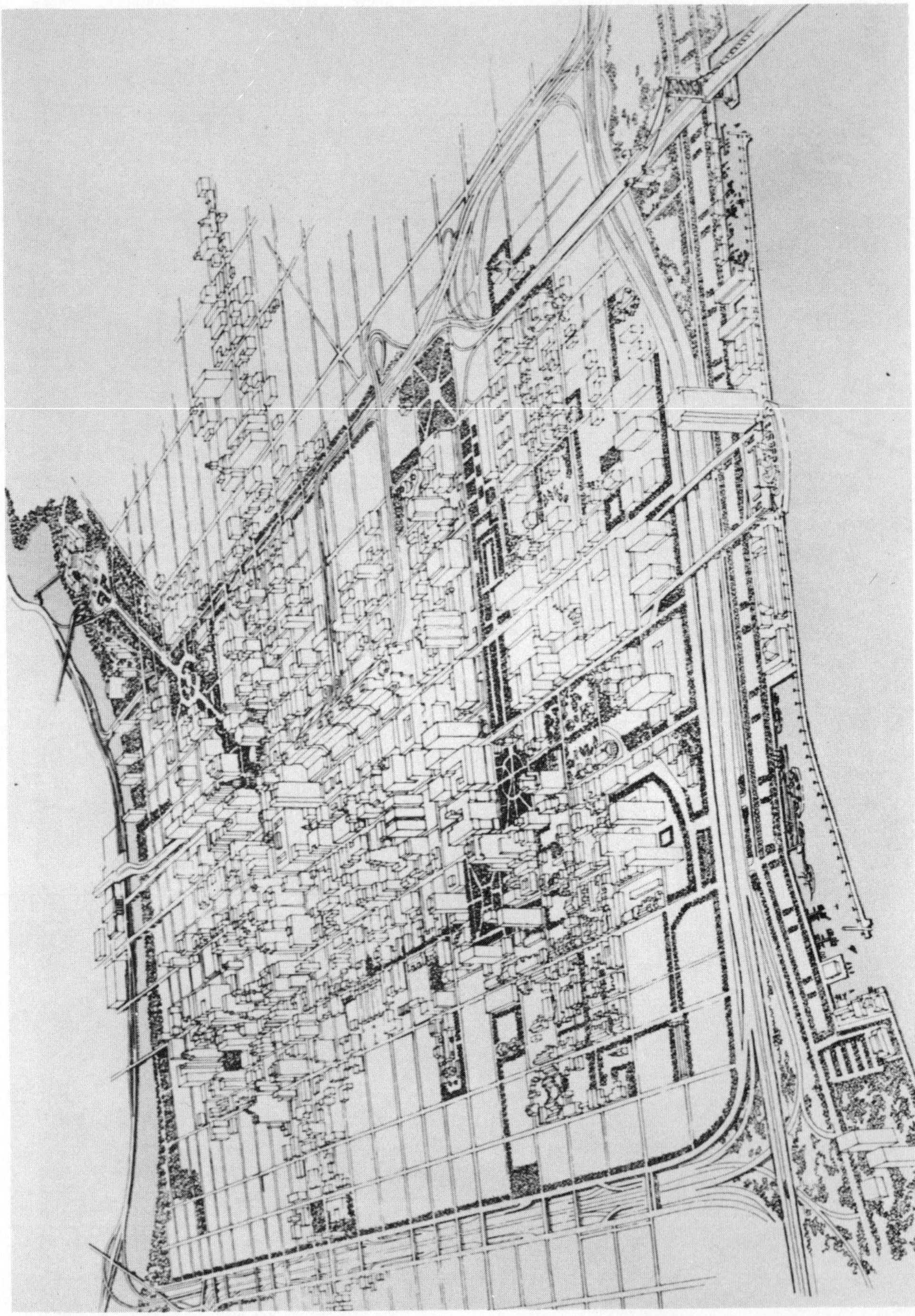

FIG. 48. The designed structure of central Philadelphia, USA

FIG. 49. Nathan Road, Kowloon.

FIG. 50. 'The Golden Gateway' development, San Fancisco.

89

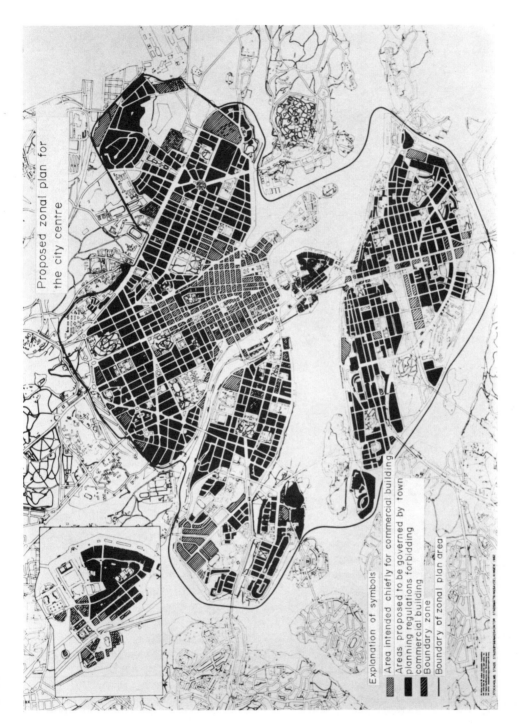

Proposed zonal plan for the city centre

Explanation of symbols

Area intended chiefly for commercial building

Areas proposed to be governed by town planning regulations forbidding commercial building

Boundary zone

Boundary of zonal plan area

FIG. 51.　Central Stockholm zoning plan.

FIG. 52. 'Outram Park', renewal area, Singapore.

FIG. 53.   'Marina City', Chicago.

FIG. 54.   Place Bonaventure complex, Montreal.

FIG. 55.   Hotel above department store, Cincinnati, USA.

FIG. 56.   Waldorf Astoria, Pan-Am and other developments, Park Avenue, New York.

FIG. 57. Washington Heights, North Manhattan—flats astride a 12-lane motorway.

FIG. 58.   High density development in the Paris metropolitan area.

FIG. 59. 'The Rows', Watergate Street, Chester.

FIG. 60.   Golden Lane redevelopment, City of London.

FIG. 61. Post-war reconstruction in Hanover.

FIG. 62. Shopping, 'Australia Square', Sydney.

FIG. 63.   Aesthetic control by 'building envelopes', Canberra.

FIG. 64. The Guggenheim Gallery, Manhattan, New York.

Chapter VI

Multi-purpose land use concepts

It is inevitable that land in central urban areas will be more costly than that located further out, in either metropolitan 'fringes' or rural areas. This is not simply due to a supply-demand market mechanism but also, and much more importantly, because land situated at the focal centre of the city is most conveniently accessible to the largest number of urban dwellers and, in turn, is most conveniently located near to other business and commercial, or residential areas—all of which provide it with a unique degree of accessibility on a metropolitan scale.

Furthermore, such land is fully serviced, in a developed environment, and provided with all the appurtenances and facilities which are the prerequisites of a civilised urban community. These have been contributed to by the local taxpayers or ratepayers, who have met the cost of streets, sewers, water supply, sanitation, police and fire protection, schools, parks and playgrounds. They have also paid for any public transport facilities which are available.

On the other hand, private enterprise has added, almost entirely through private investment, industrial facilities, homes, commercial buildings, shopping centres, theatres and other capital works. This all helps explain why, where a suburban residential block to take a single house may cost between $5000 and $10 000, or its equivalent, for a quarter-acre, a central city site may very well cost something of the order of a million dollars an acre. Obviously those who build on such central area sites consider that the capital investment in the site is well worth while. This is, of course, always assuming that it is a business or commercial undertaking facing the purchase of such land.

The high cost of land of this type seems to place a daunting barrier in the way of the development of such sites for residential purposes. If this were the whole story, it would undeniably argue for all residential provisions being made in outlying metropolitan areas. But, of course, it is far from being the whole story; that is, if the whole of the capital costs involved in the provision of comparable services to those which exist already in the central area are taken into account in connection with the opening up of new residential areas.

Over and above the more effective use of valuable central area sites, both in the form and in the intensity of development, it is vitally necessary that the waste implied in a continuation of slum and blighted areas, representing a total loss of urban opportunities and a pervasive demoralisation, be recognised. We can neither afford this type of waste from a social nor an economic point of view, and in terms of the effect on the environment, it is one of the most serious and urgent anti-city elements which cries out for attention: not by retreating from the problem into the 'broad acres' surrounding the city, but rather by tackling it on the spot. Only in such a way can there be any assurance that the city itself does not continue to decline at an accelerated rate, or, on the other hand, that the right kind of rehousing opportunities are created in the right place at economic rent levels, for the people who need them most.

It is quite inevitable that a treatise concerned with the form and pattern of central city development should also be closely involved, as one of its considerations, with the provision of housing. This is just as much so as that work concerned with urban housing must take full account of the city entity as a whole. The simple fact is that in any study highlighting housing as an important component of the urbanising process discussion of these aspects cannot be separated from the numerous other aspects of the development process. A book about housing will be a book about an essential part of cities, and, similarly, a work directed to the problems of housing and cities must also deal with the implications of the urban land problem. Housing cannot be thought of as merely the provision of shelter, but much more as part of the fundamental urban and social structure.

It is equally true that, if the city is to continue as a functioning organism, it must increasingly revert to a situation in which it is very much more closely interlocked with its residential aspects—without which it cannot be regarded as a true city. There must, moreover, be a consistency of policies and planning techniques in relation to all aspects of the city, be they in the housing segment or in the commercial and public segments. High densities and intensified land-use in one must logically be accompanied by similar forms of compact development in the other. It is a matter of simple fact, however, that, in relation to this burning question of density, more ill-informed nonsense has been spoken and written than perhaps about almost any other single aspect of urban planning. It is not intended to repeat here at length arguments which have been put forward by the writer in considerable detail and with factual support elsewhere.[95]

Nevertheless, it must be recalled that the initial and continuing illusion from which the many critics of higher densities in the city suffer, is the belief that intensified development, leading to larger numbers of people living or working in a particular area is necessarily synonymous with congestion in a pejorative sense. The further *non-sequitur* usually leads to the false conclusion that these are the preconditions which will automatically generate the slums of the future.

Of course nothing can be farther from the truth. It is necessary to repeat that the slums of the past arose, in the majority of cases, at comparatively low densities and in all cases were due to bad planning, inadequate maintenance and impoverished inhabitants who had not learned the basic requirements of civilised living. Mixed and incompatible environmental uses and planning completed the picture and led, inevitably in such circumstances, to a steady deterioration and decline until the stage was reached where these areas were the preserves of the under-privileged and the permanently poor.

On the other hand, where people have learned to live together with a degree of discipline, forbearance and a recognition of one another's needs and interests, very high densities are feasible without in any way implying slum conditions or gross overcrowding. An example of this is to be found in Hong Kong, as perhaps the outstanding example of the ways in which truly urbane people can learn to live together, albeit in conditions that most western urban populations would regard as minimal (Fig. 49).

Further confusing this question are the various methods of measuring density and the difficulties in making really valid comparisons. The fact is that the traditional concept of density in residential areas and the common use of the term to indicate a ratio between the number of individuals or families and a given area of the earth's surface, is outmoded and often fallacious—and, if so used, is in error when a formula for regulating residential densities is being determined.

The traditional concept of density is out-of-date, much in the same way as are many of the traditional concepts of land-use, zoning and related elements of land development. As urban areas have increased in population and expanded in area and as our economies, during the last hundred years, have shifted from rural to urban, the philosophy and mental attitude of too many individuals remain rural. One of the major obstructions in the way of sound and logical development and of the renewal of urban areas is the lingering nostalgia and illusions connected with traditional rural village life.

However, it must be realised that: 'logical urban development can take place only when those responsible for that development are urban-oriented in their philosophy, have a deep and positive attitude toward urban society and are willing to mould their thinking towards shaping the urban environment to satisfy the needs and desires of an urban society. Cities can be livable, they can be attractive, they can satisfactorily house many more people than they do now'.*

The truth is, of course, that it is the area which people have for their use, both within the dwelling and adjoining the dwelling, that is the measure we have to adopt, as well as a consideration of the overall layout, planning and relationship to the environment as a whole. These are the criteria that matter and the ones by which we can judge urban living conditions as well as conditions for all other urban activities. Density yardsticks and rules-of-thumb customarily adopted by planning authorities do not give reliable indications of the true conditions and can, in fact, be totally misleading. We should recognise that they are worthless as planning tools and have played, unfortunately, a very considerable part in the misdirection of urban planning policies in the past as well as the loss of valuable development potential.

The implications of policies leading to the more intensive forms of development in the central city indicate that only in this way can we expect to use to better advantage valuable sites and planning powers in a manner that promises much better prospects for a lively city. Thus, not only should we find the means, wherever practicable, to increase the total bulk of building on a given area—primarily through vertical extension—but, in addition, every opportunity should be taken to exploit the planned relationship of compatible, though different, land-uses, where these can be harmoniously linked together.

The reaction against non-conforming uses in the city some twenty-five years ago or more led to a clinical overpurification of the planning process on extremely stereotyped lines, with every different type of land-use and particular subdivision within

---

* Reproduced from mimeograph by Marshall Miller on Residential Density—privately circulated.

each of these main land-uses neatly parcelled or segregated on a two-dimensional co-planar framework. This was probably responsible for the sterile, deadly appearance and atmosphere and lack of variety and liveliness of many contemporary cities.

These purist ideas must now give way to a saner policy of highly integrated land-uses, as was traditionally the case in earlier cities with the shopkeeper 'living above the store' and the professional letter-writer and legal adviser operating close at hand to the tinker, the innkeeper and the produce merchant.

Many legislators and government officials concerned with building and city planning matters have realised, more and more over the years that, if they are to have the type of legislation which will not only act in a negative sense to prevent undesirable tendencies, but, wherever possible, also offer constructive help in the direction of encouraging new developments and enterprise of the right kind, building acts and planning control legislation must be fundamentally amended and related much more to performance standards and standard 'codes' for construction and equipment.

The advantages, both administrative and in terms of the lively variety which a city should generate, are obvious if and where such a degree of flexibility can be introduced. To mention a particular example by way of illustration, there would seem to be no reason at all why, within a single area of development on a city site, underground car parking might not be introduced at the lowest levels. Above this there might be storage or safe deposits, or the type of accommodation that does not need windows or natural ventilation. Here a link might be introduced with an underground railway system, leading into a central vertical circulation core. At ground level shops, with arcading to the street, might be planned (Fig. 50) and, if the area was of considerable depth, the internal spaces could be used either for additional storage or as parking spaces and service access routes.

At the next level, in the form of a podium, large piazzas surrounded by town houses or patio houses could be introduced, together with high-rise tower buildings. Some of these would contain dwellings and others, at least up to a level of say five or six floors above the podium, professional chambers, consulting rooms for doctors or dentists or a more prestigeous type of office accommodation.

Ideally, dwellings should be located above the level of offices or professional accommodation and, as these could be given almost equivalent open space private environment to that enjoyed by the town houses at the podium level, they would thus admirably cater for a wide selection of different types of tenant.

Planning of this type cannot be undertaken, of course, unless a sufficiently large area is under redevelopment—an area such as would permit comprehensive replanning. There is everything to be said, therefore, for the assembly of the largest possible number of freeholds at a given time and for their simultaneous, rather than piecemeal development. Not only does this provide advantages in the extent to which different uses may be interwoven without serious detriment one to the other, but, quite clearly, even greater advantages likely to accrue are in the overall design of the development and the greater likelihood that a unified treatment can be assured, virtually as part of a single operation.

Examples of this type of multi-level, mixed use development already exist and have proved immensely successful in practice. Unfortunately, however, in too many cases costs have tended to preclude from sharing the benefits any other than the middle or upper income level groups. Although more than one housing expert has commented on the great importance of bringing back into the city centre higher income level families in order to reinforce the tax base on which the city's life depends, an even greater problem is that of ensuring that housing opportunities are created for the widest possible cross-section of the population at all income levels and ages, so that a viable alternative to the suburb (and its illusions) really does exist for everyone.

If this is to be brought about then, unquestionably, the subsidies which have become a permanent part of housing policies in most western cities will have to be continued, since in no other way is it feasible to bring high density housing on high cost central sites to rent or cost levels which can be afforded by lower income level families.

Reference was made earlier to the importance of the multi-level zoning concept since, even in newly-planned communities, the values of the vitality thus generated have been rejected in favour of a design purity which obsesses certain city planners and architects. Happily it can be said that increasingly fewer city planners or architects regard this purity as a very fruitful approach to central area planning and certainly not as the means of creating a livelier form of urban design. These professions have, more frequently and generally, been in the forefront in insisting on a complete change of approach in systems that appear to have been devised by lawyers for lawyers, as the simplest to administer.

Any enlightened professional planner would take the view that possibly the most doubtful feature of contemporary planning is over-rigid zoning (Fig. 51) which, in effect, separates the place of work from housing and, in this way, breaks up the continuity of life. It is just this quality of continuity in the city that we should aim for. In this lies the hope of restoring, by means of planning, an integrated seven-day-a-week pattern of living on a totally comprehensive basis (Fig. 52).

It is some encouragement for those grappling with these problems that they can occasionally feel they have engendered a degree of understanding and support. Even in the one country of extreme planning conservatism, Great Britain, it was recently stated that while the planners who believe in the city as a focus of social life are still only partly effective their impact is growing and increasingly making itself felt on even the most hardened adherents of low densities and garden suburbs.

This leads to the well-founded belief that in the future emphasis must inevitably be towards a renaissance of city centres and on rehousing people within easy reach of them. By this means, cultural life, which now suffers such appalling handicaps by virtue of long journeys to and from work, may, once again, be stimulated.

The well-known architect and planner, Victor Gruen, helped to bring this problem into better focus when he wrote recently: 'We have centres for culture, centres for amusement, centres for education, centres for finance and finally, areas reserved for residing only. This transferral of our general, contemporary love affair with specialisation to the shaping of the urban environment, has destroyed the very sense and meaning of the urban centre. If we are to save our centres, not just physically but in their meaning to humanity, we have to reverse this trend towards specialisation and return to the all-purpose, integrated, closely knit, compact, exciting and enjoyable form of the urban centre'.[71]

Specialisation we must have in the metropolitan city since, only in this way can we expect to make available many of the services which only this type of city can provide on an economic basis. It would indeed be the ultimate irony if this basic essential of urbanism lent any kind of weight to the forces of disintegration in the city. If, on the contrary, we are sensible, we can use these very same qualities to ensure that the position of the traditional city centre remains unchallenged in the future and that its supremacy is further reinforced by a continued infusion of the same kind of qualities.

Many of the more important aspects of these arguments and considerations relating to better integrated uses and planning of the central city were crystallised in a recent publication in which, on the question of what kind of city is wanted, the writer pointed out that with our fast growing affluence and fantastically expanding technology, there is no reason why people who like high density living should not also enjoy open space and recreation quite near at hand; nor any reason why people who prefer low density living should not enjoy it much closer to where they work and shop.

Moreover: 'if (*inter alia*) we accept the simple mathematical fact that for most people urban living has to mean living close together . . . and if we stop looking backward and dreaming that tomorrow's urban life could be more like yesterday's village life, and relinquish the notion that low density is somehow better for everybody . . . and if we re-structure our big cities as radiating clusters of high density land use . . .' then we can expect to have the ideal type of city. 'High central density would help preserve close-in amenity . . . overcrowding is no problem at all on Park Avenue with up to 1000 persons per acre. Overcrowding had nothing to do with the explosion in the Californian suburb of Watts, with a density not much more than twenty persons per acre'.*

It is a fact that at the urban densities which, in the USA command the highest rents from those best able to afford to live as they like, such as on New York's Park Avenue, Chicago's Gold Coast or San Francisco's Nob Hill, there are only three American cities whose entire population could not live, work, shop, swim, play tennis, worship, attend concerts, and go to the cinema on 18 000 acres within three miles of the city centre. This would leave all the land outside that three mile circle for heavy manufacturing, golf courses, market gardening and low density suburban living. Schools would, of course, also occupy substantial parts of this green belt as part of an intensely workable and practically realistic overall urban planning solution.

We should, therefore, realise that at the density which tenants seem to like, for example in Chicago's Marina City (Fig. 53), the whole population of the area could live, work and shop, and find plenty of recreation within blocks of the Chicago River, between Lake Michigan and the Merchandise Market.

It is not, of course, seriously suggested that all our cities should be rebuilt to such a concentration, and most certainly it is no part of the recommendation that everyone in any of the larger cities should congregate at the centre. Nevertheless, the simple geometric and mathematical facts about living close are important to remember, and we must not, of course, forget the social facts, either. We should surely by now agree

* 'The Nation's Cities'. April, 1967.

that our cities must be planned for living and working as close together as is compatible with the other requirements of good business and the good life.

It would be ideal if those who want low density living could enjoy it much closer to the city than they can today in order to save them the countless hours they now waste in getting to and from their homes. It is necessary, however, to realise what should be an obvious fact—that as our urban populations increase the only way to bring low density close-in is to develop at a much higher density at the centre.

It is increasingly obvious that urban growth will be vertical, even though, in sky-scraper land: 'two generations of urban Americans have paradoxically in one sense been obsessed, bewitched, dazzled and blinded by the outward explosion touched off by the automobile, which made millions of out-lying acres newly accessible and deflated the price of close-in land by temporarily lifting the pressure to maximise its use'.* However: 'making today's urban area twice as big horizontally for tomorrow's doubled urban population would be impossibly costly in money, intolerably costly in wasted land, unbearably costly in added travel time to and from work, and to and from open space and recreation. Doubling the urban capacity by going up instead of out would cost far less, and add only seconds to everybody's travel time'.

Whether we like it or not, most urban growth in the next thirty years will therefore have to be up, not out. Even sprawling Los Angeles is finally learning the simple lesson and building three times as many new apartments as single-family detached houses. Today's greatest land waste does not lie solely in the vacant sites and unused acreage of urban sprawl, it is much more due to the failure to put more high-value, close-in land to more than one use on more than one level.

Today's high-speed automatic lifts make vertical travel much quicker, cheaper, and more convenient than horizontal movement. Whereas most real estate is thought of as being usable for a single purpose only, the economics of vertical lift transportation make it possible to simultaneously use land a considerable number of times, with each floor likely to be more sought after than those below, so that the highest, with the best views and lighting, command the highest rents. The lower levels are most useful for storage, parking and, perhaps, club-rooms, workshops and kindergartens, but the upper floors are much more suitable for offices and apartments.

Land is required in the city to house railway installations but there is no reason why such systems should not be located below skating rinks, cinemas, office buildings, shops or apartments or several of these at different levels (Fig. 54). Land used for storage on the lower floors can be used again for the purpose of holding a residential hotel on the upper levels. Chicago offers the outstanding example of this kind of stratification potential in Marina City (Fig. 53), where there are forty storeys of apartments on top of twenty storeys of parking. Below this are two levels for shopping and, at a still lower level, a marina for 200 pleasure boats, all integrated with sixteen floors of offices, a theatre, bowling alleys, tennis courts and a swimming pool.

There are other examples of the same type, such as in the Golden Gate Development in San Francisco (Fig. 50) and in the Cincinnati Hotel (Fig. 55), which is planned on top of a department store. There is the Waldorf Astoria in Manhattan over the

---

* 'The Nation's Cities'. *Op. cit.*

New York Central Railway (Fig. 56), and a number of similar developments (Fig. 57) which make the trend quite obvious. Clearly, the possibilities of making higher densities much pleasanter, more efficient, more economical and more convenient, as well as more diversified, are tremendously encouraging.

This planning technique also ensures, as has been previously emphasised, that the concentration of high density living can be maintained throughout the whole city and therefore provide really large and consistent land savings and, of course, better use of valuable land.

Also in recognition of the need for high density cluster development close-in, it is planned to build six new suburban centres in Paris (Fig. 58), each with 250 000 to 400 000 population. This French scheme of high density sub-centres close-in is almost the direct antithesis of the not too successful British attempt to create low density 'garden city' New Towns far out beyond the green belt. It closely follows, however, the precedent set in Sweden, in the development of Vällingby (Fig. 20) and Farsta.

Too many of today's New Towns have been planned just to skim off what is best in the central city, leaving behind all the residual problems such as poverty and slum areas. The greater the initial success of this wholly mistaken policy, the greater the danger that the New Towns will ultimately fail, by destroying the central city on which they must depend for many essential services, much of their employment and many cultural and educational facilities.

In the choices which appear to confront us regarding policies of urban development and as to whether central city consolidation or decentralisation are likely to produce the sought-after answers, another, most important, aspect is that concerned with taxation in the city area itself and the extent to which this provides either encouragement or discouragement to more enlightened forms of renewal. It has long been held by experienced social workers that the slums are likely to remain a continuous problem until taxation makes their ownership less profitable.

On the other hand, a real practical incentive may well be provided through changes in the taxation or rating system and, in particular, the method of levying taxes on unimproved land values, in preference to the system more frequently in operation at present of taxing the value of the land together with buildings—constituting improvements—erected upon it.

It is obvious that taxation of land values tends to encourage, speed, or even compel, improvements. The bigger the land tax, the bigger the leverage on owners of under-used property to do something to increase its earning power—or sell it to someone who will. On the other hand, heavy taxes on improvements are bound to lower the supply and raise the cost and rent for improvements. Land taxes heavy enough to bring more land on the market are, however, certain to lower the price of land. For these reasons the more prevalent type of property tax tends to discourage investment on new construction and rehabilitation or renewal.

The lesson of all this must surely be that if we want to get rid of slums, it is foolish to subsidise them by assessing and taxing slum properties only a half or a third as heavily as good housing with the same market value. Instead, we should be tying the land assessment to the building assessment and assessing land as almost worthless because the building on it is almost worthless—instead of assessing the land highly because the location is valuable and could be better used.

Of all the anti-city elements which have been referred to, or which must weigh heavily in any consideration of the future of the central city area, the effective eradication of slums is one of the most vitally important. Until this problem is tackled effectively no amount of persuasion is likely to convince the large numbers of suburban commuters that there is a better solution to their living–working problem than that which they at present adopt.

There are many other potentialities inherent in the multi-purpose zoning approach to planning which may present an almost infinitely varied means of creating a lively urban texture cityscape. These include arcaded sidewalks to permit wider streets for the passage of vehicles, with the pedestrian areas created within the curtilages of frontage buildings (Figs. 59, 60 and 61). This would, of course, have to be carried out as a part of a comprehensive planning operation if it were to be of any real value and in order to ensure a continuity of pedestrian through-ways. Such a technique, however, has the added advantages of providing climatic protection for the urban pedestrian.

Another alternative is that of creating a double level access to buildings (Fig. 27), in which the lower level caters for service vehicles and public transport, and at first floor level, pedestrian access is provided which can either be in the form of a continuous deck, allowing for the creation of pedestrian malls, or, alternatively, a perforated deck permitting light and ventilation through into the lower levels.

With the implied system of mixed uses it will no longer be either necessary or appropriate to plan schools as separate or self-contained buildings, rather they will be combined, where feasible, with high density apartment blocks. Nursery schools and crèches would certainly also be integrated in this way in order to ensure that young children were properly catered for without the need for unnecessary long journeys in all weathers.

As a part of such a planning concept, 'co-ed' bachelor apartment houses with recreational facilities, including swimming pools, would be provided for at the lower levels of large high density apartment developments. This would help meet the intractable problem of creating suitable conditions of city living for an increasing group of young people of both sexes—a group which forms an important and substantial part of the city labour force. In future it should be a relatively easy transition for such people, when they marry, to graduate, possibly by stages, from their bachelor apartments into small family apartments, without being forced to make changes involving considerable geographical dislocations and, in some cases, changes in employment.

For families with children accommodated in this type of development, outdoor play and recreation space could be created high above the streets, either on rooftops or on open floors or in interior courts (Fig. 15) sandwiched into the development at appropriate levels: and suitably protected in all cases.

Imaginative underground shopping centres, possibly linked with the rapid transit systems, such as have already been developed in a number of cities, also become practicable (Fig. 62) and these not only have the advantage of creating worthwhile, usable space, even below ground, in a way that can be developed very attractively, but may be the means, also, in a somewhat different form, of creating weather-protected conditions for the urban pedestrian.

It would be entirely wrong to assume that this multiple use of valuable city land implies, in any sense, a loss of standards or an undesirable degree of congestion. As has already been pointed out, with the right kind of planning and, more especially, with segregation of access systems, very much higher densities than anything that has hitherto been accepted in western countries are perfectly feasible without the problem of population congestion ever becoming a real issue.

With regard to the effects in terms of bulk of buildings and traffic generation it can be said that multi-level access planning, together with the application of design codes which ensure adequate spacing between adjoining substantial structures, suggests that there is no reason why any loss should be experienced in relation to environmental conditions, either externally or within particular buildings. Good planning can certainly ensure that all these matters are capable of perfectly rational and satisfactory solution.

If city development is really to be given a new lease of life in future there can be no possible question but that the stereotyped and highly unsatisfactory zoning systems must be discarded without delay. They may have succeeded in eliminating some of the evils of incompatible land-use but, in many ways, they have also been the means of preventing more enlightened planning.

Most two-dimensional, negative control systems have, in fact, been producing ever more trite city developments over the last twenty-five years and, in the process of attempting to solve one set of problems have created an even greater degree of dissatisfaction with the urban environment.

The loss of townscape is frequently referred to, with full justification, as a by-product of these methods. Many cities planned in this way still look, in their completed form, as though something has been left out or forgotten. The great, wide, windy open spaces which are apparently thought of as an indispensable part of such planning, fail to create any sort of sense of cohesion in the city—and expand the urban scale in a way that no longer makes it possible to think of these areas as being appropriate for use by the pedestrian, certainly with any degree of convenience.

Functionally, therefore, as well as in terms of convenience and sound economics, there can only be one rational answer; that is, the maximum degree of utilisation of urban land with highly integrated, compactly and conveniently planned urban complexes.

Chapter VII

Control methods and limitations

Especially in contemporary conditions, a whole panoply of control systems, methods and techniques have been applied, through the medium of building ordinances and town planning regulations in various parts of the world, with the apparent object of ensuring adequate functional, and very often, also, visual standards, in urban developments.

There is, however, an increasingly wide measure of agreement as to the failure of such systems and methods to produce wholly satisfactory forms and patterns—more particularly with regard to visual qualities. Too often these methods have proved negative in character and application and, while preventing some of the more un-desirable features and tendencies, have nearly always fallen short of expectations and must always fail to produce a really positive environmental quality or individually beautiful component buildings.

These forms of control have usually initially been directed towards adequate structural and health standards in regard to particular types of building, but the building ordinances which seek to deal with these matters have frequently extended to a consideration of the standards of street daylighting—through the application of 'daylighting angles' and the separation of adjoining buildings by means of rule-of-thumb formulae of set-backs from party boundary lines. The same building ordinances frequently lay down restrictions with regard to the planning of light courts in specific buildings and may, and frequently do, stipulate overall height limitations. They will, of course, also have some bearing on the choices and types of materials which may be used.

There will also often be reference to forms of design and construction in order to obviate fire-spread, either within a given building or between it and its neighbour. These will invariably have design implications for the exterior treatment of the building. Unquestionably there will also be stipulations regarding forms of access and egress to and from buildings, as well as in relation to the planning of horizontal and vertical circulation systems—more particularly, again, with a view to providing adequate means of escape in the case of a fire or other emergency. These are likely, moreover, to have aesthetic implications.

The quite normal stipulations contained in most building ordinances relating to minimum floor to ceiling heights in habitable accommodation, which would include most commercial and business premises—and in regard to the minimum areas of natural lighting and ventilation—are also obviously important, in as much as they tend to dictate external proportions and appearance. It may well, however, be that, in the case of air-conditioned buildings, the minimum natural lighting area, as well as the amount of natural ventilation afforded, may be reduced, or eliminated entirely in certain circumstances. Even in these circumstances of 'waivers' from building statutes the implications of aesthetic appearance are still very closely linked with acceptable techniques of planning and design within established precedents.

Methods of applying external climate or sun control, although rarely laid down in building statutes, will unquestionably play a major part in most city buildings in the external aesthetic treatment. So, too, will the economic dictates of efficient planning for specific purposes, since these have a very considerable bearing on the plan, shape and form of the building envelope as well as on the height of a building. By no means least in significance is the fact that, in some cases, acceptable design and fenestration patterns have been related to the existence of standard fire-fighting and escape appliances or the prevention of fire-spread.

More specific town planning forms of control which may be applied are those concerned with density or total volume of buildings and these are likely to be laid down in the form of a 'Floor Space Index' or 'Plot Ratio', or the less familiar 'Land Use Intensity Index'. These, in each case, attempt to provide a formula which relates total admissible floor area, as a ratio, to the area of a given site, and therefore also the provision of residual open space.

Purely planning controls may often also attempt to limit or control the form and massing of buildings and groups, not merely in relation to aesthetic considerations but also with regard to the desirability of preventing undue overshadowing between adjoining buildings, overlooking or loss of privacy, and a reduction of the risk of firespread between adjoining buildings. In one specific case, at least, building 'envelopes' have been stipulated as part of an overall aesthetic concept (Fig. 63).

Town planning regulations sometimes dictate types and colours of materials, relevant floor levels and numbers of vehicle parking spaces—although these are often treated as a bonus on the permissible bulk of a building. Most city planning ordinances, as has already been mentioned, will lay down a zoning system to stipulate acceptable land-uses. This system therefore plays a very important role in the type and appearance of particular buildings, for good or for ill. This will still be so even with an enlightened system of multiple-use zoning.

Other matters dealt with through either building or planning ordinances include standards and types of illuminations, lettering—and particularly sky signs—the use of arcading or verandahs and types of access, including those for servicing the building, which will have a very considerable significance in overall traffic planning arrangements.

In some capital cities, including, for example, London, there are special powers of control conferred on *ad hoc* government commissions, with specific responsibilities relating to the aesthetic appearance of buildings or groups of buildings having particular regard to the fact that these may be, and frequently are, likely to be located in important and prestigious locations.

It can be said, in general, that while most of these enactments or forms of control are entirely negative, in the sense that they cannot be expected to act creatively to produce beautiful buildings or confer a positive quality of inner urban environment, at least those contained in building ordinances are usually accepted as a necessary part of government or local government administration in securing safe and healthy buildings.

It must, however, be conceded that this array of regulatory and disciplinary factors tends to control buildings, although not usually in the most desirable ways. They are too often obsolete in terms of today's problems and seldom produce sounder community environmental values or more livable cities. Current zoning, set-back and minimum lot size regulations, too, often almost dictate design. Invariably they discourage artistic grouping, rhythmic spacing and skilful and harmonious juxtaposition—the essential attributes of sensitive design. At worst they have frequently produced a form of planned mediocrity or negative sterility.

There is little doubt, too, that the application of overall height control and of floor area ratio or floor space index systems tends to have an uneven, and often stultifying, effect.

Among the controls currently in use in various parts of the world through the media of building and planning legislation there is, however, one exception in which most of these strictures would not apply. This is the British Building Research Station Daylight Control System, which has been in operation in London for some years.[145]

While this system was primarily concerned with ensuring adequate standards of natural lighting into buildings in the earliest planning stages, when the proposals were still fluid, it presented a number of other advantages.

In the first place, the system replaced a formidable array of other types of controls of the negative, restrictive variety and, in their place, assumed that what in fact was basically needed, was a control over the total bulk of the buildings, one over the form and spacing of buildings and, finally, a control over the siting and design of buildings.

The bulk of the buildings would be dictated by the floor space index plot ratio, or floor area ratio system; the form and spacing of buildings would be established through the use of the BRS Control System, whereas siting and design must always remain discretionary and subject to the intuitive approach of the architect and planner.

Of course it is necessary to stipulate that these three measures are applied simultaneously, but, clearly, at the end of this process two of the sets of controls will only have been able to prevent inefficient or non-functional types of buildings and it will still remain for the third to ensure a more positive, creative approach to good urban design.

The BRS System, which formed a part of this network of controls, should, it is emphasised, on its own, not only secure adequate daylighting standards, but also bring about some improvements with regard to potential fire-spread between adjoining buildings, some reduction in noise transmission, improvements in privacy and a greater degree of freedom from overlooking between adjoining buildings. It should also encourage the spacing of buildings rather than allow canyon type developments, particularly alongside city streets.

The then London County Council concluded, however, at an early stage after the adoption of the BRS System, that the effect of the Council's standards of plot ratio and daylighting control was to encourage high buildings in the form of an open spine or tower, rather than a lower, bulky type of building surrounding internal courtyards.

It must be appreciated that any system such as this may itself run the risk of producing a new set of stereotypes, however well it avoids some of the other less satisfactory alternatives. It, too, may need continual change and variation and, above all, the overriding hand of the master urban designer, able to assert his influence to permit artistic groupings, rhythmic spacing and skilful and harmonious juxtaposition. Perhaps the most unfortunate aspect of the application of the new systems in London has been that, because they are based on a measurable numerical or geometrical method, they have tended to pre-occupy the attention of planners at the expense of other considerations, and been applied much more rigidly than was often desirable.

Those enactments arising from planning considerations which have a purely aesthetic motive are very generally resented. It is frequently argued that, as there are no absolute canons of beauty in the visual arts, any attempt to impose by legislation external qualities of fitness and taste in the living environment of a city is doomed to failure, if expected to command general approval.

There is no doubt that aesthetic controls by public regulation can find no basis of commonly accepted principles upon which to rely. It is also a fact that most of these controls to date have been unsuccessful to a greater or lesser degree in achieving the objectives at which they are aimed.

Aesthetic criteria or controls have created so much dissension and disagreement that planning authorities have tended to steer clear of them: encouraged in this attitude, moreover, by the fact that such criteria or controls are less susceptible to any precise definition or measurement and therefore to any clear-cut system of administration.

Nevertheless, even though it may be impossible to find, at any given time, an entirely and widely-accepted range of principles on which to base such forms of control with aesthetic implications, attempts must be undertaken to create such a comprehensive workable system, since, without it, a continuation of the disorder and chaos for which our cities have become notorious, will be unavoidable.

Perhaps many of the misconceptions about, and much of the dislike of, any form of aesthetic control can, to a considerable extent, be dispelled if it can be shown that such control takes place through a beneficent system which attempts to provide the best of all possible worlds for the individual developer at any given time, as well as for the community as a whole.

At present, however, and as matters now stand, no individual developer or his professional advisers have any form of protection from what are often major changes in the context into which they have conscientiously fitted their contribution to the urban fabric. The situation in which a building, designed and erected at one moment of time, is quickly superseded by ill-considered, incompatible developments taking place close to it, occurs continuously.

The individual developer or building owner, his architects or planning consultants, cannot possibly be expected to have more than, at best, a broad impression of the future aesthetic goals and objectives of the city as a whole. At the present time, unfortunately, all too often the city planning authority may have little more than such an impression. Ideally, in future, all cities must have defined aesthetic objectives. These will need to be administered with a degree of continuity and preferably under the ultimate control of a single 'master planner' or team.

Only in this way, it is maintained, can the best overall aesthetic results be achieved, and within this framework the maximum degree of aesthetic planning and design flexibility be afforded to individual developers without resort to unnecessary, negative rule-of-thumb, regulations and restrictions. These are unnecessary in the sense that they cannot ever be shown to be part of the desirable basic system necessary to establish suitable density levels—having regard to traffic generation implications—nor yet as a means of ensuring that buildings, which are either a structural, health or fire hazard, are not erected in cities.

After the design and guidance preconditions have been met, however, it will be argued here, as the main hypothesis to be examined subsequently, that full and adequate aesthetic control can still only be ultimately administered through a system of visual analysis and design simulation studies.

Obviously, stock rules-of-thumb and the negative forms of stipulation which have, to date, been enforced in relation to most city development, have not succeeded in producing, in the majority of cases, anything more than a disorganised clutter of unrelated buildings. At worst, they have produced some monstrous eyesores which, however much they may have conformed to ordinances, are an affront to the visual senses, contributing nothing whatever to a positive, pleasurable environment, but rather tending to make the city an abomination for all.

It is too much to expect that any system will provide visual satisfaction for everyone. The best we can hope for is to strive for a degree of excellence—which can reasonably be assured—resulting from the endeavours of urban designers and planners who have already proved themselves and who have both the necessary experience and intuitive sense and skill. We must be prepared to place our trust in a system of this kind rather than in no system at all, or in the often clumsy efforts of amateur administrators. Otherwise we should simply be faced with an abject demonstration of total defeat, and an admission that we are not able to do anything to rectify the muddle that confronts us in our cities.

Unfortunately, it is the lot of most architects and nearly all planners to be continually confronted with situations in which, in spite of their experience and advice, a lay committee or the public as a whole profess to know better and as frequently insist on pressing their individual and collective points of view against sound advice. It is of the utmost importance, therefore, that not only should there be a much greater degree of responsibility vested in trained and experienced professionals at both government and local government level, whether they be concerned with problems of physical development of the city or, for that matter, with other governmental problems, but also a move in the direction of a greater degree of professionalism amongst our political and government administrators and legislators.

Only in this way can we hope to have any understanding of the need for a consistent and soundly-based set of policies to be applied by the executive administrative team, working from a background of tested experience. It is difficult to understand in all the circumstances how, in some of the most important work undertaken in our communities concerned with government and local government agencies, we have not hitherto insisted on such safeguards. Any improvement in the management of our affairs in future must be wholly dependent on the progressive elimination of that inept amateurism in government at all levels for which, in the past, we have paid so dearly.

If we are prepared to accept the urgency of these changes then much more flexible systems of control, particularly in relation to aesthetic matters, become not only more important but are thereby facilitated. Only when we no longer have to depend on 'safe' sets of optimistic and too-detailed restrictive rules, which can be applied by unimaginative and ill-trained officials with the minimum of experience, can we expect to see positive and creative urban design and planning.

We need to establish the belief, if we are to do anything about the quality of our cities, that it is right and proper in aesthetic matters, as well as in other questions of moment, for those who have the training and experience to hold convictions without necessarily being required to articulate them verbally. On the contrary, we should try to accept that in aesthetic choices intuition has a vital role to play. It is still as true today as ever that with regard to matters of taste there can be no dispute. Surely, therefore, we can accept the logical corollary of putting our trust in the experienced and intuitive approach as the only workable answer to aesthetic order in the city.

Once again we return to a recognition of the fact that the maintenance, and creation of aesthetic standards in the city have increasingly become the urban 'missing link'. Even though this may be an area of conflicting opinions and frequent misunderstandings, it must, nevertheless, not be left, as is so often the case at present, purely to chance or to arbitrary sets of meaningless rules. 'Grasping the nettle' and establishing the sort of standard to apply in matters of aesthetics is, whether we like it or not, something which must both be attempted and resolved.

FIG. 65.   The 'Latino–Americano' building, Mexico City.

FIG. 66.   Piazza di Spagna, Rome.

FIG. 67. 'Little Venice', North Westminster, London.

FIG. 68. Spitalerstrasse, Hamburg.

FIG. 69. The Strøget, Copenhagen, and copper clad spires.

FIG. 70.   St Mark's Piazza, Venice.

FIG. 71. Karl–Johan's Gate, Oslo—an undulating vista.

FIG. 72. Wenceslas Square, Prague—elevated climax.

FIG. 73. Paris vista—the École Militaire and UNESCO building.

FIG. 74.   'Centre Point', St Giles Circus, London.

FIG. 75.   Toronto Civic Centre.

FIG. 76. Office development in 'The Barbican', London.

FIG. 77. SAS offices, Copenhagen.

FIG. 78.   The Reserve Bank building, Adelaide, S. Australia.

FIG. 79.   The World Trade Centre, Tokyo.

FIG. 80.   Lower Manhattan skyline.

FIG. 81. Central Manhattan.

136

FIG. 82. St Paul's Cathedral and the City of London from across the Thames.

FIG. 83.   Montreal skyline.

FIG. 84.   Sydney Harbour and city.

FIG. 85.   Kensington Gardens, London.

FIG. 86. Djalan Thamrin, Djakarta, Indonesia—open planning.

FIG. 87. Leibnizüfer ring road, Hanover—spacious layout.

FIG. 88.   Reconstruction of Le Havre, France—urban composition and balance.

FIG. 89.   The canyon street.

FIG. 90.   Chandigarh Town Centre, India.

FIG. 91. Greenwich Naval College—symmetrical perfection.

146

FIG. 92.   Piazza del Popolo, Rome—repetitive formality.

FIG. 93.   Thamesmead, London—formality belonging to a more autocratic age.

FIG. 94. Thamesmead, London.

FIG. 95. St Mark's Campanile and the Doge's Palace, Venice.

FIG. 96. Group of office towers, 'La Defense', Paris.

Chapter VIII

Aesthetic theories and applications

After all essential economic, sociological, political, administrative and functional criteria have been studied and satisfied to the fullest extent in the urban development project, the attainment of a satisfactory aesthetic quality in the environment can only be achieved by comprehensive design; relating each component to an area, to a district, and then, in turn, to the city as a whole. The time when buildings were designed as individual masterpieces, regardless of their surroundings, is, it is to be hoped, drawing to an end as this long-held attitude towards building has been almost wholly responsible for the fragmentation of city centres and their ragged, untidy, uncontrolled appearance (Figs. 64 and 65).

This attitude has persisted, apparently in the unreasoned expectation that, in the course of time, accidental associations and compositions might produce satisfactory results—not only a vain hope but a most wasteful process, lacking rationality in a rational age. It is even less likely to be acceptable, moreover, as a substitute basis for any planned future logical urban development.

What is needed is the achievement of a methodology which gives a certain guarantee of beauty with efficiency and some hope of civic excellence. In the long run, lack of control or negative methods of control of the visual qualities will be seen as capable only of preventing the worst solecisms. Worthwhile achievements will require the kind of talent that is demonstrated by the musician, the poet, or the painter, but with the additional obligation of meeting functional necessities in an artistic fashion.

Yet the beauty we know as likely to be most satisfying and permanent has a highly abstract quality, indefinable in terms of a descriptive formula but clearly perceivable to the enlightened and trained observer—surely the type of person we must cater for, knowing that by so doing we can hope to build up a high general level of appreciation. Obviously, compromises or attempts to legislate for popular levels of taste, or to please the largest majority, must be doomed to failure or a level of mediocrity.

Our starting point must undoubtedly be that of the planning team working in concert—with a continuous aesthetic check through visual media studies undertaken by skilled and experienced people. This is the only way, it is maintained, by which to produce a framework with certainty and logic and the promise of worthwhile results— one within which the 'thousand designers' who will follow can hope to act effectively.

It is as necessary to be alert against the current theories of complexity and confusion for their own sake and as a desirable end as it is against too obvious regimentation with its pejorative connotations. Controlled and deliberately designed variety is a very positive process. Complexity has no inherent automatic virtue and cannot be the basis of a rational methodology—but merely the means of confusing the civic composition, as an end in itself, in the vain gambler's hope that the pieces of the puzzle may fall

151

into place to produce a mesmerism of kaleidoscopic impressions with some positive aesthetic values.

This can scarcely be thought of as a means of establishing coherence, order and unity—the fundamental attributes of good civic design in any age and which must be derived directly from, and be consistent with, functional efficiency which imposes its own disciplines and method.

Why has it been thought necessary, it may be asked, to suggest a considerable pre-occupation with, and increasing attention to, the problem of the perceived city—the city of vision? The sole answer is that it provides the ultimate test of whether or not our complex political, social, economic, geographic, climatic, technological and engineering methods and approaches to the city are establishing, at macro-cosmic level, a single focus, aim, or objective directed towards the provision of a worthwhile environment for people to live, work and play in.

This environment will utterly fail in its purpose unless it provides that satisfaction which only comes from the human perception of a thing of beauty. A similar situation occurs in considering, at micro-cosmic level, the distinction between a merely function-ally efficient building and one that has, by contrast, the timeless and enduring qualities of real architecture.

Although architects were also invariably trained, fifty years or so ago, in the then leading English University School, as civic designers—thus preceding by very many years the recent developments in environmental design—it has currently become fashionable to decry the creative design approach as one concerned primarily with urban cosmetics, or historically-derivative town building ideas unrelated to contempo-rary needs and functions.

With the warning apparent to all of what mere utilitarianism could do to the city, when divorced from any concern for creating a humane environment, it might have been thought that a renewal of emphasis would have occurred long ago on the importance of civic or urban design.

Yet, though half-a-century has passed by, in the English-speaking world at least the quality of the environment had, until very recently, scarcely received more than a token gesture from a limited number of clear-sighted individuals. The technological vandals have for far too long had matters entirely their own way as, too, has the non-constructive school of analytical behaviourists.

In consequence of this loss of perspective, the problem is now infinitely more difficult to deal with, and we have the added complication of a multiplicity of disciplines persuading themselves that theirs is the vital role in city building, and the one which will provide the only satisfactory answers. How far this is from the truth can be judged by casual observation of most of our cities, and their utter failure to inspire or uplift the soul in anything like the way that earlier historical centres could (Fig. 66).

This is far from arguing for a process of putting back the clock, but rather for a continuation of the application of conscious aesthetic principles in the collective design of our cities. This is in contrast to advocating a devotion of all of our zeal to a similar process merely applied to individual buildings—in the mistaken belief that, because we have seldom hitherto managed to control our urban context as a whole, an *a priori* assumption exists that in future we will still be unable to do so.

The even more damaging assumption, of course, is that the slick decision-making process with which we have become involved—more redolent of the patent medicine salesman—is a preferable substitute for vitally important matters of taste which cannot be expressed in arithmetical terms.

One thing, above all, must be abundantly clear and that is the fact that decisions in regard to the planning of our cities cannot be based simply on historical precedents or derivatives if we are to establish a new scale of aesthetic values. Rather must we search for, and apply, an empiric system of control allied to such known and accepted canons of artistic merit, or aesthetic criteria, available to us—as a complementary aspect of functional efficiency.

By trial-and-error methods and using visual observation techniques, all the necessary alternatives should be tested, with a continuous 'feed-back' of experience from the actual physical construction to the model simulation. The effectiveness of this technique, however, clearly depends, to a very considerable extent, on the skill and experience of the individual designer and planner.

The required social, economic, topographical, transportation, and other functional analyses of the city necessarily stop short of giving it form—this must be the work of the creative master-mind; capable of translating the vital statistics into aesthetic satisfactions—or the diagnostic and factual data into a meaningful and worthwhile environment, fit for people to use and from which to draw their inspirations and stimuli. This creative activity must increasingly be seen as the key, and essentially the only solution to, the problem of providing a humane urban environment.

Unless trained urban designers and planners, with an acknowledged emphasis on visual education, are, moreover, accepted as the *sine qua non* in this equation, we must expect city planning to be without its essential creative quality, and instead simply to become a purely bureaucratic and negative operation, leaving a professional void in the field of urban design for non-planners to fill with, obviously, a potential for the most disastrous results.

We must increasingly be aware of the difficult fact that words alone are inadequate to analyse and describe civic design which needs to be studied by observation and experience of the ways in which people live and work in the city, as well as of the structural principles and planning and building regulations to which the designer has to conform. If we are to produce the satisfactory ultimate aesthetic objective and not lose sight of the fact that this is the principal criterion, then observation must be the all-important controlling factor.

It is no less true, whether it be said of the collective city group of buildings or the individual building, that, whatever other definition we may choose to use, undeniably, even at best these involve, in essence, the artistic expression of a scientific and functional solution to the problem of creating practical and useful spaces and volumes.

Obviously we have many other design problems to solve in relation both to the individual building and to the enlarged urban context. Nonetheless, in whatever circumstances and whether it is the work of the architectural profession or of the urban design creative field we have to consider, the essential principles can be similarly expressed.

The view of one critic is that the city can never be a work of art but the confirmation or denial of this, it might be held, must depend, to a considerable extent, on what is meant by art.[93]

If the assumption is that the urban planner or designer sets out with the principal intention of creating an artistic city for its own sake as a first prerequisite; this would be very likely to presage a measure of failure. If, however, we assume that creating a functional, efficient, city is not enough, but that the finished city must also be given an aesthetic quality, as being the ultimate and most important achievement of all, then the city not only can be, but ideally should be, a work of art.

Only some of the most recent, haphazardly undesigned American cities, which this same critic no doubt has in mind, could have led to such an unfortunate misconception. On the other hand, numerous earlier examples of worthy cities could leave us in no doubt as to their being works of art.

It is an essential part of the present thesis that a way has to be found to revive these aesthetic qualities so that the city may be more convincingly, if not an actual work of art, at least an aggregation of artistically-conceived components with an underlying cohesion and a sense of aesthetic unity and consistency. This is thus to argue for the very antithesis of the prevailing preoccupation with urban 'systems approaches' or operationally-researched cities as ends in themselves, since they are likely to be totally lacking in vitality or soul. What do we really achieve by adopting techniques with a concentration on functional efficiency at any cost, if the resulting environment is one totally lacking in any sense of beauty or pleasure?

If, as the alternative, it is accepted that art has an important role to play in city design, we are still confronted with the problem of choices and standards since, as most people will be aware: 'one cannot dispute matters of taste' (to use the well-known aphorism). This, however, is a problem we must be prepared to face if we are to have any hope of establishing an acceptable aesthetic philosophy or a workable set of criteria. Its solution is certainly not beyond the bounds of human ingenuity and innovation.

A further hurdle we have to surmount is, in many ways, much more difficult—the fact that beauty lies in the eye of the beholder. The implication that there can be no commonly-accepted 'yardstick' or set of standards which may be applied in relation to aesthetic questions, is one that needs consideration. A closer examination of the complex field of perception and the visual medium is necessary in order to understand how valid this objection is and whether the means can be found to overcome it.

In our investigation of the whole problem of perception we need first to know something of the end product of the visual, physiological, psychological process, and whether the same objects are likely to produce similar sets of intellectual responses in different individuals.

If this could conceivably be shown to be the case, then we would have a firm basis on which to undertake all design solutions, at whatever scale, with the certainty that they would be perceived in a predictable way. If, on the other hand, this appears unlikely, then we must surely conclude that standards of quality should be established by those who are trained to undertake such work and by whose precepts and creative efforts levels of popular taste may be expected to be influenced.

This process may seem to imply a form of artistic dictatorship but if clear thought is brought to bear on the question it must be abundantly obvious that there are only two alternatives open to us, broadly speaking—chaotic anarchy, in which the opinions and ideas of every individual are given equal weight, regardless of their merits, and the method of operating basically on those canons of beauty, quality and taste which, over long periods, have been established as likely to satisfy the largest number of visually-trained and artistically-sensitive individuals.

There seems to be no escaping this choice. Therefore, however precisely, and with whatever set of systems or methods we try to achieve the desired ends, it must be the second of the above alternatives which we should support if we are ever to have cities truly fit for their purpose and an effectively organised visual environment.

The importance of experience in the perception process, and therefore the justification for placing a large measure of responsibility in the hands of trained designers, is that we know that perception itself is directly affected by experience and thus can be regarded as a series of conditioned responses. In other words, people may be said to interpret what they see very largely in terms of what they are accustomed to. Much experimental work underlines this fact and confirms its importance.

Undoubtedly one of the most interesting sets of studies concerned with perceptive response has been carried out by Lynch and referred to in 'The Image of the City'.[120] However, while these carried forward our knowledge of the ways in which many different people were actually perceiving the physical form of the city, and recording the similarities, as well as the differences of approach, this analytical tool has so far not apparently led to any useful synthesis or methodology for creative planning.

Wide though the number of variables were in this study, we are still left with far too limited information from which to prepare a perceptual code, and which could be regarded as a reliable basis for informed design decisions.

Even though this detailed analysis of visual perceptual responses may not provide a workable set of conclusions, which can be more generally and reliably applied as a set of objective tools for the urban designer, it is likely, nevertheless, through an enlargement of his personal experience and awareness, to influence the subjective judgements upon which he will ultimately have to depend. To this extent, the studies have had undeniable value and have come nearer to opening the door to a better understanding of the intractable problem of the aesthetic quality of a city on an organised basis, than anything previously recorded.

There are many other facts about the perceptive process which may have a bearing on this whole problem. For example, the human ability to comprehend and process environmental clues seems to be limited genetically so that, at the outset, we have to accept that not all men are born equal, and least of all in the matter of spatial and formal sensibility and awareness. Those who have been concerned with architectural education will be well acquainted with this fact.

We also know that it is the special growth of the receptor centres for touch and sight and of the association areas, that institutes in the primates an instinctively elaborated mechanism for contact with the environment. This would suggest that, whatever the variations between individual responses, the human being is much more aware of his physical surroundings than he may be able to express in any articulate way. It cannot therefore be concluded that he is blindly unaware of the chaotic urban mess he all too often occupies. Even though he may have concluded that there is little he can do about it the planner's appreciation of order and of beauty will not go unrewarded in terms of human response.

The entire school of 'Gestalt'-psychologists, in attempting to analyse the psychological and perceptual responses more closely, came to the conclusion that the perceptual process is always one of actively organising configurations and of picking out a figure from its ground of grouping and pattern making. This is basic. Other laws, such as that relating to similarity, proximity, closure and continuation all tend to underline the concept of perceptual organisation as a means of dealing with particular sets of visually-experienced circumstances.

There may be some disagreement as to how far this attempt at scientific rationalisation helps us in understanding the whole range of perceptual responses: it nevertheless does establish the clear suggestion of an innate human appreciation of order, as against disorganisation.

Undoubtedly one of the most intangible aspects of our understanding of perception is that we need to understand that there are immense differences between the real, or physical, world as it is defined and measured by the instruments of the physical sciences, and the perceived world of normal, unaided observation. This forms the basis of the main argument, which follows, for finally resorting to a visual form of analysis or appraisal of architectural and urban planning solutions which, otherwise, are likely to defy any known form of rational enquiry, in the present state of our knowledge.

In the first place we know that different people perceive the same groups of objects differently, both as regards the image itself on the retina, and, more so, at the termination of the physiological-psychological sequence and in the mental record impressed on the brain. Beauty is not, therefore, so much in the eye of the beholder as in his mind. Even if we try to trace this process through the physiological responses in the vastly complex neural network, to the final set of images, we are still a long way off codifying visual environment in a way that would lead to predictable mental responses in fixed sets of circumstances.

There therefore seems no alternative at present to an empiric approach and frank acceptance of a set of criteria gradually built up by those trained and experienced in this work; just as, for example, most medical diagnosis is still necessarily undertaken on a basis of personal human experience—and for which at present there is also no substitute, however valuable the computer proves to be as an adjunct.

This entire question, moreover, becomes vastly more complicated and even less predictable when we bring into account the vitally important and always relevant factor of movement. We cannot think in terms of a set of static images—but rather a connected sequence of dynamic responses—as our basic equation in urban perception.

It is a fact that what we observe is never in exact correspondence with the physical situation; some aspects are omitted, some added, some distorted. Therefore, most of the qualities of the world about us which we perceive, such as size, colour and weight, are only very loosely related to the physical measurements to which we have given the same names. This is also equally true of form and shape, as is well evidenced by the illusions created by the familiar Ames room experiments.

The study of perception is primarily psychological, therefore no amount of study of the physical manifestations alone, or confined to the physiological structure, will teach us anything about perception.

On being confronted with a situation which seems to suggest a dead end and in order to proceed further, two different sets of procedures have been used to discover the inventory of different sensory qualities, or sensations, which we can observe, and to understand the differences in physical stimuli which are responsible for these differences in sensation. These have been termed sensory psycho-physics and analytic introspection.

To explain the latter first, we might think of an observer looking at what appears to be a uniformly coloured cube with right angles; which is itself a mental interpretation—and of this being represented as though it were a drawing on paper in two dimensions, with the necessary adjustment of light, shade and angles.

Our major sensory systems are not directly in contact with the objects we see. These are therefore described as distal stimuli, by which term we imply that they stimulate our nervous system indirectly by reflecting light energy, some of which may not even reach our sense organs. The energy patterns that do reach our sense organs are, however, the proximal stimuli. We can only be aware of the distal physical world—the world of space and objects and motion—through these proximal stimuli distributions acting upon our sense organs.

There appears to have been some success in tracing, from particular stimuli, the part of the nervous system termed a receptor neuron which is responsive to a particular kind of physical energy. In turn, the impulses from these areas enter the cerebral cortex of the brain in what is called the projection area.

As a physiological experiment it is enormously important to know whether a substitute for the proximal stimulus can be provided by an electrical or mechanical artificial stimulus of the sensory nerves. This has led to the conclusion that we do not see objects directly, nor do we see the retinal image, nor, in the normally-accepted sense, do we see the excitation of the optic nerve. What we claim we see is the final effect on the projection area of the cerebral cortex of this long chain of impulses or stimuli moving through a part of the nervous system.

While we have gone this far in tracing and understanding the visual perceptive process it still does not tell us much about the objective responses to those messages delivered to the relevant area of the brain—and once again we must conclude that the only approach to this at present will be through systematic empiric methods.

Efforts have been made, over the years, to extend this process of discovery and association in order to learn how our visual sensations combine with the images acquired in our past experiences and thus construct our perceptions of space and spatial position. We know that the sensation, as it is received, cannot be disassociated from knowledge and memory related to the particular object providing the stimulus.

To further complicate this whole question, it has been shown that if we ponder and reflect, the visual sensations of every object's properties appear to vary from one moment to the next. Size, shape, brightness, all change drastically in the optic array and in the retinal image, as the observer and the objects he looks at move about and so, therefore, should our observations change.

The further fact, of which most of us will be aware, is that the illusions and persistences reveal discrepancies between what we should observe if sensations are simply added together, on the one hand, and what we do, in fact, observe on the other. These well-known discrepancies and illusions become overwhelming when we consider the perception of shape and of notion. Sensations seem to become completely unobservable and totally submerged in the overall organisation of the perceived object. Moreover, familiar shape is no better a predictor of what we will see than are colour and familiar size.

Unfortunately, we have to conclude, after an examination of all the components of colour, position, shape and size and of visual perception, that sensory psychophysics data do not give an accurate prediction of the observations made when all these elements are combined together.

In these circumstances it is therefore unarguable that some form of empiricism is tenable. The only way to know what association any observer has formed is to discover what he has experienced in the past, and to perform an environmental survey of the frequented localities in order to discover what combinations of stimulus patterns are likely to confront the average observer.

It seems likely that some theory of complex perception processes of association will inevitably be devised with, perhaps, in due course the elaboration of a 'logical model'. This could at least allow the investigation of a very large number of factual variables from which, perhaps, systematic patterns may appear as between object and response.

It must, however, be appreciated that the neural circuitry in the cerebral cortex of the brain is immensely complex. An attempt to explain perception in terms of brain response would necessarily have to accept a very simplified, and therefore probably a most misleading, formula or model.

Against this it has now been realised that individual receptor actions do not produce observable elements of experience translated into combinations in the association areas of the brain. The idea of attempting to break down the complex patterns and actions into simpler components is, therefore, still an extremely forbidding one, and one about which there can be no undue optimism. This is in spite of the fact that our nervous systems appear to organise the perceived world in whatever way will keep changes and differences to a minimum, and thus avoid sensory overload.

Here we see confirmation of the instinctive desire for simplicity as against complexity. Nevertheless, while the law of simplicity looks like a very powerful principle it does not necessarily take us much further along the road of understanding how the simplification itself works and what is its end product.

This somewhat discursive enquiry is far from being a mere digression but is aimed at demonstrating the fundamental degree of uncertainty which still surrounds the complex problem of perception, and the difficulty of predicting, in any known way, how a particular individual is going to respond to a set of visual stimuli. It is therefore argued that, in these circumstances, which are unlikely to change soon, the only useful and workable approach is for the talented and experienced designer to rely on his own stock of perceptive responses as the basis of an intuitive approach to a particular problem. This would be based on the reasonably well-founded hope that it could constitute an acceptable basis, either initially or in the course of time, for those who have that special ability to comprehend and process the environmental situation.

It will never be possible to appeal with certainty to those who have been termed the 'aesthetic cripples' and we have no alternative, therefore, but to place our reliance completely on sound, subjective intuitive judgements.

The biologist, Dr Abercrombie, has referred to two levels of designing—that of putting real things together, which we perceive with our senses and manipulate in three-dimensional space, or designing in the abstract, which is a matter of visualisation. [3] She rightly observes that, 'we tend to sneer at the first. It seems too direct and simple'. Yet it appears that, sooner or later, the only way in which people can 'experience' our buildings will be by means of their senses.

Why then, Dr Abercrombie asks, should we be afraid to regulate the design of buildings in this way? She provides the answer, which is, of course: 'Plato told us to beware of using real material objects in the solving of problems'.

Plato is said to have castigated Archytes, a mathematician, for using models to work out solutions in geometry. 'And ever since we have believed, with Plato, that mental processes somehow are better than physical ones'. It has thus become fashionable to avoid the suggestion of three-dimensional manipulation. 'The inter-action chart has taken the place of the drawing as the object for final presentation'.

This contemporary tendency to want to measure everything, including aesthetic values, in terms of numbers, is indeed one of the curses of the age and must be firmly rejected if we are to find an acceptable technique for dealing, in an effective way, with the crucially difficult design problems of the city.

It is unquestionably of vital importance to obtain a better understanding of the perceptive visual process and, more particularly, the extent to which we may be able to place reliance upon this in a way which would permit a firm basis of prediction of observer responses for the urban designer. However, the further point has been made on a number of occasions by writers in the specialised field of architectural aesthetics that architecture is the outward and visible artistic expression of scientific applications of human problems. It must therefore not merely be perceived by the various senses but experienced as a totality. Any change in one aspect or component of the environment likely to affect one of the senses must inevitably influence perception by the rest— just as the overriding control of prior experiences will condition the whole perception process.

Moreover, the visual part of the perception process is dynamic rather than static, inasmuch as it is concerned both with the movement of the subject up to, around and through buildings and groups of buildings and spaces; but the eyes and the head are also in a continuous state of movement through which light, shade, form and, most particularly, the three-dimensional binocular quality, are fully comprehended.

The heightened impressions of space obtained by people with claustrophobic tendencies or those addicted to vertigo, are examples of the more obvious perceptive processes involving more than one of the senses. The physical effort of movement up or down stairs or ramps, the acoustical qualities leading to echoes or to the dead effect of a noiseless area, the clinical odour of a hospital and the very characteristic smell experienced in particular cities are obvious examples of sensory perception—

such as will heighten the effect of the visual impact—coming into play in an architectural or urban environment.

Taste is so closely linked with the olfactory sense that, while it may not be directly involved in perception, its participation in the whole process cannot be discounted. However, the tactile qualities which will be appreciated primarily through the visual image must also bear on the whole process of appraisal, largely as a consequence of a background of experience of the actual physical feel of materials and textures. This appreciation does not have to be continually renewed through physical contact.

It has also been pointed out recently that even the subtle process by which we maintain a balance, through a wonderful physiological mechanism related to the inner ear, confers a particular sensitivity to vertical alignments and, in all probability, to symmetry. The extent to which air movements can either assist in, or act at variance with, the sense of enclosure, can be of particular importance in the urban environment. One has only to think of some of the unfriendly, windy spaces in some cities on the one hand, and the protective sense of intimacy in relatively undisturbed enclosed areas in others, to realise that such impressions are not solely gained through the visual perceptive process.

All of these facts point to the inevitable conclusion that the true experience of architecture, both in individual buildings or 'in extenso' in the urban design environment, is an enormously complex process calling into operation every part of the human physiology through the various perceptual mechanisms and the metabolic process, leading to a very individual and personal synthesis. This total mental image will then be further interpreted and conditioned through a final process involving both intuition and experience. The extent to which these conditioning elements interact will also vary for each individual in any given set of circumstances.

All this shows that there appears, in the state of our present knowledge, to be no certain way in which the designer may set about satisfying all tastes and all viewpoints, and in any given culture or set of values or judgements, at any given period of history, there cannot ever be a single accepted criterion of beauty.

Clearly, therefore, the wide problem of urban design, further complicated as it is by the time-scale, can only be undertaken, as has already been postulated, either under the guidance of a single trained designer—to ensure a consistent evaluation in terms of likely perceptual responses—or by a team sufficiently in agreement with a dominant philosophy and set of techniques to impart a similar degree of consistency. Only in this way can it be hoped that standards of taste and judgement, albeit on a subjective, intuitive, basis, will ultimately find a sufficiently wide acceptance to inculcate similar standards on a far wider basis.

In view of the totality of the sensory experience involved, clearly the designer must himself understand and cater explicitly for the whole spectrum of perception, although it must be considered that the visual analysis and synthesis is the key to the whole structure of urban design and its full appreciation. Without this and the *prima facie* satisfaction which an adequate and persuasive visual image can confer, none of the perception processes occurring through the other senses can be expected to rescue it from the inevitable lack of order or cohesion.

Important though the structural abutments, such as are implied by functional considerations of an efficient urban planning system and including the recognition of the many other elements of perception, may be, without the visual keystone the whole system must collapse. This, briefly, can be said to be the cause of the plight confronting so many contemporary cities.

Once we have clearly understood the complexity of the perceptive process, it is possible to deal with the question of beauty itself and how far we may be likely to guarantee this quality in our urban design. It has been established that this is not an easily definable quality nor is it the same for everyone. In any event, its very personal interpretation is conditioned in so many ways that there seems to be very little virtue in trying to narrow down the definition of beauty, as such, by directing our further researches into the realms of theory.

It is now more clearly evident than before that 'beauty is no quality of things but of experiences',[36] and that, 'it lives in seeming'. Therefore any attempts to discriminate between the virtues of the Hedonistic-moral theory of Tolstoy or Ruskin, the Realistic-typical theory of Aristotle, the Intellectualist theories of Kant and Coleridge, the Emotionalist theories of Schopenhauer and Nietzsche, the Expressionist theory of Croce or the theories of Einfuhlung seem unlikely to be able to indicate directions in which a better understanding of applied urban aesthetics may be codified. This is due to the fact that architecture is not solely an art form but is necessarily equally concerned with function and the whole range of sensory experience.

With a somewhat clearer picture of how far we may expect to be able to introduce a design methodology or a set of systematic rules which can be applied in the urban design process, it is of particular interest to look at the views and ideas of both practitioners and critics in this field.

It has, for example, been argued as an acceptable generalisation that, 'few will quarrel with urban beauty as an ideal, but fewer still will value it highly or grant it a place in government programmes for the American city', and that, 'even some, with an enlightened social interest, who long ago accepted public intervention in a great variety of urban problems, suspect that the architect–planner seeks to strait-jacket free choice and variety in private tastes'.[46]

The same writer observes that, 'our heroes in art, like our other idols, are those who pursue the individual liberties of virtuosity, initiative or courage'. It is indeed one of the serious practical problems which we have to recognise that, in applying subjective judgements on the whole urban design framework, we must expect arguments to the effect that this implies the imposition of standards of taste on all participants, to the detriment of individual artistic liberty.

The truth is, however, that the system of visual appraisal of the individual components of the urban environment, as and when these are undertaken by particular architects or urban designers, provides enormous scope for variety through a multiplicity of alternatives. Moreover, it leaves in the hands of the individual promoter a substantial share in the final decision between alternatives. The way in which it is proposed to operate such a system will be elaborated on in more detail later.

As an important milestone it is encouraging to recall that, in at least one country—the United States—the courts have 'sanctioned beauty of urban design as a public purpose',[46] through a firmly established decision in the Supreme Court. On the other hand, it has been emphasised that there is, as yet, almost no political sanction for public programmes in urban design—certainly so far as the United States is concerned —and therefore no means of preventing the perpetration of buildings or urban groups which do not satisfy the definition of beauty.

There is, of course, the further problem of developing an awareness of, and cultivating an appreciation of, the need for aesthetic quality; if the evidence is to be taken from cities in their present condition. There seems little prospect that, even if city dwellers ultimately appear to 'possess a potent and universal theory of what makes the city beautiful and well ordered' or have a philosophy for undertaking community design, the possession of 'a systematic strategy for bringing about an aesthetic order' may be a fruitful direction for research, since it is extremely unlikely, for reasons already indicated, that general agreement, either in fact or in theory, can be expected. Certainly this cannot be the case until much more enlightened work, with the essential degree of inspired guidance, has been undertaken.

It is probably entirely true, when everything is considered, that intuition is the only source of creativity in science or anything else. We can also receive valuable reassurance by recognising the fact that, in the extremely complex operation of planning for total sensory experience, the preference of really creative individuals falls invariably and inevitably on the side of intuitive perception. Moreover, it can be assumed that it is just these people who can apply their experience in the most meaningful and positive way.

It may be most useful, in summarising this part of the present chapter, to think specifically of the perception process related to the city on a city scale. In doing so it must be appreciated that if there is to be such a thing as urban design it must be related to some perception of the city as a whole. It cannot deal simply with parts of the city at architectural scale. However, the unity of the city as an accepted fact need not be thought of solely in terms of a single snapshot view encompassing the whole urban area, but as a unified continuous experience which may take place over many miles and many days.

In further underlining the importance of this unified perceptive experience, it is clear that the essential factor is that all parts of the city so experienced must be recognisable as parts of the whole city. This need not, of course, in any way restrict diversity or variety within the overall attainment of unity of concept.

As has also been pointed out, 'perception of the city today is more than rude contact with its physical solids and voids'.[73] Such perception requires a new kind of insight— unifying personal experiences—because of the greater degree of mobility and ease of movement. Time and space are thus related in our experience and we can see whole areas of the city almost simultaneously, both in their physical appearance and as a correlation of factual, functional and sociological data.

It therefore becomes clear that in attempting to create aesthetic qualities in a city a realistic approach is imperative. When urban design means that we can begin to see a reflection of the essential urban influences compatible with social, political and economic needs, we may expect cities with a sense of purpose and the assurance of a future. It is towards these ends that we must now direct our attention in more detail.

Chapter IX

A philosophy of urban design: case studies

Although most people seem to have fairly firm views as to the appearance and design of their houses, both inside and outside, when it comes to the consideration of the centres of their cities the same process no longer seems consciously to take place, among the large majority of city dwellers in any explicit way. Otherwise how could cities have deteriorated to the condition in which we see them today? The daily preoccupations of city life, particularly for those who have charge of a motor vehicle and have to guide it safely through the maelstrom of urban traffic, may have a great deal to do with this.

Others may be aware of the city's shortcomings, and because it is not a matter which requires their individual investment or ownership, but one which is in the hands of the government of the day, they think that there is nothing that can be done about it and simply accept the situation as yet another example of the inevitable 'march of progress'. It is, of course, clear that even those who are conscious of the shoddy and unsatisfactory nature of the urban environment are not always able to express the reasons for their feelings in any satisfactory or methodical way as a prelude to a cure.

Even though, in certain circumstances, there may be the most obvious conflicts with any generally-accepted canons of beauty, or where there is an outrageous discordance in design, or, in fact, an entire lack of design, this may be only fully comprehended by those who are specifically trained to both observe and analyse, and who have sufficient experience in the field of urban design to know how the situation might be improved.

In time, it has already been suggested, this situation must rectify itself and the commonly-accepted levels of taste raised to a pitch where a better appreciation of what is possible and most desirable in city planning and urban design will enforce a realisation through progressive programmes of renewal.

In our attempts to create such a situation, urban design has, in the first place, to bring about the development of a matrix or framework, which is clearly apparent and yet which does not inhibit, to any serious extent, individual architectural expression or future development, either in general or in detail.

Profiles, forms, patterns, materials, textures, taken separately or together, may help to provide a possible common denominator outside the confines of which many variants are possible without destroying the essential unity. Unity is, indeed, the key, as in a single work of architecture or art, rather than any suggestion of uniformity, which must be firmly avoided.

However, the whole problem is a great deal more complex than this; since, in attaining these local objectives on a more limited scale, regard must be paid to the overall city pattern, as well as to a planning and functional rationale which relates local or environmental areas or developments.

Obviously the needs of movement and transportation, both of vehicles and people, are likely to play a very considerable part in establishing this overall system or network. Intelligent planning will, however, relate these transportation methods in a way which, wherever possible, distinguishes clearly their separate functions so that movement is not allowed to conflict with the uses and purposes of the buildings served. We have, in fact, to return urgently to a realisation, in the city itself, that movement is only one of the many functions which have to be catered for and that this arises from the physical development in terms of buildings and the people who either occupy them, or move in and out of them.

What has long been accepted as an entirely undesirable form of planning—'ribbon development'—demonstrates the conflict of movement with riparian land use. We now realise that it is not necessary for this conflict to occur, and must rather plan in such a way that transportation and movement still serve the buildings in the city, but do so in such a way as to segregate the pedestrian and free him from the risk and annoyance of the motor vehicle.

The service function of vehicular transportation in the city has, regrettably, been lost sight of for too long. Too often the motor vehicle, with its associated freeways and expressways, has been allowed to assume a dominant role in such a manner as to make it impossible to salvage anything worthwhile in the city, or to provide a basis for a creative environment of the right kind.

The all-too-apparent incompatibility in such circumstances, must be resolved or eliminated both by restrictions on areas of movement, as a part of the planning system, and the segregation of pedestrian and other movement systems (Fig. 67).

Until we get this whole problem into perspective there is the serious danger that urban road systems of a mechanistic and destructive variety, instead of the basis of a logical network round which the city may be expected to develop, are likely to fragment and tear the city apart and leave little hope of being able to remedy the situation within the limitations of any of the local environmental areas which result.

In fact, of course, it is becoming more and more apparent, from some of the recent development being undertaken in a number of cities, that priority provision of pedestrian precincts (Figs. 68 and 69) and movement systems, entirely independent of vehicular movement systems can offer the greatest hope of creating a meaningful and coherent system throughout the city as a whole. This is a very different matter from a policy of free rein for the motor vehicle and making the best use possible of fortuitously 'left over' areas for pedestrians.

The total ambit of this system may not often be completely apparent at any given time in view of the growth of city scale—except in those cities of very modest size and population. Nevertheless, in the course of time, the interrelated parts are likely, through a series of visual experiences and journeys within the city itself, to merge as part of a coherent pattern, quite apparent to those who find their way about on foot. In consequence there will be a continually growing realisation of the logic of the system and of the overall pattern.

We need continually to return to a recognition of the fact that, if the city is to be a viable entity, then it must be used by, and for, pedestrians (Fig. 70). This is the case whatever the scale or size of the city as a whole and even if particular journeys at particular times are only related to one limited geographical locality. Even from within the city itself, the eye can often encompass a greater distance than it is possible to cover on foot, and this is especially the case in cities built on undulating ground or with a hilly topography (Figs. 71 and 72).

This was undoubtedly one of the great virtues of the vista planning of Paris (Fig. 73) Washington and Karlsruhe. It is no less true, however, in the case of Philadelphia (Fig. 48) where the network and system is entirely based on the pedestrian, independent of what is, nevertheless, a very strongly demarcated gridiron of vehicular routes.

In progressing from this point a stage further, it should be appreciated that we have to think beyond the design of buildings and circulation systems. We must aim at establishing volumes of space which are in scale with curren needs, and are creatively compatible and in harmony with contemporary technology. These spatial volumes must be enlivened by the quality of the architectural forms which define them. Such means are the basis for the generation of variety and stimulus in a city.

It is equally important to recognise that civic architecture means assigning a form to each building so that it fits into its environment and is compatible with its neighbours (Fig. 74). This is in contrast to the attitude which regards each building as an advertisement hoarding, or as a 'prima donna' work which must assert its importance in spite of its surroundings (Fig. 75).

Not only will the functional requirements of the building itself inevitably have a bearing on the design approach, if it is to be an honest solution in architectural and technological terms, but also topography and location, as related to the urban framework and its implication on urban grouping, will be of significance in the decisions which are taken on the overall form and massing.

The building may just be one of a number, all very similar, and with nothing to distinguish it externally within the overall composition (Fig. 76) or, alternatively, it may justify the creation of a specific focus (Fig. 77), or provide a turning point for a series of axes in the urban planning system. It may terminate a vista, it may add to or support other adjoining buildings, it may act as a transitional point between one building and another or it may occupy a particularly dominant position (Fig. 78), either in relation to a topographical feature or at some other significant geographical location in relation to the city as a whole (Fig. 79).

Obviously, to all these considerations must be added the more evident ones relating to satisfaction of its internal functions, its social purpose, planning and design to a desirable density, appropriate height and other specific design criteria relating to the building's purpose. Not the least important is the recognition of the fact that, while the city may be seen at pedestrian level most of the time, it is also often viewed from surrounding areas in a manner that makes massing and grouping, leading to a satisfactorily organised skyline or profile, even more important (Figs. 80, 81, 82, 83 and 84).

Volumes of space will be occupied by buildings and will be interposed between buildings and these are all equally important positive elements in the design equation, requiring the same degree of consideration.

Order must be brought about, therefore, both between the elements of the visual scene, in the form of the buildings themselves, and the spaces between buildings, constituting the setting. Landscape gardens (Fig. 85) and intervening spaces can assist greatly to unify urban groups and compositions, just as they can be the means of providing a buffer between otherwise disparate forms of development.

It is one of the great advantages of the open planning systems, which are more generally adopted in urban planning today (Figs. 86, 87 and 88), that they create incidental, progressive and varied views throughout the whole composition, permit a greater degree of diversity and variety in the design of the individual components, create much more attractive patterns in the use of space, and firmly avoid the traditional canyon type of city street (Fig. 89), with all its disadvantages.

With the kind of overall framework which has been suggested, and the local attention to unified design and planning, much of the basis of a comprehensive and comprehensible logical urban design methodology presents itself. The fact, however, that order is being introduced to replace chaos may, unless the greatest care is taken, contain the seeds of an equally undesirable monotony of repetitive series of stereotypes (Fig. 90), which can, in many ways, be equally soul-destroying.

A number of the new cities and New Towns, designed and built particularly during the last twenty years, have not been able, starting ab initio, to produce developments which are satisfying in an urban design sense. In fact, many are indescribably dull and lack even the pleasure of older, unplanned cities. One, at least, of the newer examples has justifiably been described as having the symmetry and formality of design of an autocratic and static age—rather than of the present (Figs. 91, 92, 93 and 94).

In the unification process quite subtle ways may be far more appropriate and less likely to suggest a design straitjacket. This can be achieved by functional linkages through the establishment of structural systems, based on similar design grids, and by formal relationships which, while not similar, are in harmony with one another. In some cases, colour or geometrical proportions may be the sole common denominator. Again, in others, unification may best be indicated by the deliberate creation of local contrasts (Fig. 95).

It is likely that in future cities, whatever the processes of renewal, the local characteristics of particular precincts will still continue to be manifest through the characteristics, patterns, forms and development of the area as a whole. The ways in which this is achieved allow for a wide range of alternatives (Fig. 96) even though keeping in general conformity with an overall system or pattern (Fig. 97). Obviously there will be considerable differences in the local texture of development of an area primarily concerned with providing cultural facilities—as against one which is predominantly concerned with the provision of office and commercial development. Similarly, there will be the areas concerned with government and local government functions, where quite a different scale, rhythm, and massing of building may be appropriate. All of these can, nevertheless, be smoothly integrated into the pattern of the city as a whole.

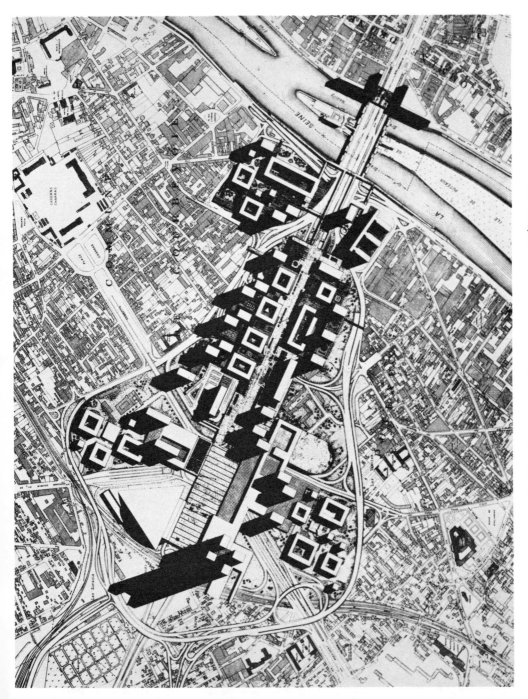

FIG. 97.   The general pattern of redevelopment, La Défense area.

FIG. 98. Oslo West renewal area.

FIG. 99.   Project for redevelopment of 'The Rocks' area, Sydney.

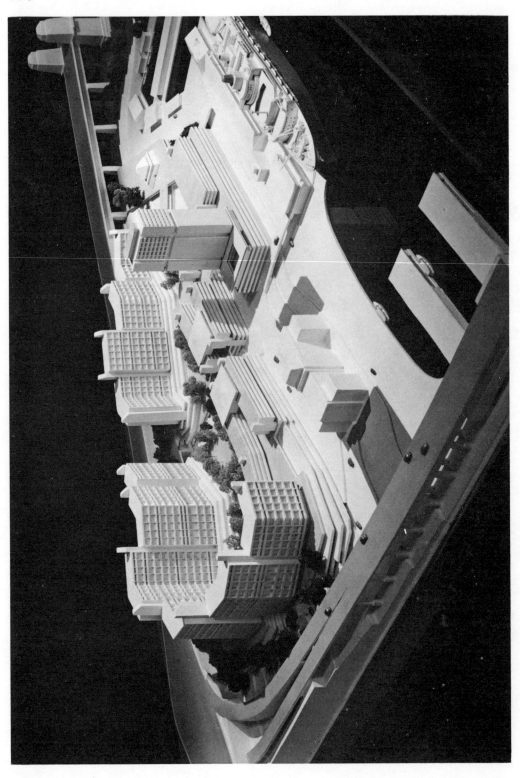

FIG. 100. Another scheme for redevelopment of 'The Rocks' area, Sydney.

FIG. 101.   Hyde Park and Tyburn Corner, London.

FIG. 102.   The Duomo and Giotto's Tower, Florence—movement and activity.

FIG. 103.   Seville Cathedral—contrast and inspiration.

FIG. 104. Peace and serenity—Edam, Holland.

FIG. 105.   Quiet seclusion—The 'Marais', Place des Vosges, Paris.

FIG. 106.   Intimate scale—Mykonos, Greece.

FIG. 107.   Environmental relief, yet truly urbane—Seville.

FIG. 108.   St Peter's Basilica, Rome.

FIG. 109. A glimpse of Amalienborg, Copenhagen.

FIG. 110. The strength and simplicity of Amalienborg permanently recorded.

FIG. 111. Sympathetic grouping—Maranouchi district, Tokyo.

FIG. 112. Marseilles from the harbour—integrated and unified.

FIG. 113.   The religious emphasis of the city—Santa Maria della Salute, Venice.

FIG. 114.   'Dominion Centre', Toronto.

FIG. 115. Oxford University Colleges.

FIG. 116.   Hradcany Castle and the Cathedral, Prague.

FIG. 117. Townscape—Chipping Camden, England.

FIG. 118. Chowringhee, Calcutta.

FIG. 119. Kowloon, Hong Kong.

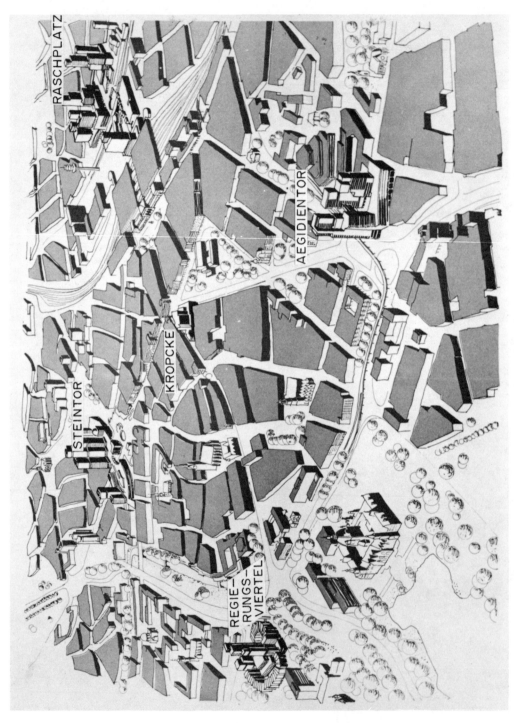

FIG. 120.　Formal structure relationships—Hanover.

FIG. 121. Concept framework for renewal area in Singapore.

FIG. 122. Organisational discipline, Geschäftsstadt Nord, Hamburg.

FIG. 123.   The Seagram Building, Manhattan.

FIG. 124. Fisherman's Wharf, Copenhagen—continuous unity.

FIG. 125. The Kremlin, Moscow.

FIG. 126.   Manhattan at close quarters—the collective quality and variety of forms.

FIG. 127. Hong Kong harbour.

FIG. 128. Galata heights seen across the Golden Horn.

The whole concept of multi-purpose zoning is itself, if applied intelligently, a firm and logical basis for a better integrated city, with a much greater natural degree of cohesion arising from purely functional considerations. This is in direct contrast to the compartmentalisation, and the much lesser likelihood of innate unity, inevitable in our contemporary traditional city planning techniques.

The burden of these arguments is underlined if we can picture the city planner faced with the increasing complexities of our city centres, constantly seeking wider terms of reference for his day-to-day decisions, since he is aware that: 'More orderly, more efficient, and more beautiful downtowns can be achieved only when each individual planning solution is seen in a larger perspective'.[55] It is in this climate that planners are constantly searching for perspective as they reach out in time and space to find a coherent body of ideas and concepts which can link their operations.

This perspective is the El Dorado we seek in our cities, and there is by now ample evidence to demonstrate that attaining these 'ideas and concepts', through comprehensive programmes of urban design, is virtually impossible unless the whole of the work is either undertaken by one individual, or, more probably, by several working together collectively, but in close collaboration (Fig. 98). There must, in all circumstances, however, be guidance from a single dominant personality or through a clear-cut philosophy. Too many of the failures in urban planning have arisen from inadequately guided or oriented team or committee operations, which have tended to produce the unwanted committee 'camel' rather than the desirable 'horse'.

Obviously most existing cities are likely to change much over a considerable period of time, and in a series of stages, which makes the restoration of maintenance of any city-wide unity even more difficult. Nevertheless, it has already been demonstrated in the last few years that much can effectively be achieved with this problem, and our best hope is that some continuity can be established as quickly as possible by means of an imaginatively devised, firmly applied guidance system (Fig. 48).

It cannot be said too often that an important part of the planning process involves, at all stages, both in the diagnostic and the analytical team, participation of the architect in his role as urban designer. He needs to be given proper status at the outset and the chance not only to act within his own specialised field but also to assist in the co-ordination and synthesis of the elements of the team's other contributors.

The architect-planner is required, it must be emphasised, not merely to add gloss, as part of a cosmetic process at a late stage, nor as a censor of others' work. His basic understanding of spatial relationships, circulation patterns and three-dimensional form can be of real value only if woven into the whole fabric of the city at every point.

This is, of course, not in any sense to deny the important roles of the many other participants in the urban design and planning operation, including the engineer, the transportation specialist, the surveyor, the lawyer, the administrator, the politician, the sociologist, the geographer, and others. We cannot, however, overlook the fact that the element which is so significantly missing from the contemporary city is the one in which the architect–planner or urban designer can make his most important contribution. It is the one basic component invariably lacking because, too frequently, these last two professions are totally unrepresented in the planning team composition.

This fundamental weakness produces the inexorable cause and effect situation of deadly cities.

It has been suggested by a critic referred to earlier that the insistence on the role of the architect implies the belief that planning or designing parts of the city is only being thought of as a larger architectural problem 'capable of being given order by converting it into a disciplined work of art'.[93] It is very much to be doubted, however, that many people would thus confuse the problem of designing an individual building with that of designing parts of a city or the whole city itself; since it is now regarded as axiomatic that the urban designer, even though basically an architect by training, must be specially equipped and experienced in the urban planning field if he is to be able to undertake the wider responsibilities he is likely to be called upon to assume.

Nevertheless, there is something of an analogy between the micro-building and the macro-city planning processes and it would be extremely shortsighted and lacking in appreciation of the architect's work to think of his achievements merely as disciplined works of art, as has been suggested by one writer. The architect's work is far more and can very much better be expressed in essence as either an artistically-conceived scientific solution to a particular set of technical problems or, alternatively, a scientifically-motivated artistic creation.

Function looms large in the architectural problem, just as in the urban design problem, and the two operations are much more closely related than has, for far too long, been thought the case. As for the city being regarded as a work of art, however, provided this contains the discipline of a scientific sub-stratum of efficient function and of meeting socio-economic criteria, there is no reason why these prerequisites should not be entirely consistent with formal artistic expression.

The city can only be great and only provide a livable environment if, in the long run, we reconcile ourselves to the fact that such qualities are inseparable from the achievement of artistic standards. It is the absence of this artistic quality that most distinguishes the great majority of contemporary cities from the best traditional cities: and it is the one element needed to drag them out of the 'Slough of Despond' and convert them into livable places, worthy of our civilisation. To believe anything else would be to accept a complete policy of despair and an admission that urban degradation is here to stay, and that we are incapable of doing any better.

The view has recently been expressed that American cities have 'designed out' pleasure by accepting efficiency and economy as their sole design criteria. This is, of course, only too obviously true of many cities in other countries also. The reasons are, moreover, often identical.

To put matters another way, it is unfortunately true that during the past fifty years city planners in general have worked with concepts which can best be described as social mechanics and many of these have assumed grossly oversimplified systems of social and economic relationships. Such approaches attempt to express urban systems in the form of 'gravitational' models, or other dubious analogies drawn from the physical sciences. Generally the plans of those concerned with these approaches give, at best, an unrealistically naïve picture of the real forces working to form central city areas.

In support of this view a distinguished planner has argued that human will can be exercised effectively on our cities so that the form they take will be a true expression of the highest aspirations of our civilisation. With the enormous improvement in the techniques of mathematical manipulations of electronic computers, applied to the problem of projecting past trends, there is danger, it is pointed out, of 'surrendering to a mathematically extrapolated future; which at best can be nothing more than an extension of what existed before. Thus we face the prospect of losing one of the most important concepts of mankind; that the future is what we make it'.[13]

One of the quite unwarranted assumptions prevalent at the present time in conditions in which a large number of variables have to be expected and in which normal methods of resolution would be quite impracticable, is that if the computer is brought into play, sufficient alternative solutions can be provided on the basis of a mathematical–logical model. Out of this welter of speculative inaccuracy, assumptions and part-truths on a mammoth scale, it is hoped that a distillation of the true facts can be produced. While this may be an oversimplification of the process involved it is, nevertheless, much closer to the truth than anything that the computer and its programmer can possibly produce when dealing with factors not susceptible to a numerical form of evaluation or to a mathematical treatment.[232]

In considering this dilemma and the evident fact that not even a veritable genius could expect to solve equations containing the number of unknowns which must sometimes be faced in planning and urban design, it is clear that resort to the mathematical model enforces restrictions on the means of creativity as the inevitable consequence in order to make manageable the very complex sets of conditions which are beyond the ability of the individual to handle. If we were to impose such restrictions on the actual-development of cities, the results would be trite and dull stereotypes, utterly failing to reflect human needs.

If we can imagine such restrictions inhibiting any part of the urban planning or design process, the results would be, without doubt, totally misleading, and dangerously so in view of the fact that the technology involved tends to create an aura of accuracy and reliability—often entirely without justification. If we embark on one inaccurate set of assumptions, and then ring the changes on this several thousand times in slightly varied forms and permutations, there is, finally, no less a distortion of the truth, posturing as a logical planning system.

This is one of the more regrettable manifestations of the computer age, and of the complete misuse—which also often occurs in other circumstances—of this wonderful technological equipment with its unique capacity for electronic operation. Its virtues have resulted, in some cases, in a pseudo-scientific technological collusion with the programmer, working on the 'sledge-hammer and nut' philosophy.

In a pre-electronic computer age, when we were confronted with the considerable range of variables, options and choices which occur in the planning equation, an intellectual discriminatory approach would have been made to the problem in a series of stages using the human 'computer'.

With the assistance of experienced statisticians and mathematicians, as well as systems analysts, we would have come close to a valid solution of the range of problems posed. Any failure in the quality of cities certainly cannot be ascribed to the inadequacy of these well-tried methods but rather to a refusal to use them.

There are, of course, situations in which mathematical–statistical measurements are simply not applicable such as where numerical measurement is not feasible. Reference has been made elsewhere to 'the fallacy of expertise in which the expert may know the needs of the situation but may fail to judge the quality of the solution as he should be doing; instead of which he will attempt to place dependence on a fallacious quantitative analysis'.[142]

These quantitative decisions or answers to particular questions will almost invariably add up to complicated patterns or formulae, too often leading in the direction of a mathematical model from which many unexpected and illogical planning decisions may emerge.

Given enough of these quantity problems, usually based on the subjective assumption of a planner whose values and preferences structure the choices, and without sympathetic understanding of the city and the local area, the final and monumental quantitative output derived from the data fed into the computer is a solution which, by the very nature of programming, must itself be quantitative, even if based on the personal predilections of the operator.

An interesting application of this technique is a study recently undertaken at an English university, in which it was reported that the simulation of alternative building forms allowed a systematic assessment to be made of minimum site area requirements, taking into account a variety of statutory and functional criteria including daylighting, fire separation and surface car parking. At a more detailed level, alternative room layouts and structural and service systems were proposed and the various schemes then evaluated in terms of cost and other significant criteria, such as internal circulation efficiency.[30]

A further part of the study involved consideration of the overshadowing of adjacent buildings, using physical models to measure internal light levels in accommodation planned and spaced in a number of different ways.

Because the analysis became tedious when performed manually, and the number of examples which could be considered was limited, computer simulations of alternative building forms were undertaken with the assistance of members of the university's mathematics laboratory.

Perhaps the most significant thing about this work is that, whether dealing with the planning of universities, with urban design problems, or in some other context, the obvious concern of such studies has become that of evaluating the most economical use of particular sites by the employment of differing building forms. Nowhere does there appear to be any explicit reference to the important consideration of aesthetic quality, or the suitability of the building forms or groups proposed to a particular location and environment or as part of a larger urban composition. Moreover, a number of other questions as, for example, those relating to aspect and orientation, appear to remain unanswered.

Granted that this form of systematic analysis can be of value, albeit in this instance in a somewhat negative sense, by proving that it cannot be employed in any search to establish aesthetic superiority, and even though it has permitted a very detailed analysis of a large number of functional variables in a wide range of building forms and planning arrangements, it has yet to be shown that it has presented any ultimate advantages, in an overall design sense, as against traditional methods of choice and analysis.

Once again, because the whole procedure must necessarily rule out the all-important and vital elements of aesthetic control and internal and external environmental quality —without which architecture cannot exist—and simply because these quantities are not numerically measurable, the method cannot be considered as anything more than a preliminary phase or tooling-up operation in urban planning and design. It still begs the question of the 'intuitive leap' which the designers must ultimately take in order to embrace aesthetic considerations and choices.

One of the remarkable aspects of this research programme is that, when it was first embarked upon, justification was found in the hitherto 'limited vocabulary of arbitrary formal decisions constituting the stock-in-trade of the typical urban designer, when confronted with a particular problem'.[128] No evidence, however, appears to have been adduced to show that the production of such new forms, described by one critic as 'ruthless formalism', presented, in any fundamental way, useful and better variants. During this process of analysis there was no way of exercising aesthetic and environmental control or refinement without applying formal preconceptions and the system does not cater for these.

We must not be deluded into thinking that, because a part of the planning process may be susceptible to an apparently more rational form of analysis and measurement, this necessarily justifies subordination of the whole to the part or implies that the part is less important than the whole. Even where the rational area of analysis is relatively easier to apply, and may thereby gain conviction, other aspects of the planning process, not depending solely on analogous measurement techniques, must be given due weight.

So far all the discussion relating to the perception process, and every effort to date to rationalise aesthetic judgements through techniques of measurement, have shown that there is no alternative to intuitive judgement. Any system or method, however efficient in itself, which tends to mask this central fact, is only taking us further away from the desirable ends we seek, namely a pleasurable environment that will appeal to all the senses, but, most particularly, through the medium of the visual process.

Certainly complete confirmation of the shortcomings of the neo-systems approach is well demonstrated by examination of the particular types of building forms suggested for the development areas studied. These follow a simple stereotype which possesses very many obvious defects with regard to mutual overshadowing, sound transmission, inconvenient internal communication and, to a high degree, unsatisfactory orientation and aspect.

The fact that what is proposed may be an economic form of development on a particular site and a means of fully utilising the area, is neither here nor there, since there are other, better, methods which could obviously be employed which, without recourse to the computer, would certainly yield preferable environmental conditions and equally promising economic returns. The arbitrariness of the formal decisions cannot be concealed by the dubious suggestions that: 'building types tend to produce their own characteristic forms', or: 'these are forms of a type and not a private language', where 'the process of discovering them is analytical, measurable, and open to rational discussion and criticism'.[128]

Regrettably it must be concluded that this is, in essence, the revival of a theory, once termed functionalism, which was exploded many years ago. The whole history of building, particularly in the last hundred years, and more especially in recent decades, demonstrates that building forms do not emerge automatically from the use for which the building was designed. While they may be, therefore, subject to rational discussion and, no doubt, to criticism, this must rest very squarely on a process of intuitive, subjective judgement or speculative reason (Figs. 99 and 100). Arbitrary or not, there is no baulking this fact and no real alternative. Perhaps, however, it may be conceded that, if the necessary aesthetic evaluations are linked with inter-related functional considerations, this would surely constitute, collectively, a desirable guidance system through analysis and synthesis.

Such studies would clearly include, as a part of the whole process, definition of the size and shape of the plot, establishment of suitable depths of accommodation related to room sizes and outlook, overall building size, masses and interspaces, floor space efficiency and population range.

It would, however, appear essential, even in the more conventional forms of design evaluation, to have regard to mutual and neighbour over-shadowing—the relationship of masses to adjoining buildings, to adjoining groups and to the city as a whole, as well as to the skyline. The provision and use of external spaces as environment, the implications of fire- and noise-spread, the incidence of overlooking and loss of privacy, the effect on the design of the street, both visually and as regards overshadowing, wall-floor space ratios, economics of height to floor areas (in relation to lifts, etc.) staging of the construction programme in regard to budgeting, and physical site problems must all be taken into account. The influence on the design by such factors as over-riding town planning considerations, such as through plot ratios or height limitations, or the operation of daylighting codes, traffic generation capacity in relation to surrounding streets, orientation in regard to solar control, shading and glare, and natural lighting levels in various parts of the accommodation, all appear to be essential to a fully comprehensive study.

When judged in the fuller context of all these parameters, which are likely to have a bearing on the planning and design operation, it appears that, in the studies referred to, a gross simplification has taken place and the warning offered in a recent methodological study has not been heeded, since the approach is obviously that of the mathematician's 'tree' concept rather than of the 'semi-lattice'. Looked at another way, in the process of simplification, in order to mount the computerised operation at all, many of the vitally important factors having a direct and important bearing on the overall design and planning concept have been left unconsidered.

In view of the evidence gleaned from another recent important attempt[120] towards rationalisation of the urban design methodology, as applied to a special component part of the city, we must conclude that we are no closer to a total system of measurement of the qualitative aspects of a particular individual building, let alone of groups of buildings or the city as a whole. Nothing new or convincing, moreover, has yet been demonstrated as a planning or designing technique which provides predictable certainty of perceptual responses. This is no less true of this highly-sophisticated technology than of any other system and the lack of development of speculative thought in this design area is, in the circumstances, only too clearly evident.

Of course, the attempt to rationalise the design process in the urban setting is not a new phenomenon and, if city administrations, and others confronted with decision-making on a city scale, are to attempt to undertake these responsibilities—often without the necessary training, knowledge and experience—or without suitably-qualified staff, there is the great temptation to look for some established canons of composition or beauty which may be arrived at, in relation to the arrangement of buildings and spaces, by means of a well understood and relatively easily applied methodology or set of rules. This would no doubt make for a situation in which it would be unlikely that the worst excesses could be perpetrated in the urban design environment, were such a set of principles to be applied. On the other hand, it is much more likely that the prevailing climate of low-level mediocrity would persist as it would through the application of any other sets of stereotyped controls or rules. In fact, if it were as easy as this our cities would not be as they are.

The establishment of such systematic methods was closely studied in Germany in the latter part of the last century, where there was a particular interest in attempts to define ideal spatial relationships by the use of mathematics. The phase which we are at present passing through—with its added lure of computer techniques—demonstrates that we have come full circle. We are thus forgetting much past experience gleaned from similar exploratory processes, and that current experiments are likely to lead, inevitably, to similar conclusions.

Without exception, all these attempts at rationalisation have overlooked not only the fact that perception is a totality of sensory experience through a series of conditioned responses and that intuitive judgements are the only means by which we are likely to be able to arrive at satisfactory design criteria, but also the essential recognition of the dynamic kaleidoscopic process through which perception takes place in relation to architecture and urban design, in which movement, scale, distance and variable patterns are of vital significance. Moreover, of course, they ignore the fact that the time element has to be taken into account in an extended sense, since it is extremely unlikely that the whole of any city area can be developed or redeveloped at any one time on a completely self-contained basis and without the need for staging.

One of the most recent and well-known efforts to codify urban design experience (and one that has substantially reckoned with some of the unresolved problems occurring in most earlier attempts at rationalisation) is Lynch's 'City Image' studies. A wide-ranging survey of individual responses to urban phenomena affecting the visual field, it represents an empiric, pragmatic attempt to distil from an encyclopaedia of experience a dictionary of visual perception.

It has, however, unfortunately failed to produce a workable design code, or a definitive synthesis of universally acceptable principles and criteria which may be used as the basis of an urban design methodology. Another such survey, undertaken by similar methods under similar circumstances with a similar size sample, but by different observers, might be expected to produce entirely different results. These studies do not appear, therefore, to have carried us much further forward, and have certainly not put us in a stronger position to ignore the vital role of the master urban designer and his subjective judgements.

While of interest technically, tachistospic studies undertaken at Harvard in order to assess visual acuity and the degree of sensitivity to, and awareness of, phenomena—

particularly during motion—in the city environment, have not revealed any knowledge which we did not already possess.[193] However, that the special growth of receptive centres for touch and sight—particularly the latter—together with the association areas related with them, have instituted, in the primates, an elaborate mechanism for contact with the environment is beyond dispute. The extent to which these faculties are, in fact, employed by particular individuals, quite apart from the variation in the level of development in different subjects as well as in the background of experience, leaves us with only one conclusion: that this is an area of total unreliability and great variance which, at present, gives little promise for the development of a method or system as a creative tool.

It seems true, moreover, that the problem is being compounded by what is termed 'the weak demand from aesthetic cripples; the indifference of fugitives from the city, and the lack of effective leadership in qualitative issues of urban form'.[73] It has been argued that, in the face of these circumstances—quite apart from other recommendations already touched on—a massive educational effort is required as a means of placing urban design on a more effective basis. This educational effort is, however, more a matter of providing worthwhile exemplars and precedents rather than any form of theoretical indoctrination.

In attempting to devise suitable overall forms and in establishing architectural quality, we must remember that we are not dealing with abstract environmental modes and illusions, but with human activities. In contemporary conditions it is a fact that unlimited and destructive access to the central areas of the cities—as has often been attempted and is still proposed in many current plans—would, even if it were practicable, result in disembowelled cities offering little or nothing in the way of a true city centre destination, so that when we arrive there would be, in truth, 'no there, there'. The activities once located there in the city centre would have been dissipated to specialised areas elsewhere in the metropolitan region, and the great radial expressways would have lost their function, except to take people more rapidly away from the city. Indeed, unless this basic fact is understood from the outset, nothing subsequently undertaken in the way of a repair operation can hope to provide a worthwhile inner urban environment.

It has already been emphasised that the most important design characteristic of a city is coherence which is, of course, much more than mere order. Indeed, order alone can readily lead to monotony and dullness, and is unlikely to provide adequate scope for the imagination. Cities are dynamic and their essential quality must therefore be evident in the articulation of their component parts and in their ability to adapt and grow. Our recognition of these facts must be reinforced by understanding, based on knowledge as well as experience.

We have begun to recognise that the systematic relationships of the city, including the interaction of transportation and land-use, as well as of people and their recreational facilities, are important basic threads in urban design. This recognition also reflects our better understanding of the city, and our individual and collective relationships to it. This, in turn, implies a quality of coherence.

The abstract, difficult and yet very practical question of how to attain an appropriate quality in the city, is epitomised in the statement that, 'while symbols are not unimportant in urban design the city speaks to us more directly as a place where opportunity is extended or derived, where life is valued or suppressed, where the common good is recognised or ignored. It is true, too, that, 'The city is also directly apprehended as a place of exultation or of seclusion, of restlessness or repose, of boring monotony or exciting variety'.[73]

It is implicit in our recognition of the nature of this problem that, in so far as buildings contribute to urban design, this is primarily a question of architecture. In urban design, however, we must allow, in addition, for what have been termed 'intellectual perceptions and satisfactions', and for our insight into such related questions as historical continuity, the vitality of urban centres, functional coherence, urbane forms and 'planning as a mirror of civilisation'. To these must be added our understanding of the social city.[73]

This understanding will tell us whether the city is consistently humane and whether it adequately reflects the individual, the family and the community; whether, too, these are adequately catered for in an appropriate form through our urban design efforts or whether humanity has been disregarded.

We can also judge, in this way, whether the physical planning decisions have been based on adequate knowledge and understanding of socio-economic and other functional implications and on such practical and inescapable problems as journey to work, educational and work opportunities, the provision of unpolluted light and air and the psychological impact of the city; whether these secure the dignity of the pedestrian in his life and death struggle with the motor vehicle, the vitality of land-use arrangements, shopper safety, late night and weekend shopping in the heart of the city, the availability of recreational facilities and access to them, and the fundamental place of garden (Fig. 101) and landscape in the 'concrete jungle' are also issues which must be resolved.

The creation of lively incident, punctuation, movement (Fig. 102), surprise, contrast, inspiration (Fig. 103), areas of peace and serenity (Figs. 104 and 105), areas intimate in scale (Figs. 106 and 107), areas of grandeur (Fig. 108), monumentality and dignity (Figs. 109 and 110), important collective qualities of harmonious grouping (Fig. 111), diversity, equally subtly organised spatial relationships, excitement, exuberance, balance, as well as the generation of variation and counterpoint—all must be part of our goal. Above all in this spectrum of the human habitat, successful integration and unification of all the components at all points must be achieved (Fig. 112), both implicitly and explicitly so as to leave no room for doubt as to intention.

Cities are no longer perceived simply as religious (Fig. 113), commercial (Fig. 114) or university centres (Figs. 115 and 116), but as formed urban localities in which such dimensions as image, symbol, perspective, structure, and all the emotional values, are brought together in the complex web of total perceptual experience. It is the very essence of the problem confronting the urban designer that he must then find the means of translating these images and needs into concrete forms as part of a unified creative concept.

Emotional needs and abstract qualities are by far the most difficult to understand and cater for, or, indeed, to create during the design process. Frequently employed generic terms like urbanity and townscape are imprecise and almost incapable of exact definition, although widely accepted as desirable ingredients in the city. As with so many other facets of this problem, it is very apparent when these qualities are missing and reasonably obvious when they have been attained (Fig. 117). Visual methods of design analysis again appear to be the only satisfactory means of pretesting the existence of these qualities in the component areas of any city development.

Because the city is also, however, dependent on an ordered consistency of treatment firmly applied urban design policies must be given continuity and be adequately policed in order to prevent the intrusion of discordant and incompatible elements at later stages (Figs. 118 and 119). This consistency in policy should extend not only to buildings and intervening spaces but must also include details such as street furniture, sky signs, and other forms of advertising, and, above all, the installation of essential public services.

Perhaps the most vital of the elements contributing to this quality of townscape or urbanity is the right kind of visual variety within the framework of an overall coherent pattern; thus avoiding, on the one hand, over-regimentation or monotony and, on the other, inevitable chaos. With the right mix and composition, however, we can expect to derive all the elements of excitement, anticipation, drama, discovery and complexity which, in attaining the established advantages of the memorable city, will equally avoid the clinical deadness of totally designed towns (Fig. 1).

Attaining these qualities is not easy, and, to complicate matters, our plans and objectives have to reckon with the need to cater for 'unspecialised settings as well as for unfinished settings'.[149] Furthermore, the uses within an area can change and, in the course of time, generate new interest due to diversity of use, unpredictability of use, and changes of use—and thus, perhaps, achieve a stimulating degree of ambiguity.

Expressed another way, what we are attempting to do, without, in any sense, sacrificing a unified approach, is to ensure that, as far as is practicable, the designed environment will be, to a certain extent, indeterminate—thus allowing for subsequent development and additions, which will, in turn, give scope for the satisfaction of many different needs, and the desirable degree of diversity and variety.

In this way it seems possible that 'a kind of complexity and even apparent contradiction, based on the need to consider the richness of experience within the limitations of the medium' may be assured, not in any way, however, resulting from arbitrariness or contrived 'intricacies of picturesqueness'.[149]

In summary, we may agree that 'there are levels of taste, and we can only hope that people who design our cities and our buildings are people who dare to say that some things are ugly'.[142] We must hope that, in supporting this process and taking this kind of stand, it will be without apologies—as otherwise our cities will inevitably decline still further from their too prevalent mediocrity and squalor. Above all, too, we must recognise the danger in 'the levelling down of Sunday School aesthetics in which "beauty" is seen in everything'.

Recognising that planning method alone is not enough and cannot produce a beautiful city, but merely provides an intellectual strait-jacket, it must now be obvious that what we need is a qualitative, not a quantitative, judgement which 'must inform all the decisions on planning, not only efficiency, popular appetite, aesthetic theorising, or replacement for the sake of newness or economic exploitation'.[142]

Chapter X

A vision of the planned city

It is now necessary to establish, even more specifically than hitherto, practical policies and principles which may be expected to guide us in dealing with the actual problems involved in the design of central city areas or their component parts.

As a starting point one useful set of criteria might be expressed as creating a non-extravagant sense of space, maintaining a quality of compactness without the suggestion of undesirable congestion, blending the contributions of numerous architects, engineers, urban designers and planners without imposing regimentation or stifling originality, and combining the qualities of new and old buildings in such a way that all the component parts enhance, rather than detract from, one another.

Another approach to the problem could be described as involving the urban designer in a search for that delicate balance between internal functional needs and those of the larger environment. In this the designer recognises that the city is not made up of buildings alone, but that these are an integral part of generally more important spaces which provide the framework and continuity for the structure around them (Fig. 120).

The more enlightened city planning authorities today seem to agree with that contention which perhaps crystallises contemporary philosophies in urban design—that the city-centre cannot be designed in the same way as an individual building, and that a finite and rigid plan is impossible. What, however, is needed is an overall conceptual framework (Figs. 121 and 122) that provides the basic discipline and the opportunity and encouragement for satisfactory development on an appropriate scale. Thus 'the plan must be conceived and administered with a flexibility that can respond to new ideas and new situations'.[164]

It must also be emphasised again that there can be no question of the desirable built form, which the city should take, emerging simply and directly as a final product of analysis and research.

It is equally important to recognise that 'dull, inert cities contain the seeds of their own destruction', but that 'lively, diverse, intense cities contain the seeds of their own regeneration'.[93] Probably the surest way of producing such dull, inert urban qualities is through a scientific methodology dealing with large numbers of variables in the process of decision-making, such as have already been referred to, in which all the resulting statistical and probability analyses can be both dangerously misleading and totally lacking in any positive creative concept.

It is imperative that the nineteenth century approach to development on a piece-meal system—with each component part unrelated to the others or to the city as a whole, without any effort at timing of operations to permit comprehensive planning and without any degree of aesthetic conformity—should be rejected as totally in-appropriate and anachronistic.

There must be increasing encouragement for architects to respect the urban environment and to recognise the existence of an overall master strategy. Rather than showing unreasoning resentment to such a strategy they should be able to ensure that each individual building asserts itself reasonably within its context. Virtue must surely be seen in a policy of designing buildings 'that stand and sing quietly rather than jump and bawl', as a desirable end and as one more likely to ensure overall harmonious relationships than any other approach.

This point has been underlined by a leading American architect who recently argued that developers must face the problem that the day of the isolated masterwork is drawing to a close. If New York had fifty Seagram buildings (Fig. 123), he pointed out, it could still be an ugly city, as great cities are not created one building at a time. This is a particularly timely reminder from one whose current task, overriding his normal professional responsibilities, has become, as he describes it, 'a major effort to impose some direction, order and aesthetic responsibility on the chaotic growth of building in America'.[144]

It is, of course, equally apparent that the sense of unity, purpose and direction in urban development must survive the changes which occur over periods of time so that growth and change take place and fit in with the existing urban fabric and so that, at any given stage, the city appears complete and without serious loss of integrity.

In stressing this need for a continuous condition of unity we are really facing one of the most severe problems confronting the urban designer and planner. Nevertheless, it is one capable of solution and there are many historic examples to show that this is so (Fig. 124). If, indeed, the sense of order which underlies unity arises from the sound functional solution of a series of independent but related problems in the individual buildings and groups of buildings, as well as in the intervening spaces and movement routes, then there is some prospect that such order will prevail over all other influences and be an inherent cohesive force.

What we still cannot anticipate in this plethora of individual practical stages of development in the physical structure of a city is any easily ascertainable urban science which will acceptably unify all programmes and operations and thus make everyone's task easier.

A much-quoted critic believes that a city cannot be a work of art, because this would imply 'selection, organisation and control, and is thus arbitrary, symbolic and abstracted'.[93] It is therefore held that such a city is 'life-killing' since it 'impoverishes life instead of enriching it'. These confused and erroneous concepts of art and the philosophy and methods of the urban designer are misleading and indeed fallacious. Significantly, such views are not accompanied by supporting evidence.

The basic error, of course, lies in not recognising that, in the fundamental process of city planning, the form of the city must be considered from the visual, as well as the economic and social viewpoints. Urban planning and urban design are inseparable parts of an integrated process. However, it is implicit and of supreme importance that the cities we build and renew should evoke lasting aesthetic responses, stemming from a conservation of physical form and urban function within a defined perceptual framework.

It is, of course, true that in city planning, until quite recently, deliberate efforts to organise the visually-perceived city were generally confined to areas of special signi-ficance (Fig. 125) or to limited scale prestige projects. It was a part of the tradition of the 'City Beautiful' that architects and landscape architects were expected to know how to design unrelated fragments of the city. These fragments, however, have con-tinually diminished in size until the main concern of designers today is generally limited to individual buildings on isolated sites, with only rare exceptions.

Generally speaking, this anachronistic approach still persists unabated, although it must be apparent that we simply have to adopt a new attitude towards the design of the contemporary city. With the opportunity to rebuild cities, more particularly on a major scale, grows the realisation of the need for a new approach and especially for what has been described as a higher order of design. This would relate architectural elements to one another—to the physical and built environment and, above all, to the dynamic perceptual impressions and images. Involved in all this is not only the design of buildings, but also open spaces, vistas and, ultimately, a basic perceptible pattern for the whole area.

It is important to recognise that amongst the apparently considerable number of alternative ways in which we might approach the practical problems of designing a city, the historical-archaeological can have only a limited role. If this were not so we might be confronted with a process of substituting the past for the present, and thus encouraging the vain hope of using examples of historic urban places as ideals for contemporary designers who work under quite different circumstances. Many of these historic cities certainly deserve our admiration and study but as purely visual models they are inappropriate, irrelevant and even dangerously misleading precepts for emulation. They may have been logical products of their own time but the lessons they have for us today relate essentially to matters of quality rather than leading to uncomprehending plagiarism.

However much we are inspired by these historic cities the eclectic has no place, merely for its own sake, in contemporary design but only in so far as we may learn, from the best of the past, a continuing philosophy of sound basic principles. Certainly, the manifest changes that confront us at the present time, particularly in the realms of movement and communication, show that the nature of the needs and problems in the city have already changed dramatically. The future is certain to invalidate historical urban resurrections even further.

It is, of course, undeniable that contemporary urban design concepts cannot be entirely original. Our ideas of space and form have been conditioned by the evolution of civilisation over a thousand years or more. Contemporary designers can now draw knowledge from a range of examples and precedents inconceivable at any earlier period. This, however, is as far as we can justifiably or logically go in our review of earlier precepts since these, we must recognise, have emanated from living conditions: and the means of encompassing such conditions differ from those of today.

Above all we must have city forms and patterns derived from contemporary func-tions which, at best, may still adequately cater for similar functions in the foreseeable future. These will arise from, and be influenced by, aesthetic, social, economic and empiric values and interests, the relevance of which has to be judged on knowledge rather than on a set of preconceptions which may be totally irrelevant.

In the implementation of development we have already established that design is not something that can simply be implanted on to the functional economic city, nor can the reverse process, of trying to create economic and social rationalisations for preconceived design decisions, be very profitable. To be entirely logical, design must be an integral part of the planning process at every stage, and for these reasons those trained in this specialised field need to be involved in every phase of the urban planning and design operations.

One of the main arguments for an overall conceptual framework relating the various parts of the city—an argument as important as functional considerations concerned with communication—is that perception and awareness of the whole is a vital part of the enjoyment of any visual image. This is no less true of the city area than of a work of architecture or a sculpture. To be at ease with a place and to enjoy it fully one must be able to orient oneself and perceive its basic form. From pedestrian eye level only a fragment of the whole area is perceptible at any one time but to someone in motion the total pattern reveals itself as one point of view is succeeded by another.

It is when the significance of movement in the establishment of this process is understood that we can appreciate that the essential cognitive link between the urban area as a whole and its component parts becomes the basis of a clear visual framework.

In recognising the importance of this cognitive link, it is apparent that the whole city is greater than the sum of its parts and only through the unifying force of a strong overall concept can a full perceptual satisfaction be obtained, even though through a related staccato of instant impressions.

If we accept that form is something belonging to the community, where architectural design provides the scope for individual diversification, we can see that the first coherent image of any city may well be that afforded by the general urban arrangement or groups of forms. Examples which readily spring to mind are San Giminiagno or Lower Manhattan (Fig. 80).

The subsequent, close-at-hand view, gained by the pedestrian in movement in the city (Fig. 126), will, however, be just as much concerned with the collective quality of architectural achievement and forms, grouping and massing. It is the form, however, rather than the detailed architectural treatment, which is likely to have much more relevance to the cohesive structure.

It will not always be immediately apparent from within the city whether or not there is system or order until, by movement and familiarity with the larger fabric, such order becomes more evident. The apparent abstraction, will then give way, as a consequence of panoramic vision from a hilltop (Fig. 127), river front, or other vantage point (Figs. 128, 129 and 130), to a recognition of the homogeneity, continuity of form, diversity, scale, composition, grouping, contrasts, regulation, direction and form, as well as the many other essential elements which contribute towards the creative image of the city as a whole.

Lynch's image survey, whatever its limitations, does confirm that, in the course of time, a great many people become explicitly aware of many of the significant cohesive linkages and urban indicators, characterised in his study by the identifiable paths, districts, edges, landmarks and nodes. Although, as has already been argued, this may not be the basis for a creative design methodology, it does demonstrate a basis of awareness of the visual environment on which we may hope to build in future.

Obviously, one of the ways in which the comprehension of the city as a whole has become much more difficult and its cohesion loosened so that interest has tended to be localised, is in the lowering of densities and the tendency for cities to sprawl while their populations have increased and the cities themselves grown in response to accommodation needs of various kinds.

The importance of a return to the compact city, designed for the pedestrian at pedestrian scale, cannot be too strongly emphasised. We must also again stress the significance of multi-level, multi-purpose zoning which would be an integral part of such a concept, lending its own additional advantages of convenient propinquity and, therefore, a heightened sense of coherence. Changes in forms of city transport which are only just round the corner and are likely to involve not only the more familiar underground rapid transit systems, but also more convenient and less space-consuming surface vehicles, must aid in this process of understanding the structural logic of the city.

The construction of even more high-rise buildings in cities also has a great deal to do with the increasing awareness of the significance of urban form (Fig. 131). This is somewhat reassuring in view of the fact that, in addition to underground rapid transit systems making direct connection with office and commercial buildings in cities, underground pedestrian routes are being introduced, for climatic reasons, in some cities.

The loss of orientation or continuity of visual experience which may be implied in these subterranean excursions makes the establishment of an overall logical pattern even more important. Progressively, then, over the course of time, all city dwellers and city workers will become sufficiently familiar with the matrix to understand its significance, in the same convincing and explicit way that one clearly understands the whole layout of the gridiron city.

Metropolitan city patterns must reflect all the communications systems in use at present or likely to be developed in the foreseeable future. It cannot be supposed that the surface operation of the motor vehicle can be discounted, any more than the large volumes of pedestrian traffic. The traffic generation concentrations and nodes and the communications and movement systems are intimately related parts of the same logical, overall, basic functional organisation, and are much less flexible than other essential services which help keep the city alive. They are, therefore, much more likely to impose their influence on the pattern of the city as a whole and this must continue to be the case however much such requirements are met at different levels or even through innovations in types of vehicle and movement characteristics.

One thing seems certain. Only when a full realisation that the unrestricted use of the motor vehicle is no longer possible in the city centre without fatal consequences dawns on all city planners, will the arbitrariness of much urban planning, dependent on the supposed mobility of the motor vehicle (let alone the horse-drawn cart, or Le Corbusier's derisory 'Pack mule'[110]) be seen at face value. Then, and only then, are we likely to see a more rational pattern of city development, integrating workable and non-destructive movement systems of all types with the physical development of component parts of the city, on which it is dependent.

All the parts of the city will then, it is assumed, have in common the elements of major, minor and subsidiary vistas (Figs. 132 and 133) views from within and without, sequences of sense of enclosure or freedom from enclosure, contrasting building materials, colours, textures and details within the overall unity of the composition and a sense of continuity—derived from moving from one enclosed space, with one predominant theme, to another. Desirably, all the individual parts will be unified in scale and in their use of building materials so that the effects of combined architectural imagination and control become apparent (Figs. 134, 135, 136 and 160).

In considering the total problem of the urban plan, we must remember that this must obviously be fundamentally affected by the topography of the area. This topography may consist of a site which is level, sloping to varied gradients, with or without a natural backdrop (Figs. 189), in a valley (Fig. 188) or on a hilltop prominence (Figs. 137 and 138), sited in a natural depression or on a ridge, or a combination of any or all of these.

These natural topographical features will, in turn, be modified or conditioned by a number of man-made features which will include urban developments, planted areas, communication facilities, formal spaces and the special emphasis of individually-significant architectural masses including particularly vertical towers and slab-like horizontal forms.

The combinations and permutations of natural and man-made features will be perceived in a number of distinctly different ways, by the pedestrian observer in motion in the city itself, by the observer located in one of the urban open spaces, either in movement or at rest (Fig. 139) from vantage points affording panoramic skyline or vista view (Fig. 140) and, increasingly important as time goes by, from aircraft landing or taking off near to the city (Fig. 141).

The useful 'check list'[211] proposed by the American Institute of Architects considers the initial approach to problems of urban planning and design under four basic headings:

THE ENVIRONMENTAL MATRIX

This consists of the setting of the city, including historical and geographical factors, the regional economic base, inter-urban transportation and other basic conditions in the environment affecting the social and physical fabric of the city.

THE URBAN FABRIC—SOCIAL

This constitutes the life of the city, including patterns of movement and congregation of people, patterns of living, recreation, shopping and working—traditions, attitudes and institutions—in short, the social form, fully dimensioned, of human activity in the city.

THE URBAN FABRIC—PHYSICAL

This means an inventory of the physical elements of the city, including transportation, the streetscape, historic features, visual features, functional concentrations for employment, shopping and recreation, residential patterns and terminal facilities—in short, the physical form of the city.

FIG. 129.   Stockholm (and the Kaknas television tower).

FIG. 130.   Vienna from the Belvedere Gardens.

FIG. 131.   Kyoto Tower Hotel, Japan.

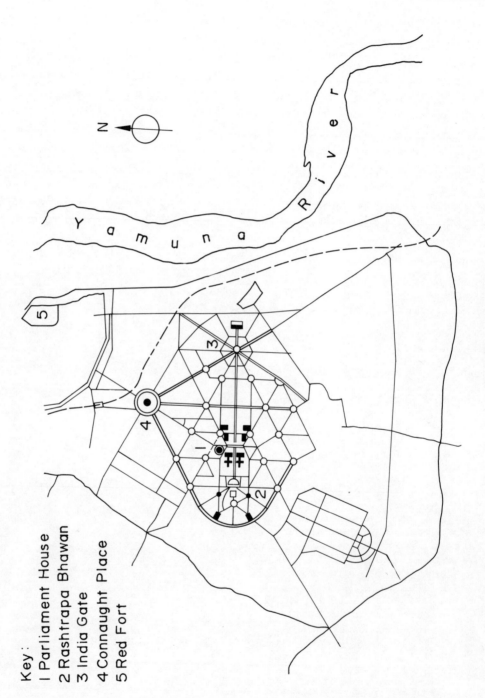

Key:
1 Parliament House
2 Rashtrapa Bhawan
3 India Gate
4 Connaught Place
5 Red Fort

FIG. 132.   The Central area, New Delhi.

FIG. 133.   The Secretariat and Great Place, New Delhi.

FIG. 134. Park Avenue, New York—uniformity of design and materials.

FIG. 135.   Fitzroy Square, London—architectural control.

FIG. 136. Whitehall, London—unified scale and treatment.

FIG. 137. The dominant image of Edinburgh's castle.

FIG. 138. The twin focal points of Paris—Sacré Coeur and Montmartre.

FIG. 139. Omonia Square, Athens.

FIG. 140. Lombard Brücke and Binnen Alster, Hamburg.

FIG. 141.   Singapore City and Harbour.

FIG. 142. St Clement Danes Church, Aldwych, London.

FIG. 143.   Strand-on-the-Green, Hammersmith, London.

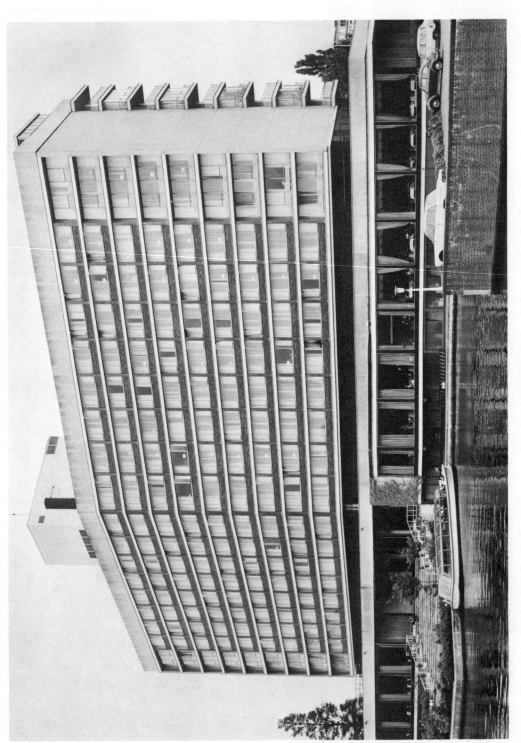

FIG. 144. Hilton Hotel, Amsterdam.

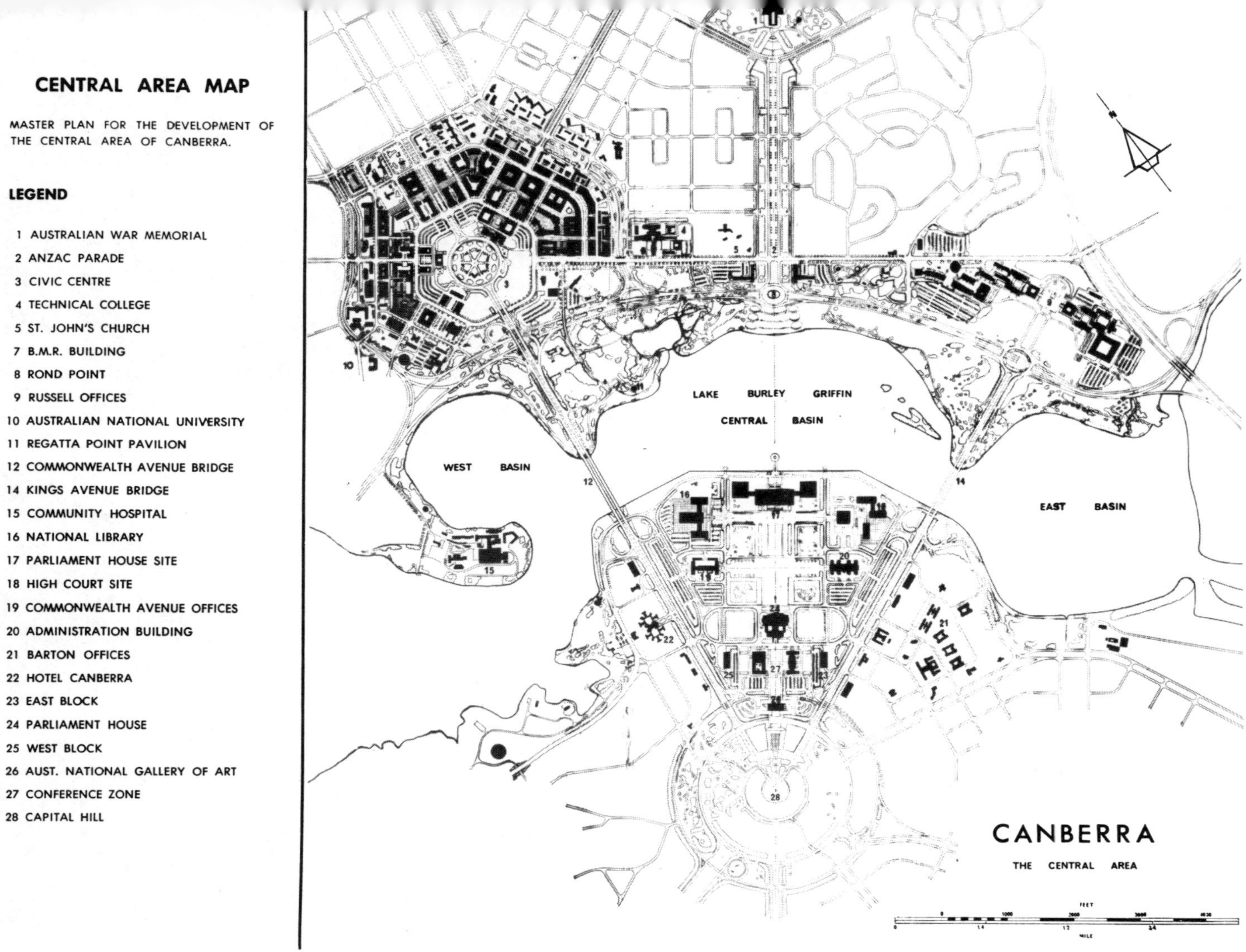

CENTRAL AREA MAP

MASTER PLAN FOR THE DEVELOPMENT OF
THE CENTRAL AREA OF CANBERRA.

LEGEND

1 AUSTRALIAN WAR MEMORIAL
2 ANZAC PARADE
3 CIVIC CENTRE
4 TECHNICAL COLLEGE
5 ST. JOHN'S CHURCH
7 B.M.R. BUILDING
8 ROND POINT
9 RUSSELL OFFICES
10 AUSTRALIAN NATIONAL UNIVERSITY
11 REGATTA POINT PAVILION
12 COMMONWEALTH AVENUE BRIDGE
14 KINGS AVENUE BRIDGE
15 COMMUNITY HOSPITAL
16 NATIONAL LIBRARY
17 PARLIAMENT HOUSE SITE
18 HIGH COURT SITE
19 COMMONWEALTH AVENUE OFFICES
20 ADMINISTRATION BUILDING
21 BARTON OFFICES
22 HOTEL CANBERRA
23 EAST BLOCK
24 PARLIAMENT HOUSE
25 WEST BLOCK
26 AUST. NATIONAL GALLERY OF ART
27 CONFERENCE ZONE
28 CAPITAL HILL

CANBERRA

THE CENTRAL AREA

EAST BASIN

LAKE BURLEY GRIFFIN

CENTRAL BASIN

WEST BASIN

FIG. 145.   Canberra central area.

FIG. 146.   La Defense renewal area, Paris.

FIG. 147. Le Corbusier's 1930 redevelopment project for Paris.

FIG. 148.   Syntagma Square, Athens—gradual change.

FIG. 149.   Model of programmed renewal, Philadelphia, USA.

FIG. 150.   Norrmalm redevelopment, Stockholm.

FIG. 151. Model of the Raschplatz area reconstruction, Hanover.

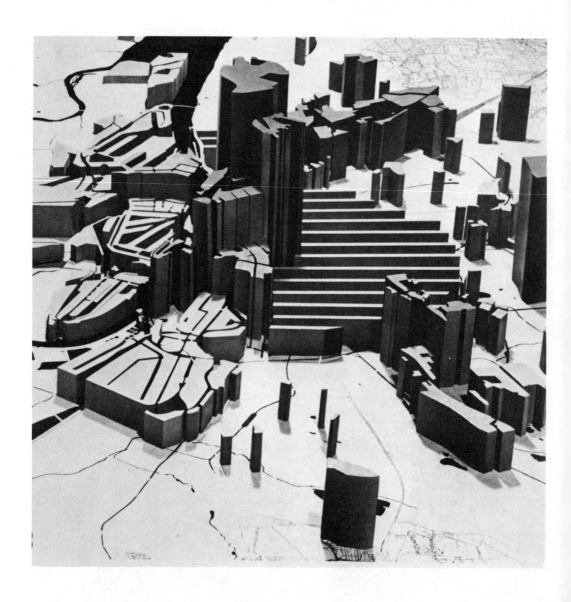

FIG. 152.   Density zoning model, Hamburg.

FIG. 153.   Planning model, Stockholm Central area.

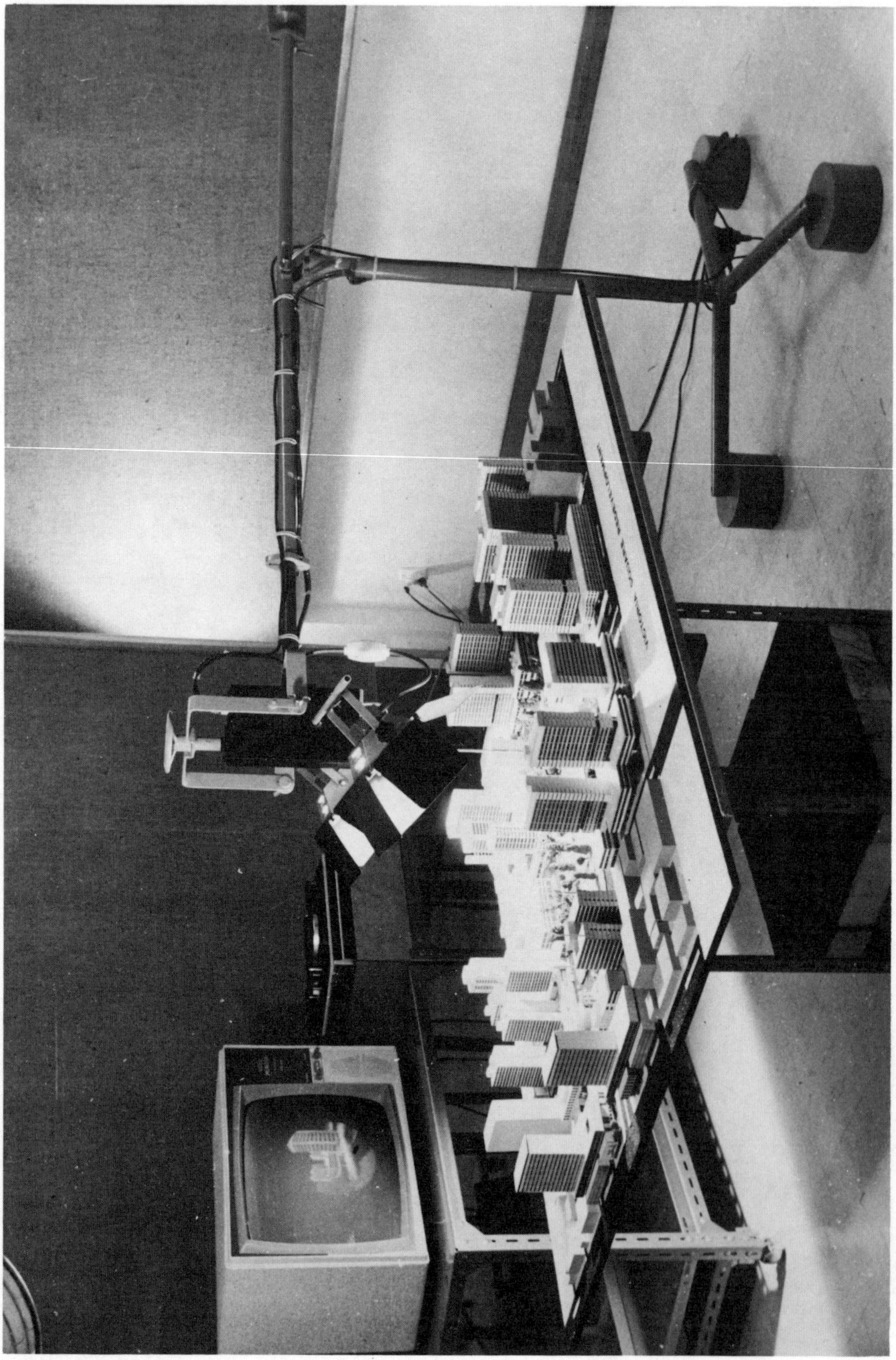

FIG. 154.   Perceptual simulation with model.

FIG. 155.   The 16th Arrondissement, Paris.

FIG. 156. Parliament buildings, Kuala Lumpur, Malaysia.

FIG. 157.   St Paul's Cathedral, London—metropolitan focus.

FIG. 158. Wells Cathedral—dominant massing.

FIG. 159.   The Acropolis, Athens.

FIG. 160. Royal Crescent, Bath.

THE FORMAL INFLUENCES
This heading covers the decision-making influencing the physical and social form of the city. Who makes the public and private decisions? How are these organised? What are the goals and enabling institutions? Thus is gained an insight into the forces now shaping the city and a knowledge of the resources that must be mobilised.

This helpful *aide-memoire* serves to emphasise the importance of the survey process and the accumulation of adequate data relevant to the planning procedures, and neatly summarises the major elements of the analytical process. Its authors also maintain, with some justification, that the process involved holds out the hope of producing order to replace our present chaos and of creating a framework for the art of architecture in place of our present artistic impoverishment. Most significantly, the statement underlines afresh, if this were necessary, the important recognition of the missing element in the urban design equation in many cities today and the need to concentrate, above all, on remedying this omission without delay as our primary objective.

The planning, as opposed to the urban design process, can be very materially assisted by a further rationalisation of method in which traditional and contemporary groupings and their locational dispositions may continue to suggest the basis of a valid approach allowing for flexible combinations and arrangements. These might occur under a series of headings such as:

COMMERCE AND DISTRIBUTION FACILITIES
Including shops (Figs. 69 and 62), markets, offices (Figs. 96 and 118) and warehousing.

SOCIAL, RELIGIOUS AND RECREATIONAL FACILITIES
Including churches (Fig. 142), clubs, theatres, cinemas, arcades, public houses (Fig. 143), restaurants, hotels (Fig. 144), dance halls, bowling alleys, coffee bars, skating rinks and swimming pools.

CIVIC, CULTURAL, GOVERNMENTAL AND EDUCATIONAL FACILITIES
Including civic centres and municipal offices, art galleries, concert halls (Fig. 86), libraries and museums, education and health facilities, telephone exchanges, government offices, car parks, bus stations, police, fire and ambulance headquarters and facilities, public conveniences and other ancillaries.

RESIDENTIAL PROVISIONS
Combined, desirably in many cases with other (Fig. 52) uses.

REGIONAL CENTRES
The method of approach to the urban design and planning problem will obviously be vitally affected by the scale of the operation, whether or not it arises from sectional renewal programmes, or whether it is concerned with the 'clean sheet' start. For convenience these have already been categorised as 'Initial', 'Superimposed', or 'Emergent'.[24]

The differences in conditions which will confront the planners in each case are at once fairly apparent inasmuch as, in the case of the 'Initial' or 'clean sheet' type of development the probability is that no city, as such, exists on the site, which will probably be devoted to some form of rural land-use (Fig. 145). It is assumed that the necessary area of land has been brought under a single ownership and therefore under some form of long-term control. It is also likely that the construction work will proceed over a comparatively short time span—as compared with the older cities—under the direction of a single organisation and in accordance with a single overall plan and development programme.

In these circumstances it is to be expected that, ideally, many of the disadvantages and inconveniences of the older cities can be avoided although this will by no means imply that determining the form and planning in the face of the uncertainty of future changes is any easier.

Interesting recent examples of this kind occur in the English New Towns, in Canberra, and in the development of Reston, Virginia, where, after prolonged consideration in the light of all our contemporary knowledge as to what would constitute a basis for an ideal city plan, it was concluded that one or more compact, unified, type of development was required rather than the 'free-standing buildings formally arranged in space-like sculptures in a garden'[215] which had been adopted in a number of other recent new town and city development projects. The argument was that 'a town has to make a strong, coherent statement', and that 'you must know when you enter it, and once inside, there should follow an intense sequence of spaces—spaces where people of different occupations meet and mix'.

It was apparent to all those concerned that the lesson we are all learning in city planning and urban design is just as valid in the case of this new city as in a refurbished city—that compactness must govern all the basic decisions and that without such compactness there can be no city. This is just as true in countries where land space availability is unrestricted, and just as important for the reasons already developed and particularly to avoid the confusion between town and country which has not, so far in the world's history, produced measurable benefits to either.

The 'Superimposed' plan (Figs. 146 and 147) calls for considerable changes in the form and character of an existing city, involving major surgery. This is obviously a somewhat unusual situation today, with limited, though noteworthy, exceptions. It is an approach that can only be justified where the most serious defects of planning and development already exist. Where this situation is brought about it is probable that there will be an assumption that bulldozer clearance will lead to a greater degree of planning freedom. In practice, however, restrictions are much more a force to be reckoned with, particularly where they relate to existing essential services.

The 'Emergent' type of development (Fig. 148) is the one we may expect to encounter in most contemporary cities and involves a more continuous and gradual planning process, with a succession of increments directed towards overall urban improvement and growth. This is far and away the most difficult type of problem to handle, for reasons which have already been stated. Nevertheless, it is a situation which we must assume to be the most prevalent, in all probability in the form of sectional urban renewal or redevelopment programmes. This is the way in which most established cities will have to meet the challenges of growth and change. In spite of the extremely complex and difficult problems imposed by these conditions, it should still be possible, by rational planning, to achieve at least some of the advantages occurring in the initial type of development of a new city.

As to the broad method of approach, from the evidence of a great deal of published work and of actual planning being undertaken in various cities, it is obvious that there are numerous angles of attack still in use. These include 'the aesthetic approach, the analytical method, the empirical approach, the architectural approach, the "ordered control" method, the organic approach, the economic approach and the accumulative method'.[167] These may appear to be arbitrary classifications and, of course, many other alternatives could be suggested. They are enough, however, to demonstrate the lack of any single clearly-defined philosophy or acceptable policy of urban planning and design which can at present be said to command the respect of a significant proportion of those involved in this work.

The alternative methods have adherents whose names are, in almost all instances, household words on the international planning scene. The importance of what they are doing is therefore not to be dismissed lightly. However, the essential question that we have to ask is: Where is the present-day city which demonstrates, in a practical way, all the desirable criteria postulated? Which of the theses or methods of approach so far put forward can be shown to unequivocably provide a completely comprehensive and workable system with the certain promise of producing the real urban Utopia of the future?

The best we can say is that while none of the efforts or approaches made to date have been entirely comprehensive or completely effective, a number have contributed usefully in particular directions to what may, in due course, become an appropriate synthesis.

The method which appears to present the nearest approach to a well-organised total system is that termed the 'ordered control' method. Even in this case, however, there are missing links in the chain, and additional vitally important stages which must be undertaken if the desired results are to be obtained. This is, of course, the method which is best exemplified in the city of Philadelphia where immensely promising results for the future of city planning are already evident.

It is one of the odd quirks of contemporary urban planning that after many have argued for so long the need for individual buildings to be subordinated to the overall logical guided framework and system—what have been termed the 'anonymous' building groups—we now see the development of a new clamour for what is termed, in contemporary jargon, 'identity'. As there can only be, at any given time or in any given physical situation, a limited number of 'jewels in the anonymous setting',[209] it is difficult to see how all component parts of the group can share in this expression of identity without a reversion to the chaotic anarchy we already have.

Rather, therefore, than heeding this plaintive cry for 'identity' which, presumably, if carried to its logical extreme, would imply each individual office in a multi-storey building shrieking a little louder than its neighbour, we must accept a self-denying ordinance in pursuance of the overall benefit. We cannot have conformity and un-bridled individuality.

For far too long the estate developer has swayed public opinion with the image of the ideal suburban house which pretends to present some form of architectural distinction from its neighbours. This is usually an entirely deceitful and misguided exercise, as many of the better moderate density housing group projects undertaken in Scandinavia or Germany demonstrate. The occupants of dwellings in such unified developments certainly appear to suffer no extreme deprivation through loss of identity, any more than the owner of a standard Ford or a General Motors automobile.

Increasingly and logically, standardisation in our accommodation requirements and in structural methods and systems must lead to a degree of external standardisation of forms. This is, however, not to suggest for one moment that we should not strive for a desirable degree of variety and diversity. Standardisation will, however, do much to procure an underlying suggestion of unity as it arises from an efficient solution of functional requirements. It cannot be considered in any way arbitrary nor, in practice, does it prohibit a form of internal identification.

An indication of how flexible a really worthwhile approach to urban planning and design can be is conveyed by one recent set of recommendations, which propose 'a free composition of slabs and towers with linking rhythms of lower structures in an open landscape. . . . From these larger scale developments . . . emerges a new vision of multi-deck movement,[194] continuous ground planes beneath elevated structures, and a spatial flow between and through metal and glass cages'. Also: 'here is an alternation of long and short perspectives interlocking internal and external spaces, contrast of horizontal plateaux and vertical slabs in asymmetrical groupings, modelled in light and shade and oriented functionally. . . . solid and void of wall and window are fused into panes of glass and masonry or the cellular anatomy of structure itself imposing a pattern on surface and space'.

This proposal contains the suggestion that 'instead of continuous street facades the new town will provide a setting for free standing buildings', as well as 'breaking up of street grids with designed traffic and parking squares as distinct from the 'Bloomsbury' type of domestic retreat'[194] (Fig. 135).

A pleasant glimpse of the possibilities afforded by another multi-purpose zoning concept is conveyed by a recent reference to a development in which it was pointed out that 'in a big project you can use high rise and low rise together in such a way that you can have your cake and eat it too: you can have very high densities and still have open space—you can have standardisation of design but still have a varied and flowing landscape; you can have rambling pedestrian walkways and still have plenty of vehicular access and parking space; and you can fit shops, offices, theatres, playgrounds, into the plan so that it would look incomplete without them'.* Here, surely, must be the strategy for the more convenient idealistic city we should be striving to build.

If the city is to persist as a viable entity its functional pattern must be strong enough to preserve its basic essentials in a way that will permit it to grow and change without detriment to its essential form. In fact, it can be said that a really imaginative system will benefit from each subsequent change and come to full maturity as growth takes place.

* The architect Wilment Vickrey referring to Riley Center, Indiana, USA.

This must be regarded as the essential starting point for any consideration of the planning and design of the city core. Within this overall concept the next step must be that of creating a logical framework of sub-systems, or more localised patterns of development, as a coherent part of the whole and within which the scale of urban renewal operations, as they are likely to be encountered, may take place without loss of context or environmental significance.

The integration of these local development or renewal programmes into the overall metropolitan context, while retaining some environmental individuality or identity, is a balance which can only be struck by the application of an overall, consistent philosophy of design, judged by the same individual or team of planners. Excellent examples of the way in which this integration can be made to work most effectively can be seen in Philadelphia (Fig. 149) and Stockholm (Figs. 150 and 151).

Within the sub-areas, and notwithstanding conformity with and respect for metropolitan systems and patterns, there will, of course, have to be provision for local and internal circulation and efficient functioning of each of the component parts, whether for business, commerce or governmental needs. Above all it has to be recognised that it is at this point that the pedestrian comes into his own. It is for him that urban planning and the creation of a suitable environment has the most significance since, as Goethe wrote, 'Only when we walk around a building, move through it, can we share in its life'. This is equally true of a single building or a group of buildings in the urban context under discussion.

Moving down to the scale of the urban superblock, an overall density and massing study (Fig. 152) in relation to known land-use requirements and communication needs will lead directly to a number of alternatives. These will be concerned with the grouping of closely interrelated, contributory developments, with a demonstrable concern for the design of related spaces and a cohesive physical linkage with all other such areas adjoining and with the vehicular and pedestrian transportation systems.

Even when all the functional and socio-economic considerations have been studied and are met, an enormous number of permissible variants exist in the solution of this more localised planning work, which is where the creation of the city, and its change and growth, are going to occur. The final decision on which of these variants is the most acceptable must ultimately be greatly influenced by the all-important consideration of the visual qualities of the environment and its contribution to this—a matter of selective, intuitive visual evaluation.

In discussing visual appraisals or evaluation up to this point, it may have been assumed that this proposal does little more than suggest a fundamental change of emphasis. It may even seem to have familiar connotations. An entirely new technique—'Perceptual Simulation'—has been developed for this purpose which, it is believed, provides a fresh and completely convincing answer to the problem of urban visual analysis and enables this vital task to be undertaken in a way not previously possible at any stage in the history of urban planning.[102]

There is no reason why a sense of spontaneity, rather than a ponderous, over-deliberate quality, should not be produced by a selective, intuitive system, based on subjective judgements. It may, in certain respects, appear to accept something arbitrary but it need not, in consequence, be in any sense illogical.

Any architect is well aware of the fact that every building must be much more than a purely functional, self-organised set of interrelated decisions in physical form. If it is worthy to be considered as architecture, it must be a strong, intuitive, artistic interpretation of the essential facts of its purpose. This is also true with the city, as has been proved through past failures and increasingly today, as a consequence of too frequent dependence on a mere 'functionalist' approach.

No sets of rules, systems or theories can effectively meet this challenge. Rather, if we try to take refuge in such methods, do they merely serve to stultify or entirely suppress individual imagination? On the other hand, while visual appraisal techniques may not involve all the senses, the perceptual simulation method has been shown as capable of coming very close to actuality. That is as close as it is possible to do, short of putting up groups of experimental buildings and tearing them down again if and when it is considered that they have failed to meet exact criteria in the build-up of the urban environment.

Many of the visual evaluation methods utilised traditionally by architects and urban planners have, unfortunately, been found wanting and, in many cases, are probably misleading. Our contemporary design problems have indeed expanded to a degree of complexity in which it is simply not possible to illustrate them in perspective. This traditional form of representation has, therefore, to be discarded as a means of communicating the planners' ideas. Equally important is the fact that the method for so long in use entirely fails to provide the designer with reliable information as a basis for decision-making.

There can be no question that the standard architectural perspective and model create notoriously false impressions, particularly in two respects—they give incorrect and unnatural viewpoints and, moreover, such viewpoints are stationary. We cannot, in this matter, hold out much hope that even in the long run the ubiquitous computer will help solve our problems for us, although programmes now exist capable of producing multiple viewpoint perspectives. These unfortunately lack that sense of realism which would make them an acceptable alternative.

The undeniable shortcomings of the traditional perspective with its single preconceived static viewpoint, mean that we know little or nothing about the changing impressions which occur as movement takes place around the building, towards it, and then within it. Far less is there any sense of involvement from a two-dimensional representation of this type, in which there is no feeling of perceptual experience.

However, the multiplicity of perspectives created by the computer's graphic display takes us very little further ahead. It provides nothing more nor less than a series of static images which, because they are in line and two dimensions only, convey little sense of light and shade or real modelling. Moreover, they are usually confused with unwanted construction lines which are difficult to eradicate within the present programming constraints.

In attempting to deal with the all-important question of movement, there have been at least two significant efforts directed towards systems of notation, which indicate both movement routes and sequential impressions. It has been said about one of these, 'In order to design for movement a whole new system of conceptualising must be undertaken'.[78] Our present design and planning systems are inevitably limited, it is argued, by our techniques of demonstrating concepts and our methods of symbolising ideas. We know only how to delineate static objects, which is the usual process. Since we have developed techniques for showing buildings and objects and outlining the spaces which they confine we plan, of course, by the use of architectural symbols projected by conventional methods on paper.

As a part of these techniques we use the plan and the elevation, the isometric or axonometric projection and, sometimes, a model. However all these accepted systems of architectural language describe only the fixed surroundings, the structures, and the spaces they enclose. Since we have not techniques for describing the activity that occurs within spaces or within buildings, we cannot adequately plan for such activity. It has therefore been contended that 'a new system should be able to focus primarily on movement and only secondarily on the environment'.

While there must be a close measure of agreement as to the lack of adequate appreciation of movement and specific design method related to it, either in architecture or in planning, it seems that to focus on movement first, and only 'secondarily on environment', is to put the cart before the horse and to get the whole urban design problem seriously out of balance.

Movement is an essential element which produces a form of kinesthetic experience, and conditions perception through the other senses, all of which, however, are directed to the total perception of the environment. It is the environment itself, therefore, which is all-important and movement merely a means to an end.

The codification of movement systems and patterns may very well help in a better understanding of the ways in which buildings are likely to be seen or used, but in so far as the pedestrian is concerned, these are no different from other communication patterns which form a part of the basic functional framework to which the layout or design of the city has to respond. The mere tracing of these patterns on paper in two dimensions can do little or nothing towards a better appreciation of the visual qualities of the environment.

If it is agreed that the traditional perspective and attempts to establish movement codes or to study visual image surveys are partial, but very limited, indicators of certain aspects of urban design, we must consider how far the use of models may be of assistance.

All too frequently, if models are constructed with the intention of producing a small-scale simulation of buildings or groups of buildings which it is intended to construct, these have already been decided in a two-dimensional form of representation and construction in three dimensions is on an entirely preconceived basis not susceptible to, or easily capable of, future change.

If, on the other hand, models of this type are to be of value, they must be in similar form to those which some cities, such as Philadelphia (Fig. 149) and Stockholm (Fig. 153), have used for this purpose. They should have completely replaceable sections so that a number of alternatives may be tried and studied. Unfortunately, the usual method of study in this case is from the bird's-eye view of an aircraft approaching the local airport. While this point of view may be of increasing interest as more and more people travel by air, it is not, it is contended, the most important.

The point has already been emphasised that the city must ultimately be considered as belonging to the pedestrian and even though its approaches and other viewpoints may have significance, by far the most important consideration is that of planning the view from the street at the eye level of the normal moving pedestrian.

When the instrument known as a 'modelscope' was first produced, it had evident potential as a design tool, although for a long time its use was confined solely to a series of static views of architectural design models. It did, however, succeed in bringing the eye level down to that of the pedestrian through the optical periscope system, and this provided valuable information from the admittedly limited viewpoints used. In this sense it was infinitely more convincing than the use of panoramic viewpoints at bird's eye level.

However, while this was, in many ways, a major advance towards obtaining true visual impressions of how future city developments will appear, the lack of the element of movement—and therefore of the ability to obtain a sequential series of constantly changing impressions—meant that a further improvement in techniques had to be found.

It has already been accepted that some of the sensory perceptions involved in experiencing particular parts of the urban environment are incapable of direct simulation although there is little doubt that, if the visual perceptive process can be sufficiently accurately replicated, by association many of the other senses will seem to react or respond as they would do in fact.

At one stage it was hoped that most of the answers could be found in the use of a movie camera linked with the modelscope but, in practice, this lacks all sense of spontaneity or personal involvement and because of the delay in preparing and developing the film and therefore in seeing the moving impressions, the latter appear to be so remote and detached from the model itself that they entirely lack conviction, nor are not of much value. There can, moreover, be no question of an instantaneous feedback in the study process to allow for the immediate correction or modification of particular parts of the model, since the time-lag involved seriously interferes with the creation of useful design information.

It has, however, now been found that, with special equipment which was designed to link the modelscope with a closed circuit television system and a videotape recorder, the simulation obtained is so close to reality as to be wholly convincing (Fig. 154). The sense of participation and actual enclosure in space and movement through it, is entirely persuasive and both the speed and direction of movement, as well as the varied selection of viewpoints and the scanning which the eye normally makes, can all be readily applied, adjusted and corrected by inspection of the TV monitor.

While this form of study is under way, the whole process is being recorded on videotape which can immediately be played back and studied more intensively on any number of further occasions. If design corrections appear to be warranted or necessary in relation to one particular part of the model or development, the videotape recorder can momentarily be held stationary so that the area in question can be accurately identified and studied.

If models are prepared on a city-wide or metropolitan scale and used with this system they can be the basis of the design master plan or general framework. Within this framework the widest possible range of permutations and combinations of every conceivable kind in relation to particular areas may be studied in model form and fully evaluated in a way that is not possible with any other system—least of all mathematical rationalisations or computerised studies. This system almost completely removes the elements of guesswork from the physical shape of city planning and provides the certain knowledge that, once a functional set of criteria have been established and met, the urban designer is provided with a tool with which he can satisfy himself and others—long before bulldozers appear on the site—that the best possible form of development will take place in the city on the consistent basis of a real evaluation of the visual environment.

One of the important advantages of this system, moreover, relates to the contemporary decision-making process which will almost always involve large numbers of members of planning authorities, or boards, of commercial and industrial concerns. All the evidence derived from these studies can be quite simply demonstrated in the most effective way, and, of course, the sound commentary which accompanies the videotape recording is invaluable for this purpose, as it is for teaching and for demonstration to students and other interested groups.

The sound track can also be used most effectively to add a background noise appropriate to the particular setting and perhaps, in time, means may be found to titillate the other senses by the gratuitous introduction of petrol fumes or clouds of city dust. It seems improbable, however, that any means can be found, of simulating the kinesthetic experience, although a strongly convincing visual image certainly helps to do this. A three-dimensional holograph development of this basic idea, as well as other improvements—including colour and anaglypta systems—are being investigated.

The techniques of the modern cinema with the wrap-around screen and the introduction of colour to accompany sound, have carried this process of simulation and sensual participation to an advanced stage. The sense of realism to be experienced with the best examples of these techniques can be almost complete, but the modelscope-television moving images of a city, with their background of sound, are scarcely less realistic.

Chapter XI

The relevance of history in city design and planning

Areas or parts of cities of acknowledged beauty or historical interest can often provide the basis of inspiration for future needs, as has already been demonstrated, but only inasmuch as we may be able to derive from them fundamental aesthetic values or truisms relating to norms in urban composition which may sometimes be equally valid in the very changed circumstances and conditions of today.

Otherwise, probing into history for inspiration becomes a mere exercise in ecletic mannerism and a quite illogical process, almost wholly superficial and seldom able to survive the time-scale of multiple and extended participation of the 'thousand designers' and entrepreneurs. Even for the large government complex such probing would seldom have validity as a means of providing a lively, workable and beautiful city core in contemporary conditions, far less for the probable future needs of its inhabitants.

A great deal of the pleasure most of us experience in cities belonging to an earlier period is due to the patina of age adding a kindly veneer to the once raw heterogeneity and, in turn, creating the suggestion of an overall comfortable unity—a picture which is really, in many respects, entirely misleading. Closer analysis will often show a quite different view—whether we are studying the Italian hill cities or the areas lying behind the impressive Paris boulevards (Fig. 155) which inspired Le Corbusier's Redevelopment Project (Fig. 147) some years ago.

Rather surprisingly, a similar situation occurs from the first distant view of Manhattan seen in the approach to the Battery (Fig. 80), or from the New Jersey flats (Fig. 81) and the subsequent, closer, impressions down in cavernous Wall Street, or in the thick of Stuyvesant Town (Fig. 43). It is, of course, these close at hand judgements of the environment which are its real measure.

Many of the historic cities become intolerable once we penetrate within the streets and buildings, as they date from a time when efficiency and functional convenience, as we know it today, played little or no part in the design and planning process. Such aesthetic values as there were arose in spite of planning, and not as an innate part of good design and planning. Perhaps this is the main difference in our contemporary approach. We must have, in our environment, both beauty and the knowledge of functional efficiency if our cities are to persist and not become the urban museums of the future.

In relating the factors of economics, aesthetics and ethics in modern urbanisation, it has been said that 'architects and urbanists used to be concerned mainly with beauty and prestige: and that their job was to build churches and castles, fortresses and ramparts. Because all these buildings housed prestigious and respected functions and people, they had to be spectacular to impress the outsider, the people passing by. A certain kind of beauty, or aesthetics, was indeed one of the buildings' functions. This past of architecture and urbanism has brought us an extraordinary artistic heritage, in fact most of the world's marvels'.[67]

This fairly presents an inescapable fact which we have to face with some humility in view of the chaotic state of many of our contemporary cities. Whether or not we can see the means of directly deriving benefit from a study of these earlier historic examples which have so much of a challenge to offer us, we cannot afford to forget that, in their way, they set standards which we have yet to emulate satisfactorily or in any reasonable degree in our twentieth century urban creations.

It is a sobering thought that in the periods to which we are referring many of the finest cities were conceived without aid from traffic engineers, sociologists, economists, geographers, or any of the other participants in the present-day planning team, each of whom is inclined to think of his professional skills as being the indispensable element in the creation and moulding of the city. Over the longest period of history, on the other hand, the one absolutely indispensable element has been the services of the imaginative architect–urbanist, however he may have been described at any particular time. Without him there would certainly have been no city and no individual buildings.

It is a fact that every city needs, as an expression of the varied facets of its community activities, a number of spectacular buildings whose materials, design and appearance reflect the importance, dignity and authority of the functions it houses, and for which it was created (Fig. 156). It also seems that those with perception still want the city to be beautiful, as well as convenient and accessible to all, but with the greatest possible degree of equality of benefit. We have to ask, therefore, whether such requirements are consistent with aesthetic criteria derived from a different age, but implanted on a contemporary substructure?

In seeking an answer to this all-important question we will increasingly become aware of the fact that the appearance and structure of cities are much more fundamental than mere responses to the dictates of custom, convenience or setting.

It is, of course, entirely wrong to assume that at earlier periods, the logic of sound planning within a framework of good functional design, in particular buildings and groups of buildings, was not equally regarded as of prime importance. The 'lords of the manor', as well as their artisans, appreciated the form and materials of the buildings they erected. Under the guidance of city fathers, church officials and other dignitaries, care was exercised in the locational relationships between the principal structures and the town. Buildings became functional in character both in form and location. They were rarely deliberately built to be 'picturesque'—that quality gradually developed with the careful aggregation of subsequent building harmoniously blended in. Very often impressive vistas occurred accidentally and contrasts of form and massing resulted from the rise and fall of the land and the ingenious selection of the sites for each structure. The dominant position of the cathedral or church established a focus and created a unity in the city (Figs. 157 and 158), and this was reinforced by the evident two-dimensional constraint of the city walls.

Subsequently, eclecticism with its catholicity of styles, tended to mask the true tradition of city building by obscuring the fact that urban forms in all great periods of history had invariably a contemporary image instinctively donated by creative artists and craftsmen in their own idiom. Order in cities, as a reflection of human culture at any period, can only be achieved through a dynamic expression of the idiom and forms appropriate to that particular period.

Whilst it is true that there were, in some cases, accidental effects contributing to the attractions of earlier cities, we can assert with confidence that such overall harmony as is to be found is not due solely to the mellowing brought about by age. There is, in good architectural grouping, a sincerity which is abiding and satisfying. The untrammelled honesty of the craftsman and his clarity of purpose provide a thread of continuity and assure a degree of harmony to creative works of whatever period.

We must surely concur in the contention that 'if we were to follow the tradition of great cultures of the past, we today would engage in the most powerful period of creative contemporary city building the world has ever seen',[65] since we have the equipment, the techniques and the industry, as well as the ingenuity, to make the finest cities of all times. Yet, tragically, to date we have utterly failed to build constructively on this past experience, or to use the talents, experience and knowledge that are available to us.

It is an unfortunate fact, which we must clearly recognise, that the urban planner and designer has to contend with conflicting interests and practical demands of a far more exacting nature than any which occur even in the most complex individual building. As a consequence, there have been relatively fewer significant achievements in city design than is the case in other arts. Thus the rare earlier masterpieces of the Golden Ages of Periclean Athens (Fig. 159), Renaissance Rome (Fig. 108), and Georgian England (Fig. 160), have not again been matched, but serve as a reminder that the city can, at its best, be one of Man's principal achievements.

A contemporary expression of a wholly satisfying urbanism may, therefore, be regarded as something for the future. In the meantime, however, we must eagerly anticipate the time when all our cities are transformed, as they can be, so as to become a pleasure and a worthy environment for urbane Man. To be sufficiently impatient about these possibilities may be the best guarantee of their ultimate fulfilment. Until that time, we have to recognise the many imperfections which exist in our cities and the magnitude of the problems we face, with an overwhelming predominance of mediocre building only relieved in limited localities by occasional significant urban achievements—but which, however, demonstrate how much may be achieved in creating order out of chaos.

These too rare examples of aesthetic urban order are the means by which we can get a glimpse of the unified city, compounded of a high degree of artistic cohesion and the uniform level of excellence consistent with a maximum of diversity.

Surely this ideal city should not be regarded as a mere figment of the imagination, or as unattainable, but rather as a perfectly rational goal at which to aim. As a first major step towards its attainment we must utterly reject those participants and critics who claim to see some kind of virtue in muddle, complexity and confusion, apparently for its own sake. Rather, we should be sharing the belief, founded on the evidence of history, that a city which is not a collective work of art is not a city fit to live in, no matter how efficiently it may function in other respects.

In some cases the accuracy of historical analogy is impressive and continually serves to remind us of the often stubborn refusal to learn from experience. With reference to the baroque period in Spain it has been pointed out that, 'the actual characteristic of Spanish city planning was unification (Fig. 161)—not to say uniformity and regularity—the belated and now conscious reaction against the manifoldness and individuality of the cities, houses and streets of the Middle Ages'.[74] Descartes has expressed this longing of the age for unity and clarity very clearly. In 'A Discourse on Method' he contends: 'there is seldom so much perfection in works composed of many separate parts upon which different hands had been employed, as in those completed by a single master. Thus it is observable that the buildings which a single architect has planned and executed are generally more elegant and commodious than those which several have attempted to improve. . . .'

Committees, Boards of Directors, Corporations and planning teams still need reminding of this fact during the inevitably protracted process of producing their compromise solutions. Rational thought now indicates, quite clearly, as has already been emphasised, that, in contemporary planning and design processes in the city, we must revert to the overall guiding hand of the 'single master', since only in this way is there the slightest prospect of obtaining the desirable unity within which the necessary degree of diversity and variety can take place. This is more especially the case with visual, subjective and intuitive judgements, which are both the co-ordinating motivating force and the all-important amalgam in the creation of appropriate urban environments.

Although the indications seem, very often, quite otherwise, it must be logically assumed that we should know more about the problems of our cities than we did before the adoption of the many current methods of research and analysis. It is particularly unfortunate, therefore, that in recent years a pseudo-scientific bias has been more evident than a concern for aesthetic values. This may be due, in part at least, to an understandable swing away from the period during which city planning was based on the superficial 'City Beautiful' concepts, which glossed over the basic fundamentals of the problem and made do with mere cosmetic effects.

It is in this area that the part of city planning which deals with the physical form of the city—namely urban design—has grown up. This is indeed the most creative aspect of city planning and the one in which imagination and artistic capacity can play a most important part. It is also, in many respects, the most difficult and controversial area and the one in which imagination and artistic capacity can play a vital role. Because of all these factors it has, relatively speaking, received less attention than it deserves.

The view has also been expressed elsewhere that, with the more recent development of a new approach to architecture, landscape architecture, highway engineering and city planning over the last decades, accepted traditions were seen to be no longer valid. However, after many years of compartmentalised work, we are only now beginning to realise the undeniable logic of an overall urban synthesis. 'Like the instruments in an orchestra these elements of urban design all have their parts to play in the total performance. The result must be harmonious and cannot be reached by individual competition'.[75] The individual parts must, moreover, be subordinated to the 'score' and to the will of a single conductor.

What, in fact, is increasingly obvious is that the desirable result may only be attained through collective collaboration through the instrumentality of a single agency and system of guidance.

Referring to the work of one of the most maligned authors to have put pen to paper in the cause of city planning, Holden expressed the view that Sitte's 'Artistic Fundamentals'[171] contributed a meaning to design and the growth of cities. It has to be confessed, nevertheless, that to a large number of people, and more especially perhaps those in North America, the use of the term 'artistic' may convey an idea of superficiality. The contemporary self-appointed role of the art historian as architectural critic reinforces this view—as a limited and entirely skin-deep approach is all he is usually qualified to take in his evaluations.

It is unfortunate that we are very often induced to believe that, because artistic merit is largely a matter of visual judgement, it is a quality which must therefore be concerned primarily with surface appearance, rather than basic and more fundamental factors. Thus most western cities including those, for example, in North America, have been much more influenced by engineering needs and ideas than by 'artistic fundamentals'. It is a regrettable fact that much of this engineering is unimaginative and lacking in a wider understanding of the humane values needed in the city if it is to be designed for people rather than for systems or machines. In such circumstances it becomes superficial in the broader sense and, therefore, to a much greater extent than where a purely artistic approach is adopted, more devastatingly inept.

While this proposition relates first and foremost to Americans and their cities it is almost equally valid when applied to the large majority of other contemporary western cities. It is a sad fact, however, that the recent growth of scepticism in relation to urban aesthetic values not measurable in mathematical terms, largely stems from approaches generated in recent years in the United States.

Referring to the persistence of three dominant systems in many of the traditional city plans and to the numerous variants on these stereotypes, Sitte offers a criticism, very often applicable in present-day circumstances, that, from an artistic point of view, the 'whole tribe' of geometric systems is worthless, 'having exhausted the last drop of art's blood from its veins'[171] (Figs. 162 and 163). Sitte believed that these systems would accomplish nothing other than a standardisation of street patterns, mechanical in conception and which would, moreover, reduce the street system to a mere traffic utility, completely disregarding the important artistic values. In these circumstances such geometrical patterns often make no appeal to the perceptive senses since their features are only discernible on a map or from an aeroplane.

In support of this contention, we may think of the chequerboard system—which originated in Mannheim as artistically bad for vehicle and pedestrian alike—with its frequent four-way intersections (Figs. 164 and 165). The fact is that the rectilinear street system was usually imposed by simple engineers or surveyors who were either too afraid or too indolent to prescribe or lay out more complicated systems. Sad to say, there are contemporary cities which demonstrate the same faults and, in addition, an unwillingness to learn from earlier experience.

Many critics of Sitte are either unaware of, or choose to ignore, his warning that modern life and building methods, 'prevent a servile imitation of old city arrangement'.

Sitte urges that, instead, we should try to glean the secrets of the essential vitality of earlier examples which should then lead to something better than mere imitation. He believed that it cannot be emphasised strongly enough, but is too frequently forgotten, that we can cater for the mandatory requirements of modern building techniques and legislation, as well as public health ordinances and traffic circulation needs, without enforcing artistic sterility. Thus, by carefully examining the best work of earlier periods to determine how much of it may be suitably adapted to present-day conditions, we may solve the aesthetic aspects of the practical problem of city building and decide what, if anything, can be preserved from the living heritage handed down by previous generations.

We can then accept specifically that any changes which may be seen as necessary, as a consequence of improved techniques or construction standards, must be carried out even if aesthetic considerations have, as a consequence, to be modified. In Sitte's philosophy there is still an utterly convincing logic and a balanced reasoned perspective to which we must return and on which we must build if we are to direct our resources and talents in order to produce worthwhile results.

Many worthy efforts have been made to distil the essence from the more memorable historical examples of good urban planning in order that the principles involved at least might be used in an examination of, and, where appropriate, as a threshold to, the solution of contemporary planning and urban design problems. In one such study[152] the emphasis is on what every architect and urban designer understands, namely the dual role of building façades as the outward expression of something more complex than at first appears, and which cannot properly be appreciated before we have perceived the relation between the interior and the exterior, between the human requirements of the occupants for which the building is constructed and the technical methods and resources available at the time of its erection. This, in contemporary terms, is to argue for an understanding of the inseparable relationship between efficient, functional internal planning arrangements in component buildings and groups of buildings as a prerequisite to their satisfactory artistic and architectural external treatment within the urban grouping.

In support of the idea of historical continuity, a number of examples of the planned city have been investigated. These include Peking (Fig. 166), built up according to a system of rules which, to a European, seem a combination of the mystic and the down-to-earth. Some parallels can be drawn between this ancient city, the French Empire period and the city building of the Third Reich all of which place the accent on city planning according to special ritual, with axes, malls and processional roads.

It was Michelangelo who saw the importance of creating a rigorous architectural unity 'out of picturesque confusion'.[152] He believed that the forms and patterns of most cities with particularly meritorious aesthetic qualities were derived primarily from quite logical underlying topographical or functional considerations in which strong artistic convictions were always present.

A contemporary urban analyst[205] has concentrated on the fundamental importance of the square as a basic factor in town planning, as the very heart of the city and the 'central formative element' which makes the community a community and not merely an aggregate of individuals.

In support of this contention, the examples of Lisbon, Karlsruhe, Florence (Fig. 167), Paris (Fig. 168), Rome (Fig. 169) and Isfahan (Fig. 170) are cited and compared with the amorphous character of the one-time Mohenjo-Daro (Fig. 171). It is maintained that all the well-known public spaces and squares in these famous cities possess qualities in common, in which space generally designates 'a three-dimensional expansion of any kind'. Such a space implies a structural organisation as a frame for human activities and is based on very definite factors, including the relationship between the forms of the surrounding buildings, their uniformity and variety, their physical dimensions and proportions relative to the width and length of the open area, the angle of entry of streets and, finally, the location of such three-dimensional punctuations or accents as monuments and fountains.

The persistence of this spatial element in both historic and contemporary cities certainly provides some justification for a preoccupation with this type and pattern of urban spaces without, however, necessarily giving it exactly the degree of emphasis which may have seemed more appropriate in the 'City Beautiful' phase.

The same sort of close attention is given by other writers to the role of the park in the town or city and we have only to think, in this connection, of Nash's Regent's Park (Figs. 172, 173 and 46) and the significance it has in the whole grand design which linked this element of London with Piccadilly Circus (Fig. 174) to understand the importance of its role in the city. Other examples are the Bois du Boulogne in Paris, Central Park in New York (Fig. 175), Riverside Park in Chicago (Fig. 176) and the central formal park created by Washington Mall. All of these play a vital part, not merely in creating recreational opportunities and a 'breath of fresh air' within the city itself, but as contributions to the essential nature of the planning framework.

Whether we ever expect to see repeated the impressive axial formalism of Paris (Fig. 73), Versailles (Figs. 177 and 178), Washington (Fig. 179), Berlin (Fig. 180), or the Mall in London, there is still an underlying continuity of such ideas in planning more recently undertaken, for example, in New Delhi or the Antipodean city of Canberra. This, of all precepts, seems to be by far the most insistent and pervasive.

In the descriptive study already referred to, the irregular layout of the Christian cities in Spain is emphasised—where, however, the streets always follow a clearly defined direction. In some of these quite enlightened examples of planning one of the most characteristic features were the arcades which offered the pedestrians protection against sun or rain and were used by the shopkeepers and artisans as a welcome extension of their workshops. This picture of a lively mediaeval city area is a reminder of something to which we might revert with advantage, as part of a renaissance of the multi-level zoning concept.

The Spanish mediaeval cities can be compared with Islamic and similar cities which grew from the simple basic element of the individual family house and thence via the ethnic or religious denominational unit. Their patterns of streets and districts were not imposed by authoritarian means; thus they developed the typical labyrinthine character with streets akin to a maze and, above all, buildings considered more important than streets, the main function of the latter being to serve buildings adjoining them, rather than establishing a prior concern for traffic movement. This further emphasis of the greater importance of buildings, and the occupants they house, as against the means

FIG. 161. Segovia, Spain.

FIG. 162.   Canberra City centre.

FIG. 163. Palma Nuova, Italy.

FIG. 164. Richelieu, France—'Chequerboard' town.

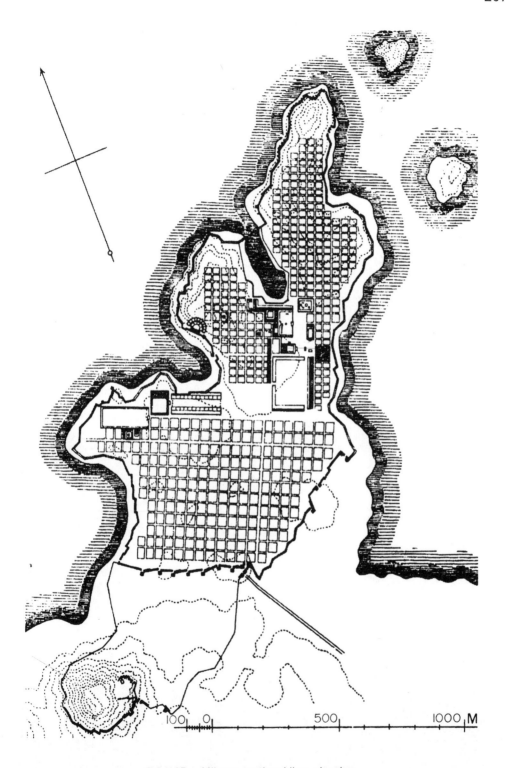

100 0   500   1000 M

FIG. 165.   Miletus—early gridiron planning.

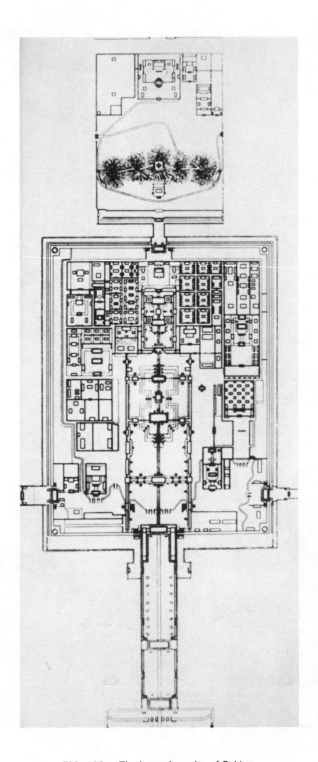

FIG. 166.   The legendary city of Peking.

FIG. 167. Palazzo Signoria, Florence.

FIG. 168. Place des Vosges, Paris.

FIG. 169. Via Conciliazone, Rome.

272

FIG. 170. The Maidan, Isfahan.

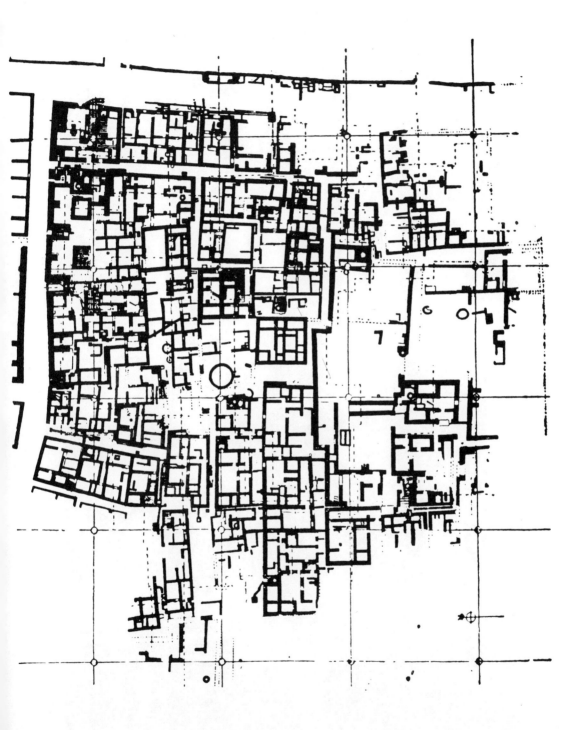

FIG. 171.   Mohenjo–Daro.

FIG. 172. Regent's Park—Nash's grand design.

FIG. 173.   Langham Place—part of the structural linkage.

FIG. 174. Piccadilly Circus.

277

FIG. 175. Central Park, New York.

FIG. 176. Grant Park, Chicago.

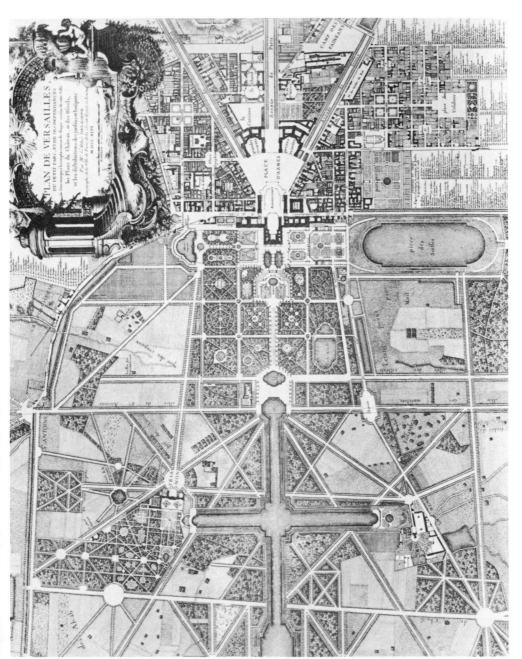

FIG. 177. Versailles—the town, chateau and gardens in 1746.

FIG. 178. Versailles chateau and Place D'Armes.

FIG. 179.　Aerial view, Washington, USA.

FIG. 180. Strasse des 17 Juni, Berlin.

FIG. 181. Hong Kong Housing development.

FIG. 182. Ellicott's 1792 Washington Plan.

FIG. 183. Organic Venice.

FIG. 184. Part of the Amsterdam Canal System.

287

FIG. 185. Aerial view showing Amsterdam's urban structure.

FIG. 186. Nyhavn, Copenhagen.

FIG. 187. Toledo, Spain, from the south.

FIG. 188.   Stuttgart—surrounded by hills.

FIG. 189. Innsbruck with mountain backdrop.

FIG. 190.   The Winter Palace, Leningrad, and River Neva.

FIG. 191.   The Danube and Buda heights.

FIG. 192.   Colonial gridiron, Adelaide, Australia.

of movement, is a complete reversal of contemporary attitudes and something we must restore if the city is ever again to reach the loftier heights of civilised creativity.

There is, of course, nothing new in the basic tenets of this philosophy, involving as it does the notion of bringing order into the city. As evidence of this we are reminded that, in the latter part of the fourteenth century, the Franciscan monk Eximenic felt that a better alternative to the spontaneous and undisciplined growth of mediaeval cities could be gained through a process of systematic planning as a means of creating and generating a satisfactory urban life. Although this was seen as the medium for, and perhaps primarily a symbolic expression of, the pre-eminence of religious ideas, it does not detract from this cleric's startling foresight and perception.

The ideal city which resulted was in every respect the very opposite of the Islamic city. The fundamental change, it is stressed—with the complete contrast from the cities of the Middle Ages and antiquity on the one hand, and from those of the Renaissance and the Baroque, as well as the following periods, on the other—must be seen and appreciated not as a superficial change of vernacular or idiom of topology, but as a revolution in attitudes to space and space relationships. Even more significant was the fact that this new feeling of space was to initiate and nurture the concept and tradition of city design which began to develop with the Renaissance.

The evolution of ideas in city planning has an interesting analogy with developments in painting in which we are reminded that the painters' point of view has been changing from proximate to distant visions throughout the history of the arts in Europe. It is further evident that there were as many points of view as there were objects represented in a primitive picture. The comparison is thus underlined and more especially with the mediaeval town. However, with the Renaissance painters such as Raphael, an abstract element was introduced into painting which created a sense of unity and this is what we term composition or architecture. Even more emphatically the painter of this period subjected all his work to an overriding form of control, namely the geometrical idea of unity.

This has justifiably been described as a Copernican revolution and it is the type of change which is, to no less an extent required today if we are to successfully re-evaluate cities in a contemporary idiom. This needs to be applied in a way that restores their aesthetic qualities and is entirely consistent with the geometrical idea of unity, but without in the process creating a mechanistic, even if smoothly functioning, urban nightmare.

Typical contemporary problems find an echo in a report that, as long ago as 1634, people in New England were complaining of a sensation of crowding, as a consequence, in the opinion of many, of towns being allowed to develop too close to one another.[68] There is more than a trace of suspicion, however, that this may have really been due simply to an acquisitive desire by the entrenched settlers to obtain more of the better land available.

Even at this period we see the all too familiar situation in which the argument of crowding is easy to advance and difficult to refute. It also leads us to ponder the phenomenon itself. Crowding may seem to become rapidly intolerable if removal is a strongly-held preconception and if those concerned do not try to find ways of accepting or alleviating such crowding locally. It is also true that if a more primitive nomadic attitude, with its insistence on continued change, is not replaced by a more civilised philosophy of settled community then any increasing sense of static neighbourliness will seem repugnant.

As most people are now beginning to be aware, but as was realised by a few researchers a considerable time ago, actual measures of the density of population do not have much significance. Indeed, density, congestion and crowding or overcrowding are all comparative and imprecise terms with emotive connotations. They may have much less significance to a Chinese living in a development at approximately 2000 persons per acre in Hong Kong (Fig. 181) than might be the case in a more than usually densely developed suburb in one of our cities in the western world at a density of, say, 40 persons per acre. Views are bound to be based on previous experience as well as on the quality and form of the planning involved.

If we are looking for a logical method by which to develop the plan of the central city area, and in which a satisfactory quality of urban design may be created, the unusual opportunities afforded by a study of the planning of a new city in the past are of interest—particularly when compared with some of the more recent, although rarely as successful, efforts in a similar direction.

The proposals for Ellicot's City of Washington (Fig. 182) give such a picture and, as might be expected, the layout of its streets played a vital role in the concept. These consist of grand avenues and streets leading to public places as the main routes. All these were intended to contain, in addition to the carriageway, footways and lines of trees. The other, narrower streets in this formal geometrical layout link up in a pattern which has a strong Beaux Arts formalism, as had l'Enfant's plan.

The method by which this city's surveyed system was established—through celestial observations—is impressive, as is the way in which its author 'ran all the lines by a transit instrument and determined the acute angles by actual measurement and left nothing to the uncertainty of the compass'. Subsequently, a procedure possessing a degree of logic was followed which would be equally applicable in comparable circumstances today. It was then that: 'the position of the different edifices, and for the several squares or areas of different shapes as they are laid down, were first determined on the most advantageous ground commanding the most extensive prospects and the better susceptible of such improvements as either use or ornament may hereafter call for'.

The link between these focal points, and development of other spaces and squares with the communication system, formed a sequence of rational operations. We should not feel they are irrelevant to today's problems merely because the overall pattern has, for some people, slightly archaic connotations. However this may be, the city's undeniable logic, directness and simplicity create a basic, but self-evident, framework which has acted as a cohesive force and, at the same time, prevented or discouraged obvious deviations from the clearly-defined and established system and order.

It is in the failure to achieve these criteria that chaos has grown up in our present-day cities and until we can find equally valid or better systems and apply them at least as effectively, we should be prepared to benefit, for the time being, from the application of proved principles and the worthwhile qualities which have resulted.

In the light of what we are doing, or more significantly perhaps, failing to do, in our contemporary cities, we cannot lightly brush aside the splendour of the no doubt formalised but entirely unified Versailles; the subtle, organic qualities of Venice (Fig. 183), the coherence of Amsterdam's spider's-web plan, with its strong functional base of the Amstel River (Figs. 184 and 185) and the canals, or the similar layout of inner Vienna (Fig. 44), the grandeur of the vistas of the Paris boulevards, the dual communication system on water and land which makes for such a wonderful sense of diversity in the city of Copenhagen (Fig. 186), given emphasis by the splendid copper-clad spires and towers (Fig. 69), or the powerful sense of climax and total integration of the Spanish and Italian hill towns and cities. This to name but a few of the perpetual sources of urban inspiration which serve to remind us of the achievement of past ages, in so many cases still continuing to offer much in the totally changed circumstances of today.

If we are wise, what we have to try to do is to extract from these inspiring historic examples some of the well-tried, essential principles of grouping and composition which wide-ranging opinion has persistently continued to accept as being pleasurable and beautiful.

This is far from suggesting that a superficially derivative plagiarism or eclecticism should attempt to influence our urban design decisions, but rather that the spirit and permanent values are once again integrated into the functionally efficient urban framework and pattern, at both city-wide and precinct level—the qualities, moreover, which simply cannot, at any time, be derived in any other way.

At the local level it has been suggested that planning direction is undertaken through a series of logical stages in which the elements of progression; framing, surprise and transition, linear perspective, contrast, scale and climax, each have a part to play as a means of creating, or contributing to, a sense of variety within the overall cohesive pattern.

It is obvious that the way in which this problem is tackled must be greatly affected by whether the city has evolved spasmodically over a period of time or whether it has been largely established during a limited number of years, or, alternatively, whether it has developed in a planned continuous sequence. The nature of the particular city will clearly have a marked influence on detail planning and on the design approaches, whether it is a city with lush landscaping or is sparsely and inhospitably planted, whether it is secluded and pleasurable or noisy, bustling and aggressive, whether it is dirty and smoke-filled, or clean and sunny. Alternatively cities can be categorised according to their situation, such as hill cities like Assissi or Toledo (Fig. 187) cities belonging to the plains or valleys, such as Stuttgart (Fig. 188), Milan or Innsbruck (Fig. 189); or sea, lake, or riverside cities, like Leningrad (Fig. 190), Budapest (Fig. 191), Prague (Fig. 116) or Rio, Stockholm (Fig. 129), Geneva or Copenhagen (Fig. 124).

This pervasive environmental quality will just as obviously be affected by the general pattern of the physical development of the city itself, either by virtue of its location or topography or by the form of growth of its communication and movement systems. This will be no less true of contemporary examples than of those historic cities which have been thought worthy of study.

Reference has already been made to the unorganised, random meander, or aggregative system, which is primarily a manifestation of a period of spontaneous growth, well evidenced in most mediaeval and many still earlier cities. This system at least had the virtue of putting first priority emphasis on the buildings and their inhabitants, as well as pedestrian movement, and both meeting places and business centres being oriented towards the needs of the pedestrian.

There are, too, many examples of the historic revival microcosmic approach, with its studied degree of informality, designed into local areas with a strong emphasis on their aesthetic qualities. Some of the more attractive spaces and civic areas, for example in European cities, have been created in this way. In the attainment of aesthetic quality while retaining the emphasis on the needs of the pedestrian, there is much of value to be gleaned from them even though the design idiom itself may be inappropriate to our present and future needs and even though, often, these urban 'incidents' may lack conviction as part of a cohesive urban pattern.

The formal axial geometrical system such as was employed in the cities of Paris, (Fig. 47), Washington (Fig. 179) and Berlin (Fig. 180), obviously possess great merit, both in the particular qualities these cities create with their impressive vistas and also in the clarity of their city-wide unifying influence. Planning systems of this type may fail, however, to generate satisfactory conditions within which local area planning can take place on an equally logical and entirely satisfying basis unless equal care is taken to resolve geometric hinterlands. The tendency to create canyons of formalism, as it were, like a continuous piece of window dressing, makes it difficult to provide overall consistent results of equal emphasis in secondary areas (Fig. 155).

Even more difficult in some ways to adapt to present-day conditions is the Roman grid-iron plan, revised in a number of one-time colonial cities as the logical setting-out method for surveyors to employ (Figs. 192 and 193). Some of these cities have succeeded in creating attractive visual environments, notwithstanding the evident problems of traffic intersections, unclosed vistas, and the limit imposed on central area extension or growth. Cities of this type can be greatly enhanced when the too regular beat of city block and intervening streets is broken by squares which are setbacks in what are otherwise continuous street frontages. Adelaide as one example has created urban identity in these conditions, through the unique development of city parklands and squares.

In a city such as Manhattan, which is almost the extreme example of the use of the grid-iron pattern, and although the pedestrian can only normally visually perceive the limited range of two or three city blocks, the unending vistas, particularly of the avenues, often appear featureless and forbidding. The value placed on the local incident of Times Square (Fig. 194) and the Rockefeller Plaza (Fig. 195) is very obvious from the way in which people congregate at these spots (Fig. 196), and the sense of locality could be even further enhanced by the creation of 'circuses' (Fig. 197) establishing well defined foci, at intervals of not more than four or five blocks.

Most other colonial type city plans suffer in a similar way from dreary, unending and relatively featureless windswept urban canals of vehicular communication. The axially-planned cities, however, rarely fell into this error as vista terminals were an important part of their overall concept.

One imaginative attempt to carry the analytical process of desirable urban quality to even greater lengths refers to the city as being, 'like a forest' with a 'delicately balanced eco-system always in transition'.[77] It may also be the case that sometimes there is justification for certain city buildings and areas to be preserved for reasons beyond the purely functional, and, although it is recognised that there is usually at present inadequate machinery for controlling change in new construction or of guiding or directing changes of character or form, it seems essential to 'avoid any implications of compositional principles, or any rulebook of urban aesthetics', as we know from an earlier close examination of the problem. Formalistic rules are no substitute for creative positive design.

The main interest in this study relates to the public open spaces, streets, plazas, parks and the private living spaces in the city but the scope of enquiry is extended to take in other ingredients, including trees, street furniture, signs, sculpture, paintings, bus shelters and telephone boxes—all important contributory factors in the overall urban physiognomy—as well as the interrelated patterns of movement and rhythm in this 'city choreography'.

Such an exhaustive examination of broad scale composition in the streets, parks, waterfronts, plazas, piazzas and interstices of the city fabric can only be given adequate depth, and permit worthwhile practical implications to be drawn if we also look more closely at the minutiae, and the never too trivial detail which forms an inseparable part of urban design excellence, including the use of flowing water and fountains (Fig. 198), the planting of streets and spaces, the humanising of parking spaces (Figs. 199 and 200) and the handling of changes of level through the use of ramps and staircases. We must consider, too, street lighting and signs, benches, flowerboxes, kiosks, the treatment of traffic islands and median strips, the statuary and sculpture, paving patterns, colours and textures, and all the incidental detail which, visually, can make for a well and consistently-organised and designed city where walking itself can become an aesthetic experience. A lack of concern with these details tends to produce a city which is simply a centre of business and commerce and an affront to human beings.

It is now perhaps more obvious that of all the threads of historic continuity which are as valid today as in any other period, the fact that no great world city has existed without a substantial part of the population living and working in the core is probably the most significant. As has been emphasised many times before, the whole quality of a city and its human environment is primarily achieved through those areas which are occupied twenty-four hours a day, seven days a week. Neither commerce nor business, and certainly not industry, the shopper or the tourist, can create the most vital element of all in a city, important though such factors may be. The populations which too many present-day cities are in process of losing, through wholly mistaken policies or sheer folly, are the one means of keeping alive the restaurants, cultural institutions, parks, pleasure places and city squares. If these populations are allowed to drift we shall be left with a hollow urban shell.

Chapter XII

Urban renewal: potential and implementation

It has already become apparent that the most likely method by which significant development opportunities and improvements in urban planning and design may be expected to take place is through redevelopment or renewal.

This process provides the means and opportunities whereby cities can be fundamentally readapted to meet contemporary and future needs, partly through replacement and partly through renovation of outworn and usually obsolete urban equipment.

Because these renewal operations take place stage by stage and within a circumscribed framework of parts of the city which must remain and continue to function, and because they must, in a very real way, provide a linkage between what remains and other developments likely to occur in future, they nearly always involve an immensely difficult and complex process—especially in so far as the necessity of combining the interests of private enterprise and public purpose is concerned.

The process can be said to start with the organisation of effective administrative tools in the private, public and government sectors—and more especially the assembly of large enough areas of land or property to permit of the most effective type of comprehensive development.

Unless cities are renewed as part of a continuing process they cannot hope to survive through periods of growth and changing needs. Fresh starts in the form of New Towns or cities make this need no less urgent, as, unless we learn quickly how to undertake the renewal process now, New Towns will inevitably go through the same stages of decline and obsolescence which we are at present experiencing in our cities.

It must be accepted that new cities will form a part of the overall programme of urban development in a number of countries, and formulating a method of effectively handling their physical development is undoubtedly an important task. It is, however, in many ways, and for obvious reasons, a great deal simpler than the problem which has to be faced in renewing the older cities and it is on this latter problem that most attention has, necessarily, been focused as it is by far and away the most urgent and, regrettably, the real core of, our biggest social problem today. Certainly this is true in most of the more developed countries.

One of our main concerns in urban renewal and redevelopment programmes must be an assurance that at any stage the old and the new, the past and future, will be able to exist in close proximity and reasonable harmony, without sacrificing the long-term objectives of the master plan. At the same time we must ensure that the new developments increasingly bring about a proper urban balance, economically, socially and functionally, with an overriding concern for maintaining the city as a healthy, living organism and a fit place for its occupants.

There must be a real recognition and understanding of the continually changing needs and ideas of urban man, by ensuring that, as far as possible, a flexible format for the city fabric is created which will allow qualitative variations without impairing the overall character and unity of the city, and will not depend on sterile uniformity.

This supremely difficult achievement has, so far in our modern urban history, seldom been really successfully performed and yet it is one we must persist in attempting since anything less will spell defeat and the end of any worthwhile idea of the city for the future.

Inevitably, one of the prime considerations in any urban renewal operation must be the better use of valuable central area land, and the better integration of urban components, through rearrangement and reordering, as products of the process of development. Present two-dimensional preoccupation in terms of land-use zoning has played a major part in the accelerated deterioration of city centres. If this is to be halted, it must give way to a four-dimensional concept with vertical, as well as horizontal, segregation of multiple uses on a planned time-scale which recognises that the city as a living entity will continue to function while undergoing facelift operations.

During this process careful planning must still find the means of providing for the most imaginative and creative urban ecology, in the least inhibited manner and through each of the sequential stages and phases of change. This need can be expressed in another way as establishing a happy medium between 'Metropolis' and the rather forbidding image this conjures up on the one hand, and the uncontrolled muddle of our present city, on the other.

The problem of assembly of land and properties arises, of course, from consideration of the question of how best to undertake renewal without all the disadvantages of piecemeal development such as are, at present, the norm in our cities. The advantages of the comprehensive approach, now widely-accepted, are demonstrated very clearly by recent work in cities such as Rotterdam (Fig. 15), Stockholm, Paris (Figs. 26, 33, 96, 97, 146) and London (Figs. 8 and 76). Obviously, it will not always be possible to reproduce the conditions which led to these more desirable forms of urban redevelopment and renewal, but such examples and others similar should act as a challenge to ensure that comprehensiveness is always sought as a priority prerequisite.

It is rare that a major urban renewal operation takes place without considerable dislocation and interruption to businesses, social life, and the community affairs of the city. It is therefore of supreme importance to show that measurable gains are likely to flow from the renewal processes, in a quite unmistakable manner, so that those involved become active and willing participants.

All the professions involved in urban renewal planning and the execution of such projects seem, regrettably, to take a sectarian viewpoint from time to time, rather than an attitude which demonstrates an awareness of the team function—in which the role of each member is fully respected and understood. Unfortunately this situation seems very often to generate beliefs that each shares equally in a general responsibility as custodians of the perceived urban environment. There might be considerable advantage if, in practice, this *were* so. The fact remains, however, that none of the participants, other than the architect–planner, deems it sufficiently important to place it high on the list of priorities for explicit treatment and concern.

It has often been pointed out, in relation to the majority of building operations today, that the technology of building and the type of development agency have changed. Governmental participation has become vital to the success of almost every project. The architect, by virtue of his professional code of ethics, cannot act as the financier or real estate negotiator and, obviously, he cannot fill the role of government administrator. Nevertheless, he must understand the reasons why these participants in development decisions act as they do and he must guide them so as to obtain the ultimate and primary objective of a more humane city. In order to bring such a situation about it is obvious that the architect himself must participate in the programming at every stage, from its initiation.

In stressing the importance in the urban redevelopment programme of the role of one of the professions, it seems necessary to give this subject special emphasis as a basis of better mutual understanding and thereby of establishing a fruitful participation in the urban planning and design team. This, however, is not to underestimate the importance of the other members of the team, although, unfortunately, a clearer appreciation of the importance of the team operation is not yet evident in the case of the many other professions involved in renewal operations. The lack of any obvious diffidence, but rather an apparent willingness to undertake roles quite outside established professional competence or experience, while it becomes increasingly frequent, is all the more incomprehensible.

A recent example was the sociologist critic who had the temerity to plead for the architect to have a better understanding of the nature and functions of the city before he could make his contribution to these new urban developments, and thus to be in a position to offer proper services to his client. Any architect who has been trained as an urban designer or planner, and thus has those qualifications and expertise enabling him to deal with matters concerning urban developments, is, without question, likely to be equipped with a reasonably good understanding of, and insight into, the city's essential problems, needs, functions and purposes. This is an indispensable part of his training and experience.

The sociologist, however, increasingly inclined to offer gratuitous opinions as to the architect's depths of understanding, needs himself, first of all, to reassure us of his knowledge and understanding of the work of the architect and his contemporary approach to the problems of urban design and planning: derived, one would hope, from those best able to tell him the facts.

In the meantime, this type of urban analyst and others of like mind may poernd over the stupidity being demonstrated in cities all over the United States, particularly, where it has been attempted to relegate architects' work to a minor cosmetic process or ignore it altogether—with the inevitable consequences of having achieved some of the ugliest and most unlivable cities in the history of Man—in spite of all the sociological aids and application of other esoteric contemporary theory.

A matter which is increasingly being overlooked or forgotten is the fact that a long continuity of experience and application, over thousands of years, has given the architect–planner a heritage of understanding of the forces that go to make the city and, more recently, of the historical, as well as contemporary, forces that have produced in the city disorder and disorganisation. It is apparent that every member of the urban planning team can undertake his role only in full recognition of the roles undertaken by others, but it must surely be increasingly evident that something has gone wrong in the structure and operation of the modern planning team, with the continued signal failure of the decision-making, analytical professions to rectify the situation.

It is in character with this situation that the senior official of the Los Angeles City Planning Department should have proclaimed, with pride, that his authority was sacking their architects and employing social scientists *instead*. The operative word here, of course, is 'instead'—as though the two professions concerned could be interchanged at will and were thus able to undertake similar roles. This statement is perhaps, on reflection, hardly surprising since the city of Los Angeles declares such a policy and outlook publicly for all to see (Fig. 23); as the extreme case of hopeless urban suicide apparently by the common consent of its inhabitants.

It cannot, therefore, be too strongly emphasised—whether in connection with urban renewal policies and activities or in relation to other parts of our urban development programmes—that these cannot hope to succeed unless all the members of the planning team are permitted to participate fully in their proper roles from the outset. As a complete reversal of recent trends it is vital that the views, policies and the contributions in the field of visual perception which the architect–planner or urban designer has to offer, are available from the earliest stages.

It seems worthy of consideration that some of the changes stimulating urban renewal programmes in the cities should be further examined as, indeed, should the hoped-for improvements, goals and reorientation that these are likely to produce. In emphasising again the need for larger sites, it should be noted that, with the advent of new forms of construction and the increase of values in central areas, from the outset the process of assembling land for an economic parcel becomes a costly exercise in patience, good fortune and guile.

The very urgent need for these programmes arises by virtue of the fact that, in general, the central city is changing and, more particularly, is frequently losing retail trade and manufactures. It is, however, still the primary source of technical skills and the main market for goods and the exchange of ideas. It is the forum for personal business contacts, usually maintaining a high proportion of comparison shopping and containing most of the elements of tourist interest. It is also certain to provide the locale and meeting place for banking, insurance (Fig. 36) and the nucleus of many other business operations which cannot be decentralised and which are an essential part of a city's lifeblood.

Moreover, during a period when governments are becoming much more involved, only the central city can provide the more intimate contacts with officials—proximity to bureaucratic services and departments, and to the legal, diplomatic and consular services. Commercial, business and trade organisations, as well as stock exchanges (Fig. 13) and newspapers remain in the city because they cannot function elsewhere and it is only some of the larger industries which can afford a wholesale move involving the removal of costly machinery and a gamble on recruiting labour in new outlying locations. It must be added that the gamble, in the case of many planned decentralisation schemes, is a very serious one, since necessarily in these instances, industry has resorted to a very much smaller catchment area of suitable types of labour, and is in serious competition with others placed in a like position, as well as with the greater attractions and mobility provided by the central city.

It is also of course true that central city attractions, including opera, theatre, cabaret, discotheque and coffee lounges, are likely to continue in these locations. Those universities located in the city, are much more fortunate in their access to human resources. The museums, art galleries and central library are there, too, and obviously this is still the chosen location of the best restaurants. There are many other types of activity and business which cannot be undertaken in any way other than on the basis of the face-to-face traditional contacts.

Renewal programmes will unquestionably be influenced increasingly by recognition of the fact that the time is close at hand in many cities when travel will have reached the maximum of human endurance, and when a multiple dwelling may seem to be a haven of urban refuge but where, by contrast, the suburb will be just another spread-city with all the headaches and none of the traditional virtues.

It will also become increasingly apparent that even if metropolitan fringe living does, in some cases, offer advantages for families, it also presents numerous problems and disad-vantages which will never affect the more discriminating city-dweller. In these circum-stances many more will come to recognise that much of a country's economic strength and personal mobility exist because of the concentration of job opportunities in cities.

It may not always be immediately obvious that one of the added virtues of assembly of land for comprehensive renewal operations is that an assembled plot is worth far more than the sum of the values of the individual plots. It is only through the machinery of urban renewal, moreover, that vacant possession is likely to be obtained over the numerous properties involved and at cost levels that prevent exploitation by sitting landlords who may otherwise jeopardise the whole of an important scheme.

Somewhat caustically it has been suggested that, in the development of most Ameri-can cities, 'the general imprint has been that of the jackpot, not the temple'. Thus, careful planning of the city was the exception, 'for the spur was land speculation and turnover, not long-term utility'.[4] The development of the railway, the machine and industry and, more recently, the car and the freeway, obliterated any interests con-cerned with a better city environment.

On the other hand, the legal and administrative powers necessary to assemble large areas of land can do much to assist rectification of defective street patterns and help create more desirable environments planned as unified entities. They obviously make possible the establishment of continuity between sites and it becomes feasible to use land in relatively valueless pockets which could otherwise have held up the develop-ment of whole areas. The relevant powers also facilitate comprehensive joint public and private developments, as well as the planning of integrated shopping and other essential facilities.

Other advantages also include the fact that it encourages the creation of more public spaces and parking facilities. It provides the opportunity for enlarging the street system, the closing of streets where necessary, the creation of traffic diversions where thought desirable, and the formation of new streets or widened intersections. It makes possible the construction of better footways and separate pedestrian systems, segre-gated from vehicular traffic by means of two-level or single-level systems.

In short, renewal presents comprehensive opportunities in place of piecemeal efforts to provide recreation areas and open spaces, to create neighbourhood amenities and new housing under both public and private ownership, and to ameliorate traffic ills.

In referring to the situation in the United States, the point has been made (with which few would disagree in other developed countries) that, since urban environment is now influenced or created by government, it is obvious that there should be objectives to guide official policies. However, except for 'a sweeping and undefined generalisation in the 1949 Housing Act, promising a suitable living environment for every American family, there is not even a semblance of any environmental objective for Federal policy; nor despite frequent references to community renewal programmes of master plans have any objectives been framed by States or Cities'.[4]

This is the sad confirmation of what is only too evident from the present appearance of many American cities—that the one principal objective of renewal, that of providing a decent home environment, has, in some extraordinary way, been entirely lost sight of, more particularly in the course of the last twenty years. One of the main purposes of the legislation in the United States which first gave rise to these programmes has, in consequence, also been utterly frustrated. This is nothing less than a tragedy when the legislation and administrative procedures could be seen as veritable models of pragmatic idealism.

Of course it is obvious that the government objectives imply resolving jurisdiction of conflicts, and passing laws. It is much less troublesome, however, to commit vast sums of money to roads and other 'improvements' without openly identifying the implications. Government programmes (and this is true in many countries) 'accelerate the move to suburbia where slum clearance and urban policies for cities affect population redistribution only within city borders'.[4] Too often this occurs from one slum area to another, as these are the least attractive areas to potential developers, presenting the greatest element of risk, and therefore the ones most likely to be allowed to persist.

The goals and objectives of urban renewal programmes must necessarily themselves be comprehensive, and could include, it is suggested: the better design of all component parts and, most particularly, those involving public funds; the better recognition of and development of natural, topographical and other features in the city which must not be sacrificed to mere expediency, such as is occurring in the present era of the urban expressway, where many of the principal assets of cities in the way of riverside areas, waterfronts, or recreation areas are disappearing with increasing rapidity under the all-pervasive concrete; wherever practicable, an increase in the amount of open space for recreational and leisure purposes and improvements in planting and landscaping, with new opportunities created for these by the better spacing and grouping of buildings. This latter is one of the most important ways of replacing a spirit of humanity in the city, and must be pursued as a vigorous part of the overall replanning policy, both on a macro- and micro-scale.

It is probable that the opportunities to increase recreational areas will occur in future only as a consequence of urban renewal programmes and if these opportunities are lost population growth will never be matched in future, either within the city or on its fringes, by necessary increases of open space suitable for these purposes.

It has been suggested that the provision of more space for parks and playgrounds within and around developments can confer on cities some of the better qualities of suburbia which have drawn people away from urban centres. It is also true that better in-city recreation is a most desirable aspect of city redevelopment and renewal, not to be forgotten in future programmes.

In arguing for programmes that make the city more attractive for tourism, diversion and leisure, it should be pointed out that there are many useful contributions which could be suggested in the way of better theatres, dance halls and exhibition areas, zoological and botanic gardens, and even skating rinks. Rivers or water-frontages provide the opportunities for boating and water sports, as well as more obvious scenic advantages. If these serve the city's inhabitants in an imaginative and attractive way then it is likely that they will also be of interest to the visitor.

The city centre is a most important contributor of funds, through taxes, for essential developments. It provides a substantial proportion of certain categories of employment, it is the centre of political action and, almost invariably, of most of the professions. These days the department store, the market, the bank and the insurance office are likely to be of even greater significance than the civic centre or the centres of religious congregation. 'The availability of raw materials, power, transport and labour are some of the reasons for the city's existence as well as its proximity to education, officialdom, other trades and finance; and the centres of talent and research. City centres are however too often places to get in to and out of quickly, and not to browse in. . . .'[4]

Every contribution made to the city's renewal and redevelopment must be in the spirit of catering, first and foremost, for the pedestrian, with the aim of creating a seven-day-a-week city for twenty-four hours of each day.

Obviously, if the city is to be an efficiently functioning entity, good bus and rail services for commuters are essential. Adequate, but not excessive, vehicle parking areas must also be provided. Within the overall diversity of the city there should be more restaurants, cafés, arcades, music centres, bookshops, art galleries, museums and secluded garden areas.

Worthwhile and thoughtfully-devised urban renewal operation must conserve the best of existing values rather than destroy them. 'Custom and tradition liven the fabric of the city which must acquire a sense of heritage'.

Room must be left for people to contribute to their own environment if only in a small way, in conjunction with the provision of schools, libraries and clubs.

Those involved in the renewal operation should be allowed to participate at appropriate stages and made to feel they are a part of it.

A traditional element in the city centre has been the clustering of like enterprises and this is still welcomed by many trades, professions and other interests.

The city should continue as a centre of education and universities, trade schools, institutes of technology and cultural facilities must find a place there.

The importance of the development of a realistic mass transportation programme can hardly be overstressed. Too often cities are becoming 'suburbia's mammoth garages', and are, moreover, the sites for the construction of new highways which will attract more motor vehicles, which will, in turn, require more highways as well as more parking spaces in the city centre. This therefore provides no solution to the problems of urban development. In the light of these unalterable facts—now realised, often too late, by many city authorities, and most recently by the US Senate Committee* which has been examining the problems of urban mass transportation—it passes comprehension that so many cities continue to ignore the self-evident lessons they teach.

As it was so cogently put by the President of the American Municipal Association, 'the plain fact of the matter is that we just cannot in any case build enough lanes of highways to move everybody by private car and then create enough parking space to store the cars without completely paving over our cities and removing all of the economic, social and cultural establishments that the people are trying to reach in the first place. Even if we could do it physically the costs would bankrupt the combined resources of city and central governments'. Moreover, it would obviously utterly destroy the life of the cities which these artifacts are apparently intended to serve.

There is no doubt that the problems associated with urban renewal are such that it becomes an infinitely more difficult task than that of establishing entirely new towns or cities in vacant open spaces. Much effort and capital has been expended on these latter programmes in a number of countries in the last twenty-five years and this, together with the direct and indirect subsidy to suburban and sprawl-types of development, has simply served to aggravate and make even more urgent the task of renewing the cores of our cities. In other ways, moreover, these programmes have aggravated the problem in the central city area by increasing the pressure from commuters.

As a good example of this we should refer once again to the metropolitan area of Los Angeles which, over a period of some forty years, multiplied its population by a factor of six. During this period, however, the central city area declined at an alarming rate and more and more miles of urban expressways have been constructed (Fig. 22). These, instead of assisting commuters to reach the city centre more readily, have facilitated their journeys to outlying areas and to the district regional marketing and shopping centres. A similar pattern is repeated in an increasing number of other cities, in North America, Australia and elsewhere.

It is therefore obvious, as is now being realised, that, 'as long as automobiles can come in without too great inconvenience and as long as Los Angeles keeps making it less troublesome to come in, by creating more and more roads, and parking lots, it will sacrifice more and more land and become a duller and more polluted place in which to gasp'.[4] The same can be said of many other cities mistakenly following similar policies.

As a generalisation it can be conclusively shown that overindulgence towards the automobile has been one of the main causes of mass transportation's difficulties as well as of the aggravation of the metropolitan problem. Governments have been willing to spend money on highways but, quite illogically and incomprehensibly, expect public transit and rail facilities to be self-supporting. Vast sums of money go into motor vehicle research programmes but with other forms of transportation a bare subsistence level is maintained. Unfortunately, the motor car lobby, with its numerous

* 'Urban Mass Transportation—1961'. Sub-committee of Senate Committee on Banking, 87th Congress, 1st Session, March, 1961.

supporters, is one of the most powerful, certainly in the majority of western countries and Japan.

It must increasingly be realised that the city cannot function unless the motorist is removed from his vehicle and becomes a pedestrian. The city must be planned for the pedestrian since it is only in this way that the shopping, commercial and cultural facilities can be used. It is also frequently forgotten that many people, including the very young or the very old, invalids, pensioners and those who prefer not to, do not drive motor vehicles and are wholly dependent on public transport.

Cities must therefore increasingly be conceived as being for the pedestrian, whether delivered there by motor vehicle or by a public transport system, and this will be true if and when we have such innovations as city-cars, travelators, or other assisted means of locomotion within the city core.

It therefore follows that the city should no longer continue to make concessions to the motor vehicle, such as has been evidenced in cutting down the widths of footpaths, the removal of street shade-trees, the increasing width of carriageways, the increasing intrusion of traffic signs, parking meters and all the other paraphernalia related to a potentially greater use of the motor vehicle. This increased use, however, is self-defeating, as already a pitch has been reached in many cities where they are literally being throttled to death, both by the vehicles themselves and by their pollutants.

We are at a stage where much more rigorous restrictions are unavoidable and must be faced—restrictions such as the introduction of pedestrian malls in place of vehicle dominated shopping streets. Undoubtedly one of the most important factors making for the charm and pleasure of the best of the older cities, is that these are designed for the walker, and, in many cases, other kinds of transit are prohibited.

It has become abundantly obvious that life in the suburbs, particularly for the womenfolk, is no life at all in most cases, but simply a continuous series of deprivations. Little wonder that such women are clamouring for 'liberation'. Urban renewal and replanning are the means by which all this can be changed, particularly if more opportunities are, at the same time, afforded for city living. A substantial part of the population is likely to benefit from such changes, but most particularly women, to the extent that their isolation will thereby be almost entirely overcome. In addition there will be places of recreation available to them as well as the customary cultural facilities. There should also be provision of accommodation for single, employed women, and clubs and other such facilities designed to meet their needs. This particular group is one for which there is seldom any kind of adequate facility, yet it is on this sector of a community that the functioning of a great deal of commerce largely depends.

There is no reason at all why children should not live in the centre of a city provided that it is intelligently planned to meet their needs. Far too few cities are planned with any consideration for this possibility, but rather as business and commercial centres, or centres of industry and government.

However, if we reflect on the living areas adjoining the London Parks and Squares (Fig. 101), the Bois de Boulogne in Paris, or Central Park in Manhattan (Fig. 175), there is abundant evidence that some cities have recognised the needs of children. Of course the provision of such open spaces and recreation areas is an essential part of the urban equipment required to meet the needs of people of all ages.

Many of these suggestions and policies are an attempt to synthesise not only personal experience, but also that of other planners. They are serious proposals in a conscious effort to reflect a realistic approach to the inescapable problems of urban renewal and in a belief that neither the creation of new cities without a new set of policies, nor running away from the problem of the centre city will provide a viable urban future—far less revive our flagging central urban areas. Unfortunately there are, at present, in city government and planning, more problems than ideas, perhaps stemming from the long period of neglect, or misdirection of effort. These factors have, in turn, deflected the talents we need in urban planning into other channels.

We have, it would seem, become more concerned with the mechanics of industry and the theories of social mechanics than with the realities of the human environment. Systems planning takes precedence over planning for people. If we consider the resources, skills and effort being channelled into the physical sciences compared with that devoted to city planning, or the vast sums of money and energy being concentrated on the dramatic conquest of outer space—as against the failure fully to comprehend the proper use of space on our own planet, we are left with a startling picture of how much remains to be done in our cities; but which nevertheless, with a better balance of priorities, could be put right tomorrow.

These are only some of the principal arguments for urgent programmes of urban renewal and a further reminder, if such is needed, of the extent to which we can gain in the reordering of our cities by replanning them to a higher degree of efficiency and functioning. Last, but by no means least, are the arguments for the overwhelming advantages of rearranging the cities so as to provide greater visual satisfaction and a more humane environment.

A particularly powerful object lesson in priorities is provided by what has occurred in recent years in the United States, which is one of the reasons that country's experience has often been cited in this book. In the US it is only too evident that if the resources and energies devoted to the construction of urban freeways—in most cases entirely fruitlessly—had, instead, been used on the clearance of downtown ghettoes and their redevelopment with the right type of housing opportunities, there could have been a solid contribution to real progress. Much misery and distress, which led inevitably to collective unrest, could also have been averted.

If these opportunities had been used to undertake a significant improvement in the overall form and shape of the cities, while undergoing the process of renewal, then the cities as a whole, as well as their inhabitants, could only have benefited. The same holds true of other countries similarly placed.

In a part of the world notable for its planning efforts, it is of special interest to study the experience of one Scandinavian capital city where a planning office has been in existence for 330 years. Here, in recent times particularly, a form of leadership has been shown which has been an inspiration to many urban authorities elsewhere.

In the approach to urban redevelopment projects in Stockholm, it has been stated that during analysis the schemes are worked into economic feasibility concepts. At the same time, physical planning studies are undertaken in which the scheme is physically defined by the use of plaster models worked on concurrently with drawings and continually revised as the concept develops (Fig. 153).

In these circumstances economic principles are not the sole guiding element in the formulation of goals. Rather, the entire effectiveness of a given programme is weighed against other standards—social, cultural and political. The nearly unique quality of the Stockholm city planning effort is that it is based largely on three-dimensional study. At the start of this process the programmed buildings and installations are represented by approximate forms. Subsequently, as work proceeds, these are elaborated on and revised. When an element or feature of special importance is planned and a design of particular merit is needed an architectural competition takes place.

The economic feasibility studies have the aim, as might be expected in the re-planning of the city, of rebuilding the city core to an improved functional standard, including the creation of better traffic conditions. Renewal of existing obsolete buildings and areas also plays an important role, with particular regard to commercial demands for more space.

In the process, the proportions of the existing volume of the street are completely changed, since streets are widened but building heights are retained, or, in some cases, building heights are increased and streets retained. Blocks are joined as larger units, and inside these quiet recreation spaces are formed. The main theme in the architectonic forming of the city townscape in one recent outstanding project is the dominating office tower blocks and multi-level pedestrian and traffic complex. In other cases quite different themes are employed to dominate the urban composition.

A particular element of interest in this process is the extent to which advantage is taken of the opportunities afforded, not only to gain improvements in functional efficiency but also to increase the emphasis on the visual quality of the environment and the method by which this is studied. The sophisticated techniques used in Stockholm for many years towards this end have certainly come closer to meeting contemporary needs than procedures adopted in most other cities.

If these techniques were to be coupled with the use of modelscope and closed-circuit television and the other perceptual aids previously described, we would have the necessary basis to undertake a proper set of simulation studies. With the aid of such studies the guesswork in future urban renewal and city planning operations would be virtually removed and it becomes possible fully to utilise the hard-won opportunities of redevelopment.

As to the whole question of urban renewal, there seems likely to be very little disagreement with at least one of Mumford's revelations—namely that everyone realises, at last, that cities are in a serious plight.[140] If, as has been suggested, we are producing an environment suitable only for machines, this suggestion supports what planners are forcefully arguing—that it is probably the inevitable consequence of our addiction to mechanical and electronic systems and methods.

Scathing comments have been made in the same vein in the apparent belief, on the part of the technological disciples of these systems and methods, in their own immortality—and that of the monster they are fathering. These same people, it is not too fanciful to suggest, are the apostles of the computer, held completely in its thrall, since they are trained to ask only the quantitative questions which this electronic moron can answer, and never the qualitative ones which are the only real measure of human values and needs.

FIG. 193.   Central Philadelphia, USA.

FIG. 194.   Times Square, New York.

FIG. 195. Rockefeller Plaza, N.Y.

314

FIG. 196. Washington Square—focus for Greenwich Village.

FIG. 197. Cuauhtemoc Circus, Mexico City.

FIG. 198.   Fountain by the Paseo de la Reforma Mexico City.

FIG. 199.   International Building, San Francisco, adjoining underground garage.

FIG. 200   Union Square, San Francisco, with underground car park.

Nor will we find it difficult to share the view, and to concur with the claim suggested earlier, that the largest and wealthiest of our cities falls pitifully short of the ideal, or of the potential now available. It is also a fact that there has been neither application of imagination nor the necessary foresight to this task of city building. However, the assertion that architects have really been responsible for this loss of opportunity by being mainly concerned with cosmetics and superficialities, and that this has occurred at the overall expense of the larger environment, is a ludicrous irrelevancy.[140]

What is quite incomprehensible is the inconsistency of this allegation which is so much at variance with a number of other protestations and denigrations since it appears to assign to the architect an unusual measure of total responsibility for the design of the city—elsewhere flatly denied. It will now be apparent that it is a vital contention of the present work that much more may be expected in the way of decently-designed urban environments only if the architect trained as planner has much of the earlier responsibility restored to him—responsibility from which, traditionally, most of our more beautiful cities have originated. It is evident that no other profession can achieve the same results.

Without any supporting evidence we seem to be expected to accept the bald statement that art and architecture are simply concerned with expediency and are opposed to any sense of order or humanity, as though it were to be understood that these are the normal consequences and inevitable by-products of the work of the architect and urban designer. It is, of course, precisely with the object of restoring qualities of rational order and humanity within a framework of efficiency that the architect–planner must be concerned in future and with which only he, in his role as a professional member of the urban planning team, is by training and experience equipped to provide.

Without belabouring the matter too much, it is apparent that the real reasons for any belittlement of order and humanity in urban design are obvious. Such lack of order arises, almost entirely as a matter of course, from the architect–urban designer's role having been spurned for so long. This process has taken place in an atmosphere of compliance and in some ways praiseworthy attempts to subordinate sectarian professional interests to those of the team.

We are much nearer to identifying the real causes of urban *malaise* when we recognise that economic efficiency is not enough and has been largely responsible for much of our urban chaos. The urgent questions that we now have to ask are: Can the economists and the sociologists be trusted any further without firm supervision and guidance of their activities, in view of past performances and failures? Can they be relied upon as effective members of planning teams without interdisciplinary training? Almost certainly the answers are 'no'! It is of interest that Mumford, in giving evidence recently before a Senate Select Committee, revealed, not surprisingly, that by profession he was a writer and 'not an architect, an engineer, or a city planner'. He claimed that he saw his vital role as one of knocking the heads of specialists together, and taking a lofty overall view of their activities which they were incapable of doing themselves. Coming from a layman who does not appear ever to have been involved professionally in city planning, this damaging and presumptuous assertion seems to stem from what might have been hoped was the long-dead fallacy of equating specialisation with narrowness. The statement was made, as might be expected, without any suggestion of evidence to support the belief that the trained professional expert was a fool who needed to be taught his business by the bystander.

To make for even further confusion, there appears from the same source the clearest evidence of an unshifting prejudice and preoccupation with a few utterly discredited theories of planning which even the discriminating mind of the layman might by now have discerned. Stress is, for example, given to Ebenezer Howard's extraordinary beliefs that a limit could be placed on the size and population of a city and that additional population growth could then be catered for in new towns. Howard thought that these towns, strung together like beads on a necklace, would together perform virtually as a metropolis, while leaving intervening spaces for recreation and agriculture.[140]

Perhaps these ideas may still appear, at first glance, as desirable. However, neither at present nor at any other time has there been a way by which the population of a city can be prevented from growing, short of pestilence, famine, war or natural disaster. Nor, except in a totalitarian society or in quite unusual and normally unacceptable circumstances, can a limit be placed on the area of the city—much as many would wish that both of these measures could be achieved, for the comfort and convenience of all. As for the 'continuous growth' theory implicit in the second of Howard's notions; this was most effectively demolished by the shortcomings which followed the attempts to make his theory work in the post-Second World War New Towns in Britain, notwithstanding energetic government support.

Unless it were possible, which, obviously, it is not, to make each of such satellites more completely independent in terms of employment, and unless they could be separated from the original city centre and metropolis, all the evils of commuting and dormitory settlement are likely to be aggravated. In this sense the idea has very little to commend it as compared with the other types of urban sprawl Mumford and others so roundly condemn.

In a number of other cases symptoms have been correctly perceived but without accurate identification of the basic cause of the malady. It has been pointed out, as an obvious fact, that no city can outstrip in growth the limits of its water supply.[140] This was, nevertheless, something which was overlooked in the establishment of certain British New Towns. It is certainly no argument for new settlements, as against larger cities, since both are certain to be affected by water limitations. It is stressed that even where the metropolis has been allowed to swallow up green-belt recreation and other adjoining rural areas, this is not an argument for trying to limit the size of the city—which is impossible—but for planning it better to incorporate green wedges. These are the means of meeting the needs of recreation and of providing trees and landscapes and they should, in turn, be integrated with a network of greenways running through the urban fabric. Obviously the more distant these areas from the city itself, the less likely are they to fill the needs of recreation.

It is too seldom recognised that these peripheral areas of countryside, immediately surrounding a metropolis, are of irreplaceable value to the city-dwellers. A policy of urban concentration is the only way of preserving them. Any other methods, whether the usual extended, totally-disorganised sprawl or attempts to organise the low density spread in the form of discrete areas are still basically land-consuming.

As to the limitations imposed on urban growth by the adequacy of water supply, it is most relevant to point out that more concentrated forms of urban development inevitably lead to a lowering of total water consumption where the sprawl type of development, or the establishment of New Towns or new urban nuclei, automatically greatly increase water consumption, by virtue of the fact that suburban gardeners are the most extravagant users of a city's water resources. If we add to this the extensive run-off from suburban roofs and roads as compared with land-areas, which can absorb natural rainfall, it is clear that both increase waste—tending to alter the hydrological balance—as well as affect the ecosystems in a manner which almost certainly reduces total rainfall precipitation.

It is therefore one of the major misdirections of government financial policies, not only in United States but elsewhere, that they have favoured suburban building and been as responsible as the car manufacturers for the ghastliness of urban parking lots. These mistaken loan policies have also, regrettably, favoured scatteration spread or sprawl, or any type of development at low density. However, it should be recognised that this policy, in the long run, costs more in terms of money and steadily produces a deterioration of the centre of the city at the expense of dreary suburban areas, too often with quite inadequate services of the kind necessary to make them at least tolerable.

It is quite mistaken to see impending doom in our traditional pattern of urban existence as due largely to congestion or to cities which have grown too large and lack order, direction and the higher values.[140] Failure to establish worthwhile and imaginative objectives and to guide growth and development are undeniably causing decline; but overgrowth, as such, hardly ever, since no one has yet decided at what stage desirable growth becomes excessive, nor can problems of deterioration be identified solely with cities of a given size. Some of the dullest towns and cities are those with populations of between 100 000 and 500 000, whereas some of the most stimulating, by common agreement, have populations in the millions.

By the same token, congestion can be, in many cases, a symptom of urban health and vitality provided, however, that this relates to people rather than to motor vehicles. On the other hand, the reverse—restrained growth and underpopulation—spells almost certain disaster or decline for any city.

It is not therefore, so much a question of urban populations developing a philosophy of resignation born of despair, but rather of ordering and replanning the cities as part of a deliberate programme of urban social reconstruction. This is needed to give point and purpose to the life of the urban inhabitant and in order that, once again, he may experience some of the benefits the city can offer, without the quite unnecessary disadvantages which seem, too often today, its concomitants.

This hangover of the long outworn mythology of congestion is given a pseudo-scientific push when the claim is again made that so many of the crudities and the ugliness of present-day cities are due to congestion. In an attempt to bolster a quite false analogy, entirely unwarranted conclusions are drawn from experiments with rats (refer to the work of Dubos and Colqhoun) which, when placed in congested conditions, may undoubtedly exhibit symptoms of anxiety, aggressiveness, perversions and lack of parental responsibility. These experiments have usually been carried out in conditions in which space was so limited the animals were forced to run over one another.

If we believe in the importance of, and necessity for, the continued emphasis on the essential humane qualities of the city and human dignity, it is little short of an insult to our intelligence to suggest that *homo sapiens* can be expected in any normal circumstances to behave like cornered rats. A mass of experience and evidence proves quite conclusively that concentration of population alone does not produce in humans the symptoms referred to. Rather do these arise from inadequate or bad planning, lack of privacy, inadequate natural light and sunshine, lack of open space for recreation and other purposes and inadequate space standards within dwellings, none of which need necessarily occur in high population concentrations.

Many of the deprivations implied in the loss of the desirable facilities, however, can, and often have, occurred in quite low concentrations of population and are almost endemic in many of the scattered suburban areas.

These oft-repeated arguments, by false analogy and the underlying misconceptions, would hardly be worth refuting again, were it not for the fact that those giving them currency appear to believe in the Goebbels' dictum: 'repeat it often enough, and everyone will believe it'. Critical analysis should, however, entirely dispose of such unproven propositions which, it must be evident, have little or no real validity.

Determined refusal to face the facts and learn from experience is similarly evidenced by the position taken up and shared by many of the 'backwoods' planners. This finds expression in warnings against further increases in already populous and 'congested' centres being met by crowding people in to high-rise buildings. Of course, congestion need have no relationship to 'high-rise' which can be, and often is, at comparatively low density. Congestion may, on the other hand, be a product of low-rise development, and very often is. The height of a building has, in fact, no direct relevance to density.

In what is seemingly a *volte face* it is also argued that there is no future in adding large areas of suburbs to cities and thereby involving even more time-wasting journeys to work. Of course the only solution to this is to develop compact cities. It is no answer to the problem to build new communities since this has usually just perpetuated the collective problem for many people, with even longer journeys to work.

The real danger lies, of course, in developing quite illogical phobias about 'congestion', and of using ill-founded arguments, as has so often happened in the last twenty-five years, to justify what, in effect, becomes suburban scatteration—or whatever pseudo-technical jargon we use to describe it. Let us be quite clear about this phenomenon. In one or other form it is the certain alternative to rational and logical city consolidation.

How can we, in fact, ensure that the newly-planned communities are better models if we have not learnt how to solve the problems of guiding and ordering the growth of established cities? What happens, moreover, to the older towns and cities when and if we pursue such a policy of proliferation? We have already seen that it is quite impracticable to restrain their growth; but if there were any way, in theory, to retain them at a static level it is virtually certain that this would be the means of accelerating the process of urban morbidity.

First-hand experience in urban housing and planning work in London after the Second World War showed once and for all that this method—if it can be so described

—of distributing population on a regional basis, completely failed to arrest the growth of cities, or to attain its other objectives—claimed as flowing from the New Towns programme—other than the simple and obvious one of creating roofs to put over the heads of people in need of housing. This, however, could have been achieved more effectively, more cheaply and more quickly in other ways.

Many of the families needing accommodation in the urban or metropolitan areas were not prepared to move away from their accustomed locality, regardless of temporary inconveniences and privations, since this was the environment they were accustomed to, and one that could, they felt, continue to serve their needs well. It was moreover evident, in a great many such cases, that families were not mobile, in the sense that they might be able and willing to change existing employment. Whatever the defects of their existing dwellings, there was at least the assurance that they were conveniently located to the widest range of job opportunities—a consideration not to be lightly dismissed.

The older cities in Britain continue to increase in size and population, and much of the growth of the New Towns came from relatively distant provincial areas—with the consequence that no relief whatever was afforded to the metropolitan problem. There was, moreover, no way of preventing further immigration into the cities from other parts of the country and the current, government-backed 'South-East Plan' in Britain which is attempting to put a good face on the situation, indicates just how serious the problem has become and how complete has been the failure to arrest metropolitan growth, particularly in London.

Working on the Howard–Stein formula, the New Towns were placed far too close to existing metropolitan areas, and because they, too, at an early stage, failed to provide balanced employment of all types, and particularly in secondary industry and commerce, commuting to and from the older cities began at the outset and has since increased considerably. The addition of a second generation of white collar workers has added to the number of commuters.

If these facts are examined dispassionately and the flat refusal of many city-dwellers to wait for suburban utopian promises to materialise—but rather to settle for an urban 'bird in the hand'—we must entirely concur that no planning strategy is likely to be acceptable unless it accurately measures, and is geared to, human needs.[140] Recognition of this simple fact, which is almost in the nature of a platitude, should have prevented the attempts to apply merely theoretical nostrums, or at least have helped to identify their shortcomings, without prejudice, as soon as they became evident. Regrettably it has done neither.

It is indeed true that if our urban civilisation is to avoid total collapse we shall have to effectively carry out a complete reconstruction job. Such an operation would, of course, bring about a general transformation which would in turn affect every aspect of life. Obviously, urban politics and planning must be closely and significantly involved. It is with urban planning and design, more particularly, that we are at present concerned, and, of these functions, it can be accurately claimed that they are the 'formative, stabilising, coherent, order-making forces' involved in the whole process, and should undeniably be specially encouraged.

It is most specifically and directly the self-evident and perceivable forces of order and coherence in the planning of a city with which this book is primarily concerned, but only if and when these forces are organised in a way that is also compatible with functional efficiency.

It is obviously not possible here to deal comprehensively with every aspect of the development and design of the city centre, nor to discuss in detail all of the issues, principles and policies which must be dealt with as contributory elements of the overall problem. It is certainly, however, very much a central objective to demonstrate that beauty, order, spaciousness and clearly-defined intentions are some of the goals worthy of our aspirations for their buoyant effect on the human spirit. While, therefore, no one would claim that soundly-conceived and well-designed buildings are everything in city planning, however much the architect is blamed for the cities' shortcomings, we must avoid the conclusion that high-quality architecture is unimportant.

The suggestion that the typical unplanned disorder of the urban street and the district it serves should be regarded as desirable elements of the city and a virtue in themselves and the idea that the city is inconsistent with artistic principles, are, however, propositions which are entirely unacceptable as a basis for the creation of any sort of decent and orderly environment for urban man. For uncivilised animals they may suffice. It is of some significance to remind ourselves that part of the justification for this process of better order in the design of the contemporary city must stem from the clear recognition of the evident advantages of a well-planned, coherently-integrated city. Moreover, we can still find inspiration, surely, in the urban cathedrals and palaces, in the uncluttered directness and simplicity of the monasteries and the older universities and in the dignity and grandeur of the fine piazzas and squares of the older cities, where many of their essential qualities have been retained over a period of history.

It is also true that these are, moreover, the tangible evidence of the firm guidance administered by talented urban designers—not economists, not sociologists, not geographers, not engineers, but architects working in their enlarged role as urban specialists.

If today it appears appropriate to some labouring under the persuasion of theories of complexity and confusion, that, 'the mess is in the message', then we should remember that Jung was one of many who drew attention to the manifest advantages of the traditional city, compared with the formless sprawling modern conurbation. In doing this he probably identified some of the elements which have been lost sight of in city growth and which might, even now, be the means of a return, at least in part, to rationality. Therefore, since, as Sophocles said long ago, 'the city is the people', this must be the final, absolute, and most convincing proof of the need for perceptible order.

If we can recognise that this is still very much the case in contemporary circumstances, it may help to rectify the present position of an almost total absence of any environmental specialist, specifically concerned with the visually-perceptible aspects of town building and civic design in all but a few urban development operations. This phenomenon, of recent vintage, arises from the pressure of team operations in the often pseudo-scientific myopia of systems analysis, operations research and from the transportation lobbies. We are suffering, too, from an overdose of contemporary decision-making and management techniques, data assembly, processing and manipulation—until it seems to have been forgotten that, what the city looks like, what it is and how it functions, are of paramount importance. All the methodological techniques and management paraphernalia should simply be the means to that end. In so far as they may assist in this way their elaboration of the obvious may be justified.

Chapter XIII

Politics, policies and programmes

Underwriting the arguments already advanced that subjective, intuitive decisions will have to be applied as the last part of the urban design process, and therefore reinforcing the case for better design techniques at this point and for employment of top level, skilled and sensitive designers, a more than unusually enlightened sociologist has observed that when, and if, planning occurs it should not be justified by entirely arbitrary principles, 'such as aesthetic fashion, or religious dogma, or military convenience'. The view was also expressed that no plan could ever be defended on the grounds that it represented the only sane sociological solution as social theory is not yet able to specify appropriate courses of action. Thus, in these circumstances, it is apparent that 'sociologists cannot produce the answers and they will always opt out'.

It is evident, moreover, that human beings adjust themselves to the conditions they are born into, and people are far more adaptable than the man-made environment. There is thus a much better case to be made for the converse proposition to that normally held; namely that 'people are for planners'.[108] This unorthodox evidence of planning iconoclasm (as it will be considered by many), with its demolition of some of the pervasive contemporary mythology, helps restore the whole problem, and the approach to it within the urban design field, to a better perspective.

It must indeed be conceded that all the best planners in history were despots and that urban planning and design, today, if it is ever to break away from the prevailing chaos and mediocrity, must increasingly become the responsibility of individuals vested with a sufficient measure of authority.

In support of this, it has to be said that planning decisions are always a matter of opinion and the planner must be prepared to assume responsibility for personal judgements which are moral or aesthetic but not national in the pure sense. The fact is that planning is a professional skill with its own identity, depending on its own logic and its own expertise.

Predictably, there are still many of the hard-line sociologists of the more traditional school who would categorically disavow such statements. One recently admitted, however, that, 'sociologists have many deep-rooted codes and emotional blocks which limit their integration into a "dialogue" with planners and architects'.[21] This leads them into areas and conclusions based on a total misconception when it is argued that there exists a widespread fallacy in the thinking of architects—what has been called 'vulgar physicalism' or the idea that particular physical forms create standard and automatic social and behavioural responses.

The same sort of lack of comprehension is demonstrated in the unfounded belief that the architect finds it difficult to accept the fact that, 'phenomena with such potent qualities as the tendency to anthropomorphise form, do not have an important immediate influence on patterns of social action'.[21] Not so difficult, however, for us to accept is the generalisation that the sociologist concentrates his energies on what are termed 'inferential activities'.

It must be categorically stated that the initial proposition is a complete fallacy, since no architect trained as an urban designer or planner would recognise, as a part of his ethos, anything resembling 'physicalism', but rather that the forms he visualises are intended to provide a framework within which these responses may take place, obviously an entirely different proposition.

If it is a fact that the sociologist views with suspicion anyone who takes the simplistic view that visual qualities are of abiding importance, then there are the best of reasons why the architect–planner, attempting to come to terms with the urban design situation, may see the sociologist solely in his role as researcher, student or analyst, and within a quite limited context. He is also one therefore who regards himself as being immune from any immediate social obligation. The architect–planner will thus recognise him as an entirely unpractical theorist, by his own actions and philosophy, less and less useful as an ally in dealing with important urban planning and design decisions. It is not inferential activities which are likely to solve these problems in a realistic and positive way but a totally different approach, which may, perhaps, be more appropriately that of the urban ecologist.

Emphasising the view that social scientists ought to provide specifications for architects and planners to use rather than 'opting out' into their analytical hideouts, a spokesman for the human ecologists has recently said that, if sociologists are unwilling to accept this role it is perhaps because they are not the right type of social scientists to be making such specifications. 'Their academic position and training has been observational and analytical and has concentrated on methodological refinement—not on postulating theory and social specifications and testing them'.[162] It is therefore suggested that there are two different groups of professional people to distinguish between—the innovators and the analysers—and sociologists have joined the latter.

The reason for the presently developing gulf of understanding is therefore obvious. It is because architects and planners, who are by background and training essentially innovators, expect their briefs to be compiled by other innovators, or those who are at least inclined towards innovation. If the sociologist is unable or unwilling to participate in urban design in this way then perhaps we should look to the ecologist or to other disciplines who may possess the creative, and much more appropriate, approach.

To turn again to the broader picture of the city. Almost every aspect of the familiar metropolis is a composition of structures and spaces, these themselves being the products of a number of decisions, each made virtually without relation to any of the others. It is, of course, a fact that most urban communities have zoning laws and other city planning controls over the use of land and buildings. These, however, do not enable the authorities to impose an overall design framework upon the private and individual builders or, for that matter, even on an education department or other government agency, considering only its own building programme. Where public regulation has had any effect at all it has been preventive and negative, rather than positive and constructive.

Furthermore, most of this multiplicity of separate decisions takes little account of aesthetic considerations. In fact it has rightly been said that, 'the cityscape is the visual expression of the compromises and accommodations in a society, and it reflects the market and political choices of many decision-makers'.[131] The decisions referred to reflect fashion, the profit motive, political pressures and contemporary influences and values.

Any current attempt to find out why our cities are not more attractive, provides a disturbing, yet inescapable, consensus of many reasons for the present urban malady. However, it would be a considerable simplification, and often entirely untrue, to suggest that a major cause is the conflict which arises between the practical needs of a building and aesthetics. It is the architect's main function in life to resolve such aspects of his work.

Good design and good urban planning need not involve sacrifices and it has yet to be shown that Sitte's recommendation of having, 'all plans for joint building prepared in advance so that these may be an attempt at achieving the desired harmonious collective effect . . .'[171] costs more or is necessarily at the expense of other things, any more than the chaos which we appear to accept as the present alternative. However, if we are to provide acceptable philosophies and policies in the field of urban design we must be able to show, quite clearly, that of the many alternatives theoretically open to us, our choices will include some which combine the advantages of sound, functional purpose and good aesthetic quality, without incurring any significant disadvantage.

Only when we have a general recognition and realisation of these facts can we begin to expect an eradication of the pathogenic factors leading unerringly to dissolution of the city or to its disintegration, or both. Then perhaps a start may be made on the desirable regenerative and constructive processes, through positive regimens for urban health, combined with imaginative insight.

Undoubtedly some of the crucial questions that have to be asked at this stage are: How, in practice, in cities varying in size from populations of 100 000 to 10 000 000, can we ensure that effective planning control and systems are brought into operation? How are we to establish and legislate for the desirable aesthetic standards in relation not only to individual buildings but to groups of buildings? How do we engage suitable talents and the necessary skills and perceptive judgements to order and guide the planning process, and to have the wisdom and experience to do this, with the willing co-operation of all the professionals and their clients?

How, above all, can we expect to be able to find the means of spanning the time element; the growth and changes in styles and forms and the manifestly different and varied expressions of individual architectural talent and particular functional needs, in a way that will provide coherence and a sense of unity, without, at the same time, sacrificing variety and diversity?

Obviously, we need to have a new breed of government and local government official at every level and of an entirely new professional caste—with part-time amateurism recognised as the anachronism it is. If there is one thing we should have learned in our recent experience of the changes and growth which have taken place in our cities and in the failure to guide these effectively, surely this is that our machinery for undertaking this work has been totally unsatisfactory. This may be through weak and incompetent government, through untrained, inexperienced and tasteless official-dom or, as much as anything in some countries at least, the pathetic belief that entirely untrained lay members of the public, acting through citizen groups, can be regarded as an effective substitute for trained, skilled and experienced government, undertaken in an informed and enlightened way, albeit with firmness, conviction and taste.

To paraphrase John Donne, no city is an island, and we cannot consider urban problems without becoming closely involved in those of the metropolitan region, and even with national planning policies. It has already been demonstrated that this is so, when we considered the alternatives of concentration or decentralisation.

A more rigorous policy, moreover, of constructing new towns and cities in countries such as the United States, Australia and Canada, could have beneficial effects on the national economy as a whole, and on existing cities in particular, only provided that these were soundly-based economically, socially and in regard to future trade and industrial potential and were also cognisant of modern transportation needs and systems—and, above all, provided they were not in competition with, but truly complementary to, existing urban centres.

Obviously in the location of such developments close regard must be paid to existing natural resources, especially of water, and the means of disposing of human wastes, and there must be adequate sources of power, of raw materials, associated industries and equipment and recognition of the fact that, if such areas are to survive, let alone develop, they must contain amenities and attractions which will help them to vie with some of the better and bigger established cities.

Somehow or other we must, without further delay, reverse the present trend of urban population outflow, which leaves the centres of cities to rot. By all the means in our power, and particularly by a redirection of urban policies in regard to the creation of new living areas, we must bring back into the city most of its traditional lifeblood. If, at the same time, new urban concentrations, with suitable safeguards, are developed, there is some hope that we could realign the whole of our metropolitan, urban, regional, and national planning policies into a correct relationship with cities, which might then become even more economically viable.

It hardly needs emphasising that, unless there is the awareness of defects in, and impatience with, our urban surroundings, the means will not be found to put matters right. This implies that neither the people nor the machinery—administrative and otherwise—will be available, unless entirely new comprehensive programmes of education in the arts and the environment, on the Scandinavian pattern, can be introduced into other countries. The sooner this happens, the better, since the process will inevitably be protracted before the real benefits of a truly enlightened and informed public, at responsible adult level (where the decisions on the cities are likely to be made) can be seen.

Perhaps the one major defect, basically underlying all the deficiencies which this book has attempted to expose, in relation to the human urban environment and the lack of effective action to rectify them, is the regrettable fact that all but an insignificant proportion of many of our urban populations are visually untrained and artistically unenlightened. They are lacking in awareness of perceptual and visual matters and therefore, all too often, are totally unconcerned in any explicit way with their environment.

Nothing so far argued as an essential basis for the development and redevelopment of our cities can become a practical possibility unless, as a first stage, we recognise that the physical problems of reordering these cities in all their complexity must be related to a realistic politico-administrative framework of development programmes.

Referring again to the particular situation of the United States, the view has been expressed too often to be ignored that American cities are ugly or depressing but that much could, nevertheless, be achieved through the staged development of strong, formal patterns of visual relationship. It is such visual form, and the satisfactions that it can bring, which is the most imperative of all the ingredients of the renewed city.

It is, however, clear that such an achievement can occur only as a consequence of the actions of the people who live and work in the city and of those who govern it. They, in practice, make the several contributory decisions which, in turn, create the particular urban quality we experience. They must have the enthusiasm and drive to introduce the necessary machinery and to stipulate the desirable goals and objectives, if the form of the city is to be regenerated in a manner which makes a worthwhile contribution towards the creation of a humane habitat.

As to the acutely difficult problem of time-span, this largely arises from the fact that most urban construction and redevelopment occurs within areas which are already largely built-up. The designer needs supreme skill and artifice in order to create something in a contemporary idiom without devaluing the work of his predecessors, and therefore to create a harmony between the two.

In such circumstances visual contrasts can be achieved in such a way as to provide perceptible pleasure and variety. When a satisfactory juxtaposition of old and new is achieved, it is likely to be the result of carefully-contrived and imaginatively-controlled relationships in scale, proportion, colour, texture and materials.

We shall only attain this sort of image of the city if we understand that democratic policies depend upon the awareness and knowledge of the electorate, and that similarly good urban design depends upon the education and taste of people living in the cities. It has been said that in 'a democracy of taste that permits delegation of certain responsibilities to design experts, the public must possess sufficient acumen to choose among experts'. This is the crux of the problem.

Since there seems no way of avoiding the conclusion that more and more responsibility must be delegated to design experts, their choice and investiture with the necessary powers is a vital part of the success of any future urban planning and design operation, as has previously been emphasised.

Unfortunately, not only is there a lack of the requisite type of educational experience to enable those with the power of decision to recognise beauty where they see it and to understand and have the confidence in those who are trained to produce it, but there is a cultural 'hang-up' relating to visual rather than verbal evaluation, and as a reflection of this, education and communication are directed towards language and numerals. Few people, on the other hand, are taught to use, understand or appreciate pictorial or graphic communication, far less aesthetics or formal composition. It is equally a fact that, 'few rise to prominence through visual creativity, and men of power therefore are rarely men of visual taste, since verbal skills rather than visual ones are the resource of influence'.[131]

We are thus, most regrettably, confronted with a situation in which only relatively few businessmen commission, and just as few consumers seek, good architecture, landscape architecture or, for that matter, urban design.

While it is true that, in the long run more can be expected in the way of improvements in architecture and urban design from private individuals and firms than from public bodies, if for no other reason than that most of the building in our present-day cities and much of that in the suburbs is done under private auspices, more government action and concern is urgently needed. Governments, local government organisations and agencies grow in size and proliferate in number each year, and this means an increase in both building programmes to house new departments and in the armies of what have been termed 'the paper shufflers'.

This being so, more positive government action could be taken to improve the quality of urban design, both through improvements in its own developments, financed directly from government sources and through offering direct inducements to developers. This might be done through taxation relief and other such means in order to compensate for additional land or building costs directly incurred in improvements in the quality of architectural and urban design, or the standard of amenities in an area. It has also been suggested that much more might be done in the way of influencing those who commission buildings, in the vital matter of the engagement of the finest architects. One way of ensuring this would be through international competitions, held much more frequently than at present.

In all of these ways government agencies can assume the role of the chief patron of the best architects and thus occupy a place traditionally taken by the rulers and wealthy potentates who were responsible for so many of the splendid historical cities.

Since urban design, architecture and landscape architecture are 'the only arts that cannot be avoided'[131] they are of profound concern to the 'man in the street'. They should therefore, in consequence be of especial interest to all community-minded citizens, whether they guide the destinies of big business, public institutions or government. The essential combination of good taste and community-inspired leadership is the means by which we may hope to develop a fruitful and practical quality of urban design.

One of the most convincing documents to have attempted a comprehensive analysis of the urban design problems confronting the city of New York and which dealt with some of the specific ways in which these might be tackled most effectively, is the report entitled 'The Threatened City'[228] and compiled by the Mayor's task force in February, 1967. Almost all the general conclusions contained in this report have wide application in many other cities, as have some of the particular references, problems and objectives indicated.

This report, which was prepared in response to a request from the Mayor, 'to make a study of urban design in New York City, and how to improve the physical presence of the city for its residents and workers', makes the point, at the outset, that 'design is not a small enterprise in New York City today, nor should it be considered narrowly as merely a matter of aesthetics'. Furthermore: 'in our increasingly crowded man-shaped urban world, aesthetics must now include not only the marble statue in the garden, but the house, the street, the neighbourhood and the city as an accumulative expression of its residents'. Thus: 'the designs of man can shape a city well or badly, but the old method of merely designating streets, installing conventional zoning regulations, and then letting the city grow, is no longer adequate. Positive consideration of three-dimensional design relationships is necessary; shapely cities no longer happen by chance, if they ever did'.[228]

The report also refers to an English critic who pointed out that: 'by the eighteenth century Europe had discovered that cities must be designed before they are extended, since mere pragmatism in planning will not do'. Moreover, it was concluded that: 'it absolutely will not do if left to engineers, soldiers, or what are called developers'.

Underlining the somewhat disquieting state of affairs which prevails at the present in this same city is the statement of belief that 'at times it appears to be spinning towards Mumfordian doom; overgrown, over-congested, ill-managed and ill-kempt, usually solemn, sometimes violent, and scarred by enormous grey areas': indeed, 'a malignant weariness'.[228] To some of us, however, it is, in many ways, still a very exciting city with enormous potential.

These observations stress the urgent and undeniable importance of placing a renewed emphasis on the creation of a better visual environment in our cities now, and in the face of the present frequent and overwhelming anti-city elements which discourage every kind of civilised activity and even occupation of the city itself. They thus succeed very succinctly in confirming much of the basic argument which led to the preparation of this book: and in particular dismissing 'Mumfordian doom' as unacceptable.

This report mentions the committee's study directed toward offences to the eye, such as 'depressingly blank architecture, arid street scenes, and baleful housing'—conditions which, 'frustrate conventional law enforcement and may even be compounded by conventional engineering solution'. These are, it is pointed out, some of the manifestations of a situation in which those in New York know that, 'the natural environment of the city, like most large American cities, is sick', and where, too, 'an ominous pall of smog too frequently obscures the skyline and burns our throats'.

Referring to practical methods by which such conditions may be radically improved and the urban design problem grasped firmly, the present complicated procedure which, in this and other cities, does so much to frustrate positive action or instil confidence in the administration is condemned. It will be realised that, in many cities, this machinery is so ponderous and clumsy that, in the long run, it defeats its own purposes. It must therefore be streamlined if any kind of intelligent policy of creating a desirable urban ecology or a worthwhile perceived environment is ever to become effective.

Lack of design competence is, here again, given emphasis, as is the fact that, in the practical politics of dealing with urban design, a serious part of the problem arises from the situation in which, all too often, 'city departments are largely staffed with people who are able to cope with normal daily tasks and problems, but without the glimmering of hope of helping to create or commission a worthwhile environment'.[228]

There are also the associated problems of conflicting controls and their negative implications, as well as divided authority on a departmental basis, and, perhaps most serious of all, the quasi-planning functions and responsibilities increasingly being arrogated to themselves by a number of service departments and the like—of which the most noteworthy examples in recent years have been highways and transportation agencies.

This particular situation has generally resulted through a deliberate fragmentation of overall responsibility, accompanied by a lack of any sense of co-ordination or cohesion in planning, and, even more seriously, by some of the worst examples of officially-sponsored urban vandalism. These are nearly always much worse in degree and nature than any perpetrated by private individuals or corporations.

Perhaps one of the most outstanding recent examples of such a state of affairs occurs in an Australian city where a Wild West atmosphere of overhead cables and poles survives, and is even expanded year by year right into the heart of the city itself. Because of mounting criticism the electricity supply authority, the chief offender, set up what it chose to call an 'aesthetics committee'. This, which should have more accurately been called a 'camouflage committee', has done precisely nothing to improve the situation, but instead acts as an effective bureaucratic buffer for the time being, to enable legitimate public criticism to be sidestepped. It is a technique which has been repeated on many occasions in relation to environmental questions, and at varying scales of seriousness.

Concurrently another quasi-planning agency in the same city, this time the Highways Department, proposed to carve up the centre of the city with an insensate and entirely obsolete network of urban expressways; a policy which even those American cities which tried this 'remedy' for their transportation problems now know to be totally ineffective. In order to sugar the pill and to persuade the public to accede to this large-scale vandalism, an alleged study of 'community values' was made (but with staff having no training) in order to see these problems in their full planning implications. Inevitably the recommendations made only served to bolster up preconceived decisions. Thus we have another typical example of government ineptitude and cynicism, rating public opinion as not worthy of serious consideration.

Fortunately, in one sense, American cities have invested their Mayors with unusual powers and although, in practice, these have seldom been used to the extent that might be desired by some people, in relation particularly to urban design questions, perhaps this is largely because this kind of planning has been far too responsive to pressure from ill-informed, amateur citizen groups. In theory, at least, enormous improvements might be expected if, as in the report referred to on New York City, recommendations for the increased exercise of Mayoral authority were accepted.

These include suggestions that: 'the Mayor should appeal to the public, with all the prestige and strength of his office, to join with him and to support him in demanding an elevation of design standards in private construction throughout the city',[228] and that he should: 'direct his staff and all city agencies to achieve qualitative improvements in the design of physical changes brought about under their responsibility in any sector of the city, and that he should provide them with new sources of design assistance'.

In support of these proposals and as one of the first and most vitally important steps, the need for quick action by the city to acquire more expertise in design in order to establish higher standards is emphasised.

The urgent importance of: 'directing the chairman of the city planning commission to create within the city planning department an urban design force of trained professionals of the highest competence, to be headed by an architect–planner of proven ability and personal force' is stressed.[228] This group: 'should be charged with the developing—or commissioning—of concept designs for rebuilding special use sections of the city; the conceiving of neighbourhoods of residential buildings in close working collaboration with the planning section of the housing and development administration; the locating of promising areas of offices and commercial buildings . . . and the preparing of plans for area development; the preparation of renewal plans . . . and other such assignments'.

As the initial major task at what is termed 'the first level of design' the completion of a comprehensive master plan must be the first priority in any city. 'This plan should include judgements on suggested transportation and land use patterns . . . it should be revised each year in the future to provide a current set of physical assumptions for the city as an entity'.

Equally important are the 'designation of proper land use for all the areas of the city in order to keep growth in balance . . . and the attempt to anticipate the physical problems of the future in order to provide solutions before the problems get out of control'.

This level of problem-solving, it is rightly believed, 'demands the kind of vision and imagination which can sometimes change the entire physical destiny of the city or create its character'. In this way, it is suggested, l'Enfant planned Washington.

This valuable and comprehensive document, which is a model for all city authorities to study and which contains a great deal of additional detailed material and many far-reaching proposals, demonstrates that the concern for the plight of the cities and the belief that something practical can be done to rectify matters is no longer the misguided aberration of a few but the increasing conviction of all thoughtful people.

Another version of the strategy for urban design and planning, based on a rational *modus-operandi* and commanding immediate respect because of the effective results accruing from it, is that developed in the city of Philadelphia.[14]

Here, in what is called 'the seven essential steps in the cyclical comprehensive planning process', the first obviously consists of drawing up 'the comprehensive plan' which, it is emphasised, must be 'deeply rooted in an understanding of the community, based on both experience and research', and which 'sets forth an interrelated, sensitively balanced range of community objectives'.

This is followed by the 'functional plan' which sets out 'the physical organisation on a regional basis of a manageable number of factors in their primary inter-relation with each other'.

These stages are succeeded by 'the area plan' which establishes in 'a limited geographical section of the city, the three-dimensional relationships between the full range of the physical factors correlated with the functional plan, which bear on the problems to be solved in the area, in order to achieve comprehensive plan objectives'.

As the final piece of this physical planning mosaic we have 'the project plan' which sets out 'in explicit three-dimensional terms the essential nature of the project or projects which are necessary to achieve the objectives of the area plans'. Thus, down through a series of interrelated stages to the scale of operations which, particularly through urban renewal, are likely to change the face of the city, for good or for ill. If they are to be beneficial they must not only be related to what Edmund Bacon calls, 'a design idea'[13] but they must also have an inherently satisfactory environmental quality of their own and contribute positively to the make-up of the city as a whole.

The remaining steps in this process relate to 'the architectural image', 'the money entity' and 'the capital programme' and are the necessary further stages to give practical effect to the development implications of the various levels of the physical plan.

Following this process of preparing a logical physical development plan in more detail, and in conformity with 'an overall design concept' for moving, living, working, shopping, learning and playing, a whole range of initial surveys must obviously be made. It cannot, however, be stressed too often that these will not necessarily provide the basis of straight-line predictions as to future needs, but quite often and much more likely will act as a planning springboard for future proposals, sometimes intuitive, sometimes logical, but, in many cases, necessarily involving judgement rather than implicit deduction.

These surveys will include those related to existing topography, streets and highways, parks and recreation areas, generators of activities of all kinds, landmarks, connectors and barriers in the physical development, building forms and grouping and foci, population changes, income patterns, educational attainments, employment status, housing ownership and quality, overcrowding, types of occupancy, social groupings and overall land-use patterns.

A number of desirable criteria may then be established as general objectives:

Safe and secure environment for living—including access and transportation provisions.

An environment of quality—with the establishment of the relationship between community district and city.

Definition of mobility and freedom of location—with particular reference to variety of housing needs and opportunities.

Conditions of expansion of employment opportunities—including interchange points and definition of places of work.

Creation of the necessary educational opportunities—with convenient location and accessibility.

Generation of an overall quality of variety and individuality—with the greatest degree of flexibility of land-use.

The design concept itself, proceeding from these objectives and goals, establishes first its linkage with the overall pattern of development and with local area planning and other project planning, in ways which reinforce linkages and cohesion, through the explicit use of unifying elements or patterns. Clusters of activity and their spacing and location will then be defined, as will the location of high-intensity activity groups and high-rise development.

A pattern of greenways and pedestrian routes will be established as will a locational accessibility system—through region, district and community to the local or neighbourhood area. Internal and external traffic provisions of all types, and movement systems will be built into the concept at this stage.

At the district and sub-area level, residential treatments, dwelling density patterns, socio-economic areas, the location and planning for industry, shopping on a regional district and local level, and educational facilities, cultural institutions and recreational facilities, will all be integrated into the single planning functional process.

Much of this process, only outlined very briefly, underlies what has already been suggested as the basis of a logical pattern of functional analysis and plan, and precedes the more detailed considerations of the local or project area in centre city, such as is the immediate concern of this book. The fact, however, that in Philadelphia this is producing significantly workable results and one of the few really successful examples of a creative approach to a better urban design concept, makes it worthy of consideration as a case-study of workable urban planning policies.

An alternative approach to the creation of workable programmes and procedures stems first from a recognition that perception of the environment depends not only on its visible form and its objective nature, but also on the nature of the individual seeing it—his history, his needs and purposes and his social environment—in other words, as much on his experience and background as on the objects he is looking at. The same object will therefore be seen in quite different ways by different people from different backgrounds of experience and with different visual acuity, or even different objectives and tasks.

As has therefore already been emphasised, it is thus only too obvious that the consequences of appearance are only partially predictable—some of the effects perceived are due to the individual as a biological organism; others are, however, more firmly based on common ground and are acceptable to large groups of people with similar standing, experience and backgrounds, as well as environmental histories or with similar cultural philosophies.

Though such groups may be identifiable this fact does not necessarily bring us any nearer to a solution of predicting the responses to appearance of perceptual values since the taste or need of a particular group cannot be assumed to provide the basis for universal aesthetic standards.

The designer, as has already been emphasised, has particular responsibilities and must, almost by definition, be a person with special qualities as well as special temperament and training, since his intuitive judgements are likely to have a decisive influence on the ultimate outcome and decisions in urban design projects, even though they may frequently be at variance with those of other individuals or groups.

While it is not possible to draw up a comprehensive set of criteria, with universal application, which will meet all the needs of any problem concerned with aesthetic standards, it is possible to proceed part of the way, and the greater the extent to which this can be achieved, the more it is likely to help in the acceptance of judgements and recommendations, and therefore to lead to the right decisions.

Such criteria, if they are to be valid, must embrace the multiplicity of needs—and must be directly related to form; their principal object must be that of enabling a series of proposals to be evaluated in comparison with one another. Unfortunately, neither psychology, systems analysis, nor operations research, any more than contemporary or previously-expressed norms or ideas in the field of art criticism, or a professional consensus of opinion on particular design situations, form a reliable dictionary on which to base such standards.

What obviously compounds the difficulty and places it on even shakier ground is the limitation of semantic definition, and a totally inadequate vocabulary, relating particularly to the perceptual, aural and olfactory senses.

The major problem, however, is recognition of the fact that any communication, discussion or analysis, in an attempt to define these criteria as a basis for design agreement and establishment of objectives and goals, largely depends on experience of past and present environment. Without special training there is little likelihood of a better understanding or appreciation of what innovations may imply or what could occur through creative and imaginative design application.

An illustration of this problem is that of the elaborate 'image surveys' which have been undertaken in a number of cities but which cannot be the basis of predictive planning, since it is impossible to apply this data, as we have seen, as a workable synthesis.

Some of the design criteria which have, from time to time, been suggested as useful might include: ensuring that perception and experience should be within ascertainable limits likely to ensure comfort and convenience; that there should be a diversity of experience and a physical setting to give a choice of environment; that all parts of the planned area should have a clear perceptual identity and character, which is both coherent and distinctive and thus creates 'a sense of place' without the city becoming confusing and claustrophobic or dully monotonous. In addition, identifiable areas, places and localities should be part of a recognisable overall pattern and the links with this pattern should be clearly comprehensible, however dominant or subtle this may be.

Simplicity may, in certain localities, give way to a degree of complexity although this should never be at the expense of the overall sense of coherence. The local areas must, moreover, be flexible and responsive to growth and change and be particularly related to centres of activity which are of paramount importance.

Reinforcing this system will be a circulation or movement system linking together basic functional and social areas as a part of the urban and metropolitan system. Assisting in this creation of a cognitive urban pattern may be visual emphasis on particular groups or building foci, which may also help to establish a historic continuity.[121]

The environment should be seen to have meaning—function, response to social needs, economics and the establishment of political patterns—as well as being a reflection of topography and perhaps reinforcement of an historic role. The environment plays a symbiotic role in fostering intellectual, emotional and physical development of the individual—thus it must be inspiring and stimulating, as well as reflect practical needs.

Lynch has referred, in relation to the local and project design problem, to the important 'sensuous' elements, in which he includes spatial form as illustrated by writers such as Sitte. Reference is also made to the fact that visible life and the activity of people in the course of their affairs, contributes to the vital warmth and bustle varying over periods of time and season; ambience changing with the particular sensuous qualities of light, noise, micro-climate and smell and visibility with particular skylines, land forms, building masses, key viewing positions and landmarks. Also significant are the qualities of surfaces and the all-important visual and tactile textures on both walls and pavings and, finally, the emphasis on, and means by which, communication proceeds.

The view already expressed that, 'we must rely more and more on the observation of real or simulated behaviour to disclose how the environment is perceived' is further emphasised, and thus again underlines the importance of the development of the simulation system, through a total process of perception.

Of course even the method of simulation through the techniques already described, using modelscope, television and sound, still needs the exercise of imagination, knowledge, skill and experience. However, it is possible to display most facets to the uninitiated or the amateur, through the use of the visual image, movement and sound.

The olfactory sensations and those of touch, or of feeling, such as are generated by the movement of air or wind through the street or space, or the sensation of the heat of the sun, must be through the association of experience and the development of a kinesthetic sense and will be solely derived from the exercise of imagination, based on visual images. The sense of enclosure, or of exposure as its converse, will become increasingly apparent with familiarity through the use of larger and better moving images, such as has occurred with some of the contemporary cinema techniques.

However much it may be possible to convey essential aspects of these studies and demonstrations to the layman, it has to be appreciated that the designer must use his own subjective judgement in analysis as, unless the whole process is to be seriously inhibited, the value of his wider experience, knowledge and greater ability to visualise the three-dimensional consequences of his decisions, must be given free rein wherever it is practicable to do so.

Lynch goes so far as to suggest that, 'the designer can develop a system of visual sequences through an area, even before he looks at circulation requirements; or may play with silhouette before he understands requirements for enclosed space; or may work out a desirable image structure while still in a functional vacuum. . . .' This, he holds, 'is neither more nor less reprehensible than the other way round'.[121]

The design which is generated for a large environment may contain a spatial pattern of visual performance characteristics, such as space and form, visibility and texture, and it will specify form, as well as locating major paths and a rhythm of views from them, principal visual centres, axes of view and barriers of view, landmarks, consistent district characteristics—boundaries, the form of dominant open spaces, land and building masses—in fact, a comprehensive visual programme.

In general terms it may be accepted that there are three ways of ordering the appearance of the city. These are: (i) by asserting the quality of urban design consistently and comprehensively, (ii) by regulation and ordinance (that is the 'police power'), (iii) by indirect encouragement or persuasion.

Of these the first, on any comprehensive basis, requires dictatorial powers and unusual perception, but is much more likely to be practicable at superblock level. It is most likely to prove a workable system when based on the establishment of a series of nodes or foci, as, for example, the important public buildings or public areas, or through a standardised series of related patterns—with, however, a strong enough overall framework to avoid a patchwork appearance.

The second alternative through regulation will rely on a series of controls which may include those applying to visual form as well as to zoning, heights and other parameters. It is, of course, already evident that this cannot promise a fine environment, but it may prevent the worst and is, in effect, negative in value.

The establishment of appellate machinery can do much to reinforce the more flexible and creative application of such regulations and controls but if these are to be most effective they should operate from the earliest sketch design stages, with the use of three-dimensional models and the perceptual simulation system of appraisal.

The third alternative is, in one sense, closely linked with the second, inasmuch as encouragement may be gained through application of a guidance system or merely by example, or both. Obviously, in either case, when sensitive and experienced designers influence the final decisions or participate in some way while development planning is taking place, there will be innumerable benefits in the levels and quality of design, as well as on overall imaginative qualities. It is important that this should apply to government building agencies with equal force to that exerted over building in the private sector.

One of the very useful suggestions which have been made in this connection is that the influence of the good designers, who are likely to be in official or government employment, could be extended to public agencies by making their services available to these or at least to smaller developers who do not have the capabilities within their own departments or staffs. Such designers could work for a purely nominal fee.

Perhaps it is unduly optimistic to imagine that such a situation could come about at an early date, and certainly not until city authorities make it compulsory for every developer and builder to employ suitably-qualified people on their own staffs or to obtain the equivalent services through consultancy arrangements. Obviously, government departments concerned with building and development should not be exempt from such provisions, any more than from compliance with overall planning objectives and the obligation of being subject to the scrutiny and approval of all their proposals by the city planning department.

For the departmental structure involved in the practical problems of urban design and planning, it has already been emphasised that visual design cannot be set up as a separate section but must be integrated with the whole of the planning process at every stage. This implies that suitably-trained and qualified people must be given a significant role in every part of the team operation at all stages.

There should, however, also be what has been termed 'a visual intelligence section' in the city planning organisation, with the specific purpose of evaluating, testing and analysing projects, both for the department itself and for other developers and individual members of the public. There should, in addition, be a liaison and review section in the planning department in order to improve communication with project and system designers as well as with other government departments and agencies.

Finally, we should hope to reach a stage at which we can look forward to 'design task forces' certainly in the larger city planning authorities, with the responsibility of undertaking strategic or tactical design projects and developing prototypes or examples of worthwhile quality on which specific developments may be based.

This section of planning departments would have a very close link internally with the visual intelligence section and would form the core of research in executive urban design at a point at which it is likely to have the most immediate and beneficial results, and the most effective feedback of knowledge.

Rarely, at present, is there to be found a city planning department with this degree of comprehensiveness—and more particularly one equipped to understand and apply the whole range of knowledge relating to the perceived form of the city. It is certainly no answer to suggest that this may be better solved by employing sociologists rather than architects in the team, since this indicates an abysmal lack of understanding of even the rudiments of the problem.

It cannot be repeated too often that, 'city form is a critical aspect of the human environment, and design it we must'. Until we understand this and set about organising our plans and policies to give it effective recognition and expression, our cities will continue in their present chaotic state of 'malignant weariness'.

Selected bibliography and references

1. ALEXANDER, C. A City is not a Tree, *Architectural Forum*, April/May, 1965.
2. ALEXANDER, C. The Pattern of Streets, *AIP Journal*, September, 1966.
3. ABERCROMBIE, J. Design Methods in Architecture, *Arena*, February, 1968.
4. ABRAMS, C. *The City is the Frontier*, New York, Harper & Row, 1965.
5. ABRAMS, C. *Man's Struggle for Shelter in an Urbanising World*, Cambridge, Mass., MIT Press, 1964.
6. ABSE, W. *Some Psychologic and Psychoanalytic Aspects of Perception, Perception and Environment: Foundations of Urban Design*, Ed. R. Stipe—Inst. of Govt, Univ., N. Carolina.
7. AHLBERG, C. F. *Problems of the Urban Core*, Lecture to Royal Swedish Acad. of Eng. Sciences, November, 1963.
8. ANDERSON, N. *The Urban Community*, London, Routledge & K. Paul, 1960.
9. APPLEYARD, LYNCH & MYER, *The View from the Road*, Cambridge, 1963.
10. AREGGER, H. & CLAUS, O. *Highrise Building and Urban Design*, London, Thames & Hudson, 1967.
11. ARNHEIM, R. *Art and Visual Perception*, Berkeley, University of California Press, 1960.
12. AUERBACK, H. C. *et al.* Downtown in 3-D, *Architectural Forum*, September, 1966.
13. BACON, E. *Design of Cities*, London, Thames & Hudson, 1967.
14. BACON, E. Urban Design as a Force in Comprehensive Planning, *American Institute of Planners Journal*, February, 1963.
15. BANFIELD, E. C. & WILSON, J. Q. *City Politics*, Cambridge, Mass., MIT Press, 1965.
16. BARTHOLOMEW, H. *Land Uses in American Cities*, Cambridge, Harvard University Press, 1955.
17. BAUER, C. ed. *The Future of Cities and Urban Redevelopment*, Chicago, University of Chicago Press, 1961.
18. BAUER-WURSTER, C. in *Cities and Space*, RFF Wingo, ed., Baltimore, Johns Hopkins Press, 1963.
19. BENDTSEN, P. H. *Town and Traffic in the Motor Age*, transl. E. Rockwell, Danish Technical Paper, 1961.
20. BEST, R. H. *Land for New Towns*, Town and Country Planning Assoc., Publications, 1964.
21. BLAIR, T. L. *Official Architecture and Planning*, February, 1969.
22. BLAKE, P. *God's Own Junkyard*, New York, Holt, Rinehart & Winston, 1964.
23. BLUMENFELD, H. The Urban Pattern, *Annals of the American Academy of Political and Social Science*, March, 1964, p. 81.
24. BRANCH, M. C. *Planning Aspects and Applications*, New York, Wiley, 1966.
25. BRENNAN, T. *Reshaping a City*, London, House of Grant, 1959.
26. BRETT, L. The Environmentalists, *Architectural Review*, May, 1959.

27. BUCHANAN, C. Report of the Public Inquiry Concerning Development on the Monico Site at the Piccadilly Circus, *Town Planning Review*, January, 1961.
28. BUCHANAN, C. *et al. Traffic in Towns*, Harmondsworth, Penguin, 1964.
29. BUCHANAN, C. *Mixed Blessing: the Motor in Britain*, London, Leonard Hill, 1958.
30. BULLOCK, DICKENS & STEADMAN, A Theoretical Model, *Official Architecture and Planning*, April, 1968.
31. BURCHARD, J. E. in *Man and the Modern City*, Univ. of Pittsburgh Press, 1963.
32. BURCHARD, J. E. The Limitations of Utilitarianism as a Basis for Determining Urban Joy, in *Man and the Modern City*, University of Pittsburgh Press, 1963.
33. BURCHARD, J. E. *Land, House & Home*, June, 1962.
34. BURCHARD, J. E. The Urban Aesthetic, *Annals of the American Academy of Political and Social Science*, November, 1957.
35. BURNS, W. *New Towns for Old*, London, Leonard Hill, 1963.
36. CARRITT, E. F. *The Theory of Beauty*, London, Associated Book Publishers, 1949.
37. CARVER, H. *Cities in the Suburbs*, Toronto, Toronto University Press, 1962.
38. CHADWICK, G. F. *The Park and the Town*, London, Architectural Press, 1966.
39. CHAPIN, F. S. JR. Selected Theories of Urban Growth and Structure, *AIP Journal*, February, 1964.
40. CHAPIN, F. S. JR. ed. & WEISS, S. T. *Urban Growth Dynamics*, New York, Wiley, 1962 (extract from *Livability of the City* by R. L. Wilson).
41. CHAPIN, F. S. JR. Urban Land Use Planning (ref. Williams, S. H., Urban Aesthetics), *Town Planning Review*, July, 1954.
42. CHINITZ, B. ed. *City and Suburb*, New York, Prentice-Hall, 1965.
43. CHURCHILL, H. S. *The City is the People*, New York, Norton, 1962.
44. CHURCHILL, H. S. Urban Aesthetics, *AIA Journal*, October, 1958.
45. CRANE, D. The City Symbolic, *AIP Journal*, November, 1960.
46. CRANE, D. The Public Art of City Building, *Annals of the American Academy of Political and Social Science*, March, 1964.
47. CRANE, D. Alternative to Futility, *AIA Journal*, May, 1962.
48. CULLEN, G. *Townscape*, London, Architectural Press, 1961.
49. CULLINGWORTH, J. B. Housing and Local Government, p. 153.
50. CUNLIFFE, M. The Eye and the Mind's Heart, *TPI Journal*, April, 1969.
51. DAVIS, KINGSLEY. The Origin and Growth of Urbanisation in the World, *American Journal of Sociology*, March, 1955.
52. DE JONGE. Images of Urban Areas, *American Institute of Planners Journal*, November, 1962.
53. DE MARS. Townscape and the Architect, in *The Future of Cities and Urban Redevelopment*, ed. Woodbury, C. Part I, Univ. of Chicago Press, 1961.
54. DOXIADIS, C. Today's Cities: Have they any Tomorrow? *Newsweek Global Report*, May 27, 1968.
55. DURDEN, D. & MARBLE, D. The Role of Theory in Central Business District Planning, *AIP Journal*, February, 1961.
56. DUHL, L. The Ecology of Urban Space, in *Cities and Space*, RFF Wingo, ed., Baltimore, Johns Hopkins Press, 1963.
57. DUGGAR, G. ed. *The Next Big Tasks in U.R.*—1961, Library of Congress, 1961.
58. ECKBO, G. *Urban Landscape Design*, New York, McGraw-Hill, 1964.

59. ELIAS, C. E. JR., GILLIES, J. & RIEMER, S. *Metropolis: Values in Conflict*, Belmont, Wadsworth Publishing Co., 1964.

60. FITCH, J. M. The Aesthetics of Function, *Annals of New York Academy of Sciences*, **128**, September 27, 1965.

61. FLOYD, H. *Building Shapes in Central Areas*, Cape Town, Balkema, 1963.

62. FOLEY, D. L. *Controlling London's Growth*, Berkeley, University of California Press, 1963.

63. FRIEDEN, B. J. *The Future of Old Neighbourhoods*, Cambridge, Mass., MIT Press, 1964.

64. FUTTERMAN, R. A. *The Future of Our Cities*, New York, Doubleday, 1961.

65. GALLION, A. B. & EISNER, S. *The Urban Pattern*, New York, Van Nostrand-Reinhold, 1950.

66. GOODMAN, C. & VON ECKHARDT, W. *Life for Dead Spaces*, New York, Lavanburg Foundation, 1963.

67. GOTTMAN, J. Economics, Aesthetics and Ethics, in *Modern Urbanization*, New York, 20th Century Fund, 1962.

68. GOTTMAN, J. *Megalopolis*, New York, Macmillan, 1964.

69. GREBLER, L. *Europe's Reborn Cities*, Washington, Urban Land Institute, 1956.

70. GREGORY, R. L. *The Psychology of Seeing—Eye and Brain*, London, Weidenfeld & Nicholson, 1966.

71. GRUEN, V. Are Centres Necessary? *Byggekunst* (2), 1968.

72. GRUEN, V. *The Heart of the City*, New York, Simon & Schuster, 1964.

73. GUTHEIM, F. in *Cities and Space*, RFF Wingo, ed., Baltimore, Johns Hopkins Press, 1963.

74. GUTKIND, E. A. *International History of City Development, Vol. III—Urban Development in Southern Europe, etc*, New York, Free Press, 1967.

75. HAAR, C. M., Sasaki & Sert, *Land Use Planning*, Boston, Little Brown, 1966.

76. HALL, P. G. *London* 2000, London, Faber, 1963.

77. HALPRIN, L. *Cities*, New York, Van Nostrand-Reinhold, 1963.

78. HALPRIN, L. Motation, *Progressive Architecture*, July, 1965.

79. HARRIS, B. Plan or Projection, *AIP Journal*, November, 1960.

80. HASSID & JACOBS, *An Annotated Bibliography on Urban Aesthetics*, University of California, Department of Architecture, April, 1960.

81. HAUSER, P. M. & SCHNORE, L. F. *The Study of Urbanisation*, New York, Wiley, 1965.

82. HEATH, T. F. Problems of Measurement in Environmental Aesthetics, *Architectural Science Review*, March, 1968.

83. HESSELGREN, S. *The Language of Architecture*, London, Applied Science Publishers [Studentlitteratur], 1967.

84. HIGBEE, E. C. *The Squeeze: Cities Without Space*, London, Cassell, 1961.

85. HILBERSHEIMER, L. *The Nature of Cities*, Chicago, Theobald, 1955.

86. HIRSCH, W. Z. ed. *Urban Life and Form*, Washington University, St. Louis Institute for Urban and Regional Studies, New York, Holt, Rinehart & Winston, 1963.

87. HOCHBERG, J. *Perception*, New York, Prentice-Hall, 1964.

88. HOFFMAN, N. The Outlook for Downtown Housing, *AIP Journal*.

89. HOGG, J. ed. *Psychology of the Visual Arts*, Harmondsworth, Penguin, 1969.

90. HOPPENFELD, J. M. Towards a Consensus of Approach to Urban Design, *AIA Journal*, September, 1962.

91. HOPPENFELD, J. M. The Role of Design in City Planning, *AIA Journal*, May, 1961.
92. HORWOOD, E. M. & BOYCE, R. R. *Studies of the Central Business District and Urban Freeway Development*, Seattle, University of Washington Press, 1959.
93. JACOBS, JANE. *The Death and Life of Great American Cities*, New York, Random House Inc., Alfred A. Knopf Inc., 1961.
94. JELLICOE, G. A. Motopia, *Studio,* 1961.
95. JENSEN, R. *High Density Living*, Hill and Praeger, 1965.
96. JENSEN, R. Aesthetic Control in the City, *Australian Journal of Science*, June, 1968, and *NZ Inst. of Architects Journal*, **35**(7), 1968.
97. JENSEN, R. *Urban Redevelopment in Inner City Areas: Planning & Design*, Planning & Research Centre, University of Sydney, 1966.
98. JENSEN, R. *The Compact City*, Paper to ANZAAS Congress, Adelaide, 1969.
99. JENSEN, R. Density Control in Australian Cities, *Architectural Science Review*, November, 1961.
100. JENSEN, R. Planning Urban Renewal & Housing in Singapore, *TP Review*, July, 1967.
101. JENSEN, R. Freeways or People, *Proceedings of Royal Geog. Soc. of Australasia*, **66,** 1965.
102. JENSEN, R. Bringing Reality to Model Cities, *Architect & Building News*, April 16, 1970.
103. JOHNSON-MARSHALL, P. *Rebuilding Cities*, Edinburgh University Press, 1966.
104. JONES, B. Design from Knowledge not Belief, *AIA Journal*, May, 1962.
105. JONES, B. Prolegomena to a Study of the Aesthetic Effect of Cities, *Journal of Aesthetics and Art Criticism*. June, 1960, **XVIII** (4) pp. 419–29.
106. JONES, E. *Towns and Cities*, London, Oxford University Press, 1967.
107. KEPES, G. Notes on Expression and Communication in the Cityscape, *Daedalus,* Winter, 1961.
108. LEACH, E. *Official Architecture and Planning*, February,1969.
109. LEAN, W. Economics of Town Centres and Urban Shapes, *Town Planning Institute Journal*, September/October, 1966.
110. LE CORBUSIER, *The City of Tomorrow*, London, Rodker, 1929.
111. LEWIS, H. M. *Planning the Modern City*, New York, Wiley, 1961.
112. LEHMBROCK, J. City Organisation, *Bauen & Wohnen,* July, 1966.
113. LING, A. Skyscrapers and Their Siting in Cities, *Town Planning Review*, April, 1963.
114. LLEWELLYN-DAVIES, R. Town Design, *Town Planning Review*, October, 1966.
115. LOGIE, G. *The Urban Scene*, London, Faber & Faber, 1954.
116. LYNCH, K. *Physical Environment—Metropolis*.
117. LYNCH, K. City Design and City Appearance, in *Principles and Practice of Urban Planning*, Washington, International City Management Association, 1968.
118. LYNCH, K. The Pattern of the Metropolis in the Future Metropolis, *Daedalus,* Winter, 1961.
119. LYNCH, K. & RODWIN, L. A Theory of Urban Form, *Journal of the AIP*, Autumn, 1958.
120. LYNCH, K. *The Image of the City*, Cambridge, Mass., MIT Press, 1960.
121. LYNCH, K. Quality in City Design, in *Who Designs America?* L. B. Holland, ed., New York, Anchor Books, 1966.
122. MCCONNELL, S. Planning Control in City Centres, *Official Architecture and Planning*, April, 1968.

123. McConnell, S. The Future of City Centres, *Official Architecture and Planning*, September, 1967.
124. McConnell, S. Civic Design, *Official Architecture and Planning*, May, 1968.
125. Marshall-Miller, J. *Residential Density*, privately circulated notes, July, 1960.
126. Marshall-Miller, J. ed. *New Life for Cities Around the World*, Books International, 1959.
127. Martin, J. L. An Architect's Approach to Architecture, *RIBA Journal*, May, 1967.
128. Martin, J. L. Developing a National Centre, *RIBA Journal*, September, 1965.
129. McQuade, W. Boston: What Can a Sick City Do? *Fortune*, June, 1964.
130. Meier, R. L. *Science and Economic Development*, New York, Wiley, 1956 (and MIT Press).
131. Meyerson, M. *Face of the Metropolis*, New York, Random House Inc., Alfred A. Knopf Inc., 1963.
132. Meyerson, M. ed. *et al.* Metropolis in Ferment, *Annals of the Academy of Political and Social Science*, **314** (Philadelphia, 1957).
133. Morris & Zisman. The Pedestrian Downtown and the Planner, *AIP Journal*, February, 1961.
134. Mills, C. W. Referred to by A. Rockman, *Art Gallery of Ontario Catalogue*, Ottawa Centennial Commn., 1967.
135. Moses, R. Are Cities Dead? *Atlantic Monthly*, January, 1962.
136. Moholy-Nagy, S. *The Matrix of Man*, Praeger, 1969.
137. Mumford, L. *The City in History*, New York, Harcourt Brace, 1961.
138. Mumford, L. The Future of the City, *Architectural Record*, October, 1962. pp. 121–128—Dodge Corporation.
139. Mumford, L. *The Myth of the Machine*, London, Martin Secker & Warburg, 1967.
140. Mumford, L. *The Urban Prospect*, London, Martin Secker & Warburg, 1956.
141. Neutra, R. J. Human Setting in an Industrial Civilisation, *AIA Journal*, pp. 69–75.
142. Organisation of Cornell Planners, *Planning for Urban Aesthetics*, Cornell University Department of City & Regional Planning, 1961. (Anderson, Bacon, Goodman, Hoover, Jacobs, Kahn, Parson, Reps.)
143. Owen, W. *Cities in the Motor Age*, New York, Viking Press, 1959.
144. Owings, N. *Time*, 2 August, 1968.
145. Pound, G. T. Planning for Daylight, *Town Planning Institute Journal*, May/June, 1947.
146. Ponte, V. Montreal Gets a New Heart, *Architect & Building News*, 24 April, 1969.
147. 'Pragma', *Town Planning Institute Journal*, March, 1967, **53**(3), p. 86.
148. Rannels, T. *The Core of the City*, New York, 1956.
149. Rapoport, A. & Kantor, R. E. Complexity and Ambiguity in Environmental Design, *AIP Journal*, July, 1967.
150. Rasmussen, S. E. *Experiencing Architecture*, Cambridge, Mass., MIT Press, 1964.
151. Rasmussen, S. E. *London, the Unique City*, London, Pelican, 1957.
152. Rasmussen, S. E. *Towns and Buildings*, Liverpool Univ. Press, 1951.
153. Rawson, M. *Property Taxation and Urban Development*, ULT Monograph, No. 4, 1961.
154. Reichek, J. On the Design of Cities, *AIP Journal*, **27**(2), May, 1961.

155. ROBINSON, V. J. Changes and Trends in American Central Areas, *TPI Journal*, June, 1962.
156. RODWIN, L. ed. *The Future Metropolis*, London, Constable, 1962.
157. ROSE, S. W. & PIERCE, M. S. Television as a Design Tool, *Architectural Education*, March, 1967.
158. ROSENAU, H. *The Ideal City*, London, Routledge & K. Paul, 1959, p. 148.
159. ROWLAND, K. *The Shape of Towns*, Melbourne, Cheshire, 1964.
160. SAARINEN, E. *The City*, Cambridge, Mass., MIT Press, 1943.
161. SCHMID, K. O. *A Philosophy of Urban Design* (see 6).
162. SCOTT, J. *Journal of the Royal Town Planning Institute*, March, 1969 (letter).
163. SCULLY, V. J. *The Earth, the Temple and the Gods*, New Haven, Yale University Press, 1962.
164. SHANKLAND, A. *City of Liverpool Planning Report*, 1964.
165. SHARP, D. Dreaming Spires and Teeming Towers, *Town Planning Review*, January, 1963.
166. SHARMAN, H. Creativity in Architectural Design, *AIA Journal*, September, 1964.
167. SHERMAN, S. M. On Forming and Reforming Towns and Cities, *AIP Journal*, May, 1963.
168. SHULZ & SIMONS. *Offices in the Sky*, Merrill, 1959.
169. SIMONDS, J. O. *Landscape Architecture*, London, Iliffe, 1961.
170. SITTE, C. *City Planning According to Artistic Principles*, London, Phaidon, 1965.
171. SITTE, C. *The Art of Building Cities*, New York, Van Nostrand-Reinhold, 1945. (Original ed. 1889.)
172. SMIGIELSKI, W. K. London—A Metropolis in Disintegration, *TPI Journal*, July/August, 1960.
173. SMITHSON, A. & P. Urban Structuring, *Studio Vista*, 1967.
174. SPREIREGEN, P. For the Urban Design Committee, American Institute of Architects, *Urban Design: the Architecture of Towns and Cities*.
175. STONES, R. C. Housing and Redevelopment, *Town Planning Review*, January, 1967.
176. STONE, E. D. Are Most Cities Too Ugly to Save? *US News and World Report*, November 30, 1964.
177. STRAUSS, A. L. *Images of the American City*, New York, Free Press of Glencoe, 1961.
178. STRONG, E. W. The Amplitude of Design, *AIP Journal*.
179. TANGE, K. Planning for Tokyo 1960 (The Nature of a City of 10 Million), *Japan Architect* and *Bauen & Wohnen,* January, 1964.
180. TANKEL, S. B. in *Cities and Space*, RFF Wingo, ed., Baltimore, Johns Hopkins Press, 1963.
181. THIEL, P. Processional Architecture, *AIA Journal*, February, 1964.
182. THIEL, P. A. Sequence—Experience Notation, *Town Planning Review*, April, 1961.
183. THOMPSON, R. *The Psychology of Thinking*, Harmondsworth, Pelican.
184. THORNLEY, D. Space and Form in Civic Design, in *Studies in Architectural History*, York Institute of Architectural Study, 1955.
185. TUNNARD, C. & REED, H. H. *American Skyline*, Boston, Houghton Mifflin, 1955.
186. TUNNARD, C. & PUSHKAREV, B. *Man-Made America: Chaos or Control?* New Haven, Yale UP, 1963.
187. UNIVERSITY OF CALIFORNIA. Department of City Planning: *The Compact Metropolis*, January, 1961.

188. VAN GINKEL, B. The Form of the Core, *AIP Journal*, February, 1961.
189. VALENTINE, C. W. *The Experimental Psychology of Beauty*.
190. VERNON, R. *Metropolis* 1985, New York, Doubleday, 1963.
191. VERNON, R. *The Myth and Reality of an Urban Problem*, Cambridge, Mass., Joint Centre for Urban Studies, 1962.
192. VERNON, R. *The Changing Economic Function of the Central City*, Committee for Economic Development, New York, 1959.
193. VIGIER, F. C. An Experimental Approach to Urban Design, *AIP Journal*, February, 1965.
194. WARD, D. C. *The City Beautiful*, Report to 7th Australian Planning Congress, Hobart, 1962.
195. WARNER, S. B. ed. *Planning for a Nation of Cities*, Cambridge, Mass., MIT Press, 1966.
196. WARNER, S. B. JR. ed. *Streetcar Suburbs*, Cambridge, Mass., Harvard University Press, 1962.
197. WATTS, K. Functional Controls and Town Design, *Architects Journal*, 23 October, 1963.
198. WEAVER, R. C. *The Dilemma of Urban America*, Cambridge, Mass., Harvard University Press, 1965.
199. WEISS, S. The Downtown Mall Experiment, *AIP Journal*, February, 1961.
200. WHIFFEN, M. *The Architect and the City*, Cambridge, Mass., MIT Press, 1966.
201. WHYTE, W. H. JR. The Anti-City, in *Man and the Modern City*, ed. Geen, University of Pittsburgh Press, 1963.
202. WILLIAMS, S. H. Urban Aesthetics, *Town Planning Review*, July, 1954.
203. WOODS, S. The Man in the Street, *Bauen & Wohnen,* July, 1966.
204. WRIGHT, H. M. The Motor Vehicle and Civic Design, *RIBA Journal*, January, 1957.
205. ZUCKER, P. *Town and Square*, New York, Columbia Univ. Press, 1959.
206. ZUSNE, L. *Visual Perception of Form*.
207. Editorial: Aspects of Urban Management, *Official Architecture and Planning*, September, 1968.
208. Editorial: High Building in London, *Architect and Building News*, 17 May, 1956.
209. 'IMR'. Exterior Volume, *Progressive Architecture*, June, 1965.
210. Editorial: Upgrading Downtown, *Architectural Record*, June, 1965.
211. Editorial: *Checklist for Cities*, Committee on Urban Design—American Institute of Architects, January, 1968.
212. Editorial: Who are the Planners? *Official Architecture and Planning*, December, 1968.
213. Editorial: What Kind of City Do We Want? *The Nation's Cities,* April, 1967.
214. Editorial: How to Avoid a Slab City, *Progressive Architecture*, February, 1968.
215. Editorial: The New Town and Major Spaces, *Progressive Architecture*, June, 1965.
216. Intro: *Man and the Modern City*, University of Pittsburgh Press, 1963.
217. *The Urban Promenade Network*, International Research Centre for Urban Anthropology, Freiburg, 1966.
218. *Rating of Site Values*, Rating and Valuation Assoc., London, 1964.
219. Paris, *L'Architecture d'Aujourd'hui* (138), June/July, 1968.
220. Urbanisme, *L'Architecture d'Aujourd'hui* (132), June/July, 1967.
221. Back to the Waterfront, *Progressive Architecture*, August, 1966.

222. *The Lighting of Buildings*, Ministry of Planning, HMSO, 1944.
223. *Planning for Daylight and Sunlight*, Ministry of Housing and Local Government, HMSO, 1964.
224. *The Living Town*, Report of Symposium, *RIBA Journal*, May, 1959.
225. *Cinderella City* (*Pittsburgh*), National Association of Manufacturers, 1962 (No. 12).
226. Hamburg, *Urbanistica*, Nos. 36–37, November, 1962.
227. La Defense Area, Paris, *Bauen & Wohnen,* July, 1966.
228. *The Threatened City*, Report of City of New York Mayor's Task Force, 1967.
229. *Town Centres*, Ministry of Housing and Local Government, HMSO, 1963.
230. *The Planning of a New Town*, London County Council, 1961.
231. WORLD HEALTH ORGANISATION, Technical Report Series No. 297, Geneva, 1965.
232. MOORE, G. T. ed. *Emerging Methods in Environmental Design and Planning*, Cambridge, Mass., MIT Press, 1970.
233. MEIER, RICHARD L. *A Communications Theory of Urban Growth*, Joint Centre for Urban Studies and MIT Press, 1962.

Index